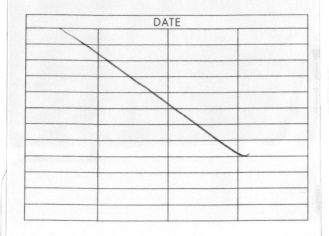

DATE			

WISDOM:
TWELVE ESSAYS

JOHN WISDOM   Photograph: Judith Jarvis Thomson

WISDOM:

TWELVE ESSAYS

Edited by

Renford Bambrough

Without Contraries is no progression
BLAKE, *The Marriage of Heaven and Hell*

The Holiness of Minute Particulars
BLAKE, *Jerusalem*

BASIL BLACKWELL
OXFORD

ISBN   0   631   14690   3

Library of Congress Catalog Card Number: 72-95692

PRINTED IN GREAT BRITAIN
BY A. T. BROOME AND SON, 18 ST. CLEMENT'S, OXFORD
AND BOUND BY THE KEMP HALL BINDERY, OXFORD

CONTENTS

Frontispiece

Foreword

FOREWORD

There is no special occasion for this collection. It is an expression of gratitude to John Wisdom from some who have worked closely with him for many years and from some others who have read his writings but have little or only recent personal acquaintance with him. But this tribute is not the book's only purpose. I hope that the essays will serve the ends of philosophy both directly and by stimulating the reading and discussion of Wisdom's own books and papers. His work, widely influential though it has been, has not even now had the attention it deserves.

His articles in the 1930's and 1940's were an indispensable source of information about the work of Wittgenstein. Since the appearance of the *Philosophical Investigations* and the *Blue and Brown Books* the impression has sometimes been given that *Philosophy and Psycho-Analysis* and *Other Minds* are more dependent and derivative than a judicious reading shows them to be. In his paper 'Teaching and Training' Gilbert Ryle has written:

> The supreme reward of the teacher is to turn out from time to time the student who comes to be not merely abreast of his teacher but ahead of him, the student, namely, who advances his subject or his craft not just by adding to it further applications of the established ways of operating but by discovering new methods or procedures of types which no one could have taught to him. He has given to his subject or his craft a new idea or a battery of new ideas. He is original. He himself, if of a grateful nature, will say that his original idea just grew of itself out of what he had learned from his teachers, his competitors and his colleagues; while they, if of a grateful nature, will say that the new idea was his discovery. Both will be right. His new idea is the fruit of a tree that others had planted and pruned. It is really his own fruit and he is really their tree.

Wisdom has always been of a grateful disposition—ready to see more of Wittgenstein, Moore and McTaggart in himself than there was, ready to see less of himself in his own pupils and

followers than can be found by the bystanders. This generosity to
other philosophers is only one of the moral qualities to which, as
much as to a powerful mind and fertile imagination, we are
indebted for Wisdom's achievement in philosophy.

All the essays in this volume are newly written for the book,
except Professor Gasking's well-known review article from the
Australasian Journal of Philosophy of 1954, which is reprinted by
kind permission of the author and the editor. Some of the essays
are studies of Wisdom's work; others extend or apply his work to
new themes; and others are more independent contributions by
philosophers who have learned from him and from the spirit of
his writings.

John Wisdom is now Professor of Philosophy at the University
of Oregon at Eugene. Until 1969 he held the Chair at Cambridge
which had earlier been held by Moore and Wittgenstein.

I hope that the essays in this book show something of the
connections of philosophy with other studies and with questions
and problems that fall outside all academic studies. Wisdom
himself has insisted on these connections, though he has always
remembered that philosophy is a branch of knowledge in its own
right, and need pay no tithes to logic or science or any other tax-
gatherer.

The differences between *Problems of Mind and Matter* and
Other Minds are sufficient to show that John Wisdom would have
been unlikely to make his distinctive contribution to the progress
of philosophy if he had not felt when he did, and as deeply as he
did, the impact of Wittgenstein's middle and later work. But
neither this fact nor Wisdom's sometimes over-generous acknowledgement of it should hide from us the size of his contribution.

He has made Wittgenstein's work accessible, not by repeating
it, but by transposing it into something nearer to the traditional
idiom of philosophical discussion. In the 1930's and 1940's he
was a spokesman and a witness, but even since the *Philosophical
Investigations* were published he has continued to perform
the invaluable service of relating Wittgenstein's enquiries and
conclusions to the context of philosophical debate which gives
them their point, and to which Wittgenstein rarely and only
obliquely refers. In doing so he has been able to display the unity
and coherence of what Wittgenstein himself had at least tried to
represent as a series of isolated 'remarks'. He has made substantial

modifications and corrections of his own. He has shown that the paradoxes of the traditional philosophers have virtues as well as defects; that while there is madness in them there is also method. Even here there are hints in Wittgenstein that might have been developed, but the achievement remains of the first importance.

Wisdom was enabled by his more systematic presentation of the issues, and by his greater attention to the philosophical context, to relate Wittgenstein's work to the writings of the great philosophers of the past. His British Academy Lecture 'The Metamorphosis of Metaphysics' is the most explicit statement of a recognition, which informs all Wisdom's philosophising, that we are all engaged in a continuing conversation in which we have much to learn from what was said earlier by others who spoke different languages from our own.

He has striven in another way to restore philosophy to a condition from which it seemed to many to have fallen. Wittgenstein remarks in a letter to Malcolm that philosophical learning and skill are useless unless they help us with our thinking about the real problems of life and the world as well as with abstract issues. But with Wisdom one does not need to go to a private letter for an acknowledgement of this need. Without ever compromising the logical distinctness of metaphysical enquiry from scientific, moral, theological and other forms of substantive enquiry, Wisdom has seen the philosopher's task as extending over these other fields as well as over metaphysics, whenever (as often) the problems that tax the practitioners of these other studies have the structure that typically belongs to philosophical problems.

One of Wisdom's stories about Wittgenstein illustrates the kinship and the difference between the two men and their methods. Wisdom reports that on one occasion he said to Wittgenstein that a conversation he had had with another philosopher had not gone well. 'Perhaps,' said Wittgenstein, 'you made the mistake of denying something that he asserted.' When Wisdom tells this story he endorses Wittgenstein's comment. He momentarily adopts Wittgenstein's own guise of the mere surveyor or inspector who has no axe to grind, no doctrine to preach, no paradox to propound. But in his own philosophical work, both written and oral, he has repeatedly shown how well he knows the value of the clash of doctrine against doctrine; how well he knows, in fact, that Wittgenstein's opposition to the idea that there are opinions or

B

theses or doctrines in philosophy was itself a paradoxical philosophical doctrine which fulfilled the characteristic functions of such doctrines in helping to convey by the saying of something false the truth of something that it did not say.

In a generation given to what has been called 'linguistic philosophy' Wisdom has been aware both of the dangers of the idea that philosophical questions are verbal questions and more generally of the inadequacies of words for some of the purposes we obsessively call upon them to fulfil. I have tried in my contribution to this collection to clarify and extend his insight that we may see and convey how things are even where there is no form of words available to us, and no form of words that *could* be available to us, that would express a true proposition to the effect that things are thus and so. My essay barely mentions his name and quotes few of his words, but he will see how much of it is due to him and also (with the generosity that has prompted him to acknowledge and exaggerate his debt to Wittgenstein) that some of it does not come from him. That essay and this book are offered to him on behalf of all who have learned from him to combine a recognition of the value of the thought of others with the necessity of thinking thoughts of their own.

RENFORD BAMBROUGH.

THE PHILOSOPHY OF JOHN WISDOM

D. A. T. GASKING

IN THESE two books* are collected some of the most important and exciting papers published in the last twenty years. Every philosopher should have them in his shelves, and few could fail to profit by an occasional rereading of them. *Other Minds* contains the eight papers under that title from *Mind*, 1940–1946, with four related papers. Its main theme is what Wisdom once described as the 'worst of all' (99)[1] philosophical problems, that of the relation between psychological and behavioural sentences. It also has important things to say on the nature of scientific theories, explanation, analogy, induction, knowledge and the nature of philosophy. *Philosophy and Psycho-Analysis* contains Wisdom's other papers from 1934 on. It has discussions of knowledge, logical analysis, the verification principle, mathematics, and the similarities between philosophy and psycho-analysis. But the main theme is perhaps: 'What is a philosophical question?'

Other Minds is well worth reading (or rereading) in order to find out (or remind oneself) what it is like to try to grapple really thoroughly with one problem. From the two books together one can, I think, learn two main things. First, one can learn a lot about the nature of philosophical issues, and how they differ from other sorts of issues. Secondly, the books constitute an excellent (if somewhat unsystematic) compendium of what is sometimes called 'the logic of language' to distinguish it from formal logic (whether Aristotelian or Russellian). From the detailed contrasting of philosophical with other questions one can learn a lot of 'logic' in that sense of the word in which Wisdom writes: '. . . the logic of the soul, that is . . . the way questions about the soul are settled'

**Other Minds.* By John Wisdom, 1952. Basil Blackwell, Oxford.
**Philosophy and Psycho-Analysis.* By John Wisdom, 1953. Basil Blackwell, Oxford.
[1] Numbers in parentheses, e.g. '(99)', are page references to *Philosophy and Psycho-Analysis*. Numbers prefixed by 'M', e.g. '(M170)', are page references to *Other Minds*.

(278). Many use the techniques of 'logical analysis', though few so skilfully as Wisdom. But Wisdom is unrivalled at letting you behind the scenes in the philosophical workshop.

But Wisdom's remarks on any one point are liable to be scattered through several papers, and his conversational style and use of dialogue, although it has considerable virtue, also tends to have the corresponding defect of making it hard to grasp the main outlines of what he wants to say. I shall therefore try to summarize what I take to be some of the main points he makes.

(1) *Empirical questions, questions of strict logic, conflict questions, and paradoxical questions*

(*a*) A typical empirical or 'betting' issue would be the dispute 'Is this inflammable?' where you say No and I say Yes, and where we both agree that the way to settle it would be to put a match to it and watch what happens, and where we moreover both agree, concerning every imaginable outcome of the experiment, in whose favour that outcome would settle the matter.

(*b*) Besides using 'logic' in the wide sense, as in 'the logic of the soul', Wisdom very often uses the word in a much narrower sense, which I shall distinguish as 'strict logic'. An issue is one of 'strict logic' if it can be definitely settled by showing that there is a generally accepted and fixed usage of some expression (M26). It is, for instance, a point of strict logic that ' "$326 \times 3 = 988$" is not a rule' (115). For it is correct usage to say that '$326 \times 3 = 988$"is false, and it is not correct usage to call a 'rule' that which one could properly describe as true or as false. Or again (M139) 'It is nowadays logically impossible for both a standard-bred trotter and his parents to fail to trot a mile in two minutes thirty seconds. But this wasn't always so. This bit of logic was made quite recently in America. For a standard-bred trotter was defined as a horse 'with a record of 2.30 or less or whose parents have a record of 2.30 or less" '. It is a point of strict logic that if this bursts into flames and rapidly burns to a fine ash after a match is put to it then it is imflammable.

(*c*) Questions of the two previous sorts are straightforward; they have in principle a definite yes-or-no answer. Conflict questions do not. They call for a decision, rather than the finding of the right answer, since, although in some respects they resemble questions of strict logic, there is no settled linguistic convention to decide the answer (M26). Wisdom gives as an example (95): 'If when a dog attacks her, a cow keeps her horns always towards him, so that she rotates as fast as he revolves, does he go round her?' Here, when we have rehearsed all the considerations in favour of the answer Yes, and all those in favour of No, we are in the position of a judge who, having heard opposing counsel state their cases on a tricky point of law on which there is no clear precedent, has to make the law. There is no settled linguistic convention governing this case. Some would hesitatingly say Yes, some give a doubtful No, and most would not feel that they could give either answer. So if we insist on giving an answer to the question we must make a convention for ourselves. And if someone decides on a different answer—prefers to adopt a different convention—we cannot say that in strict logic he is wrong. Compare 'Can one keep a promise unintentionally?' (M33).

(d) Sometimes a person asks a question which, regarded as a question of strict logic, has a definite and pretty obvious answer. The questioner knows this answer perfectly well and in spite of this persists in asking the question. And sometimes to such a question an answer is given which, in strict logic, is false. The speaker knows this perfectly well but nevertheless persists with his statement. He gives a paradoxical answer to a paradoxical question. For instance, the word 'mad' correctly applies only to people who think, feel and behave in certain rather uncommon ways: it would be a misuse of this word to apply it to people whose ways of thinking, feeling and behaving were like yours or mine. That is, as a matter of strict logic it is false that we are all mad. But one who knows this perfectly well may nevertheless say 'Aren't we all mad, really?' (M27 ff.). Such a person is 'suggesting a logical reform'. He 'wishes to draw the line less sharply between the mad and the sane'. Philosophers' remarks of this sort are (41): 'We can never know the causes of our sensations', 'Inductive conclusions are never really justified', 'The laws of mathematics are really rules of grammar', Such remarks are tantamount to suggestions such as: 'Let us agree to apply the word "mad" also to people who behave like you or me', 'Let us use "rule of grammar" in such a wide sense that it shall apply to laws of mathematics as well as to what is to be found in grammar-books'. The maker of such a remark may be unaware, or not clearly aware, that this is what his remark comes to. To that extent he may be confused.

Moreover, if his notational reforms were adopted something would be lost. There is a difference between those ordinarily called 'mad' and those ordinarily called 'sane', and one between laws of mathematics and what one ordinarily calls 'rules of grammar'. These differences our unreformed language records by having pairs of contrasting expressions. If we adopted this new way of talking we should have only one expression, 'mad', to cover both those inside mental hospitals and those outside, and one expression, 'rules of grammar', for both the contents of a Spanish Grammar and those of Hardy's *Pure Mathematics*. And this would tend to make us lose sight of the differences. But the suggested reforms would have merits too. They are also 'symptoms of linguistic penetration' (41). For there are similarities and continuities, which such paradoxical remarks bring out, between the mad and the sane and between grammar rules and mathematical laws.

Questions of strict logic, conflict questions, and paradoxical questions have something in common that distinguishes them from empirical ones. They could all be called *a priori* (cf. M20; 148) for they are either requests to be told what the existing linguistic convention is, or requests for one to be made where it does not exist, or concealed suggestions for a change in the convention. Conflict questions and paradoxical questions have something in common which distinguishes them from the straightforward empirical questions and questions of strict logic. They could both be called 'puzzle questions'. They are requests or suggestions for the making of a new convention, either to replace an existing one or to fill in a gap.

(2) *The interpenetration of different types of issue*

The different types of question are not always in practice sharply cut off from each other. There can be questions on the borderline between two types and debates centring round a single interrogative sentence, and so ostensibly about a single issue, where in fact issues of different types are mixed up together.

(*a*) The question 'Is S P?' is clearly one of strict logic if there is a settled linguistic convention, if there is an established and definite custom of calling something 'P' in virtue of its possessing the characteristic of being an S. If such a custom is entirely lacking the question is clearly a conflict question. But the definiteness of the custom is a matter of degree. It may be more or less universally followed with less or more hestitation. So between the two clear-cut cases there is a range of intermediate cases. 'The more indefinite custom is, the less is the question a matter of logic and the more it calls for a decision' (M26).

(b) If you and I are debating a question in relation to which certain possible tests or observations have not yet been made, we may be disagreeing in either or both of two different ways. We may have different expectations about the outcome of the yet unmade tests. Or the difference between us may be that I say that if the outcome of the tests were to be such and such that would make it proper to answer our question by saying 'so and so', whereas you deny this and say that if the outcome were as envisaged it would then be proper to say something different. If the difference between us is of the former sort only, our dispute is purely empirical. If our difference is only of the second sort it is purely *a priori*, perhaps one of strict logic, perhaps a conflict case, or perhaps intermediate in character. But in a given dispute we may differ in both these ways at once. And then the debate will be partly empirical, partly *a priori*. 'When one doctor disputes with another as to whether a child who coughs and vomits but doesn't whoop has whooping cough, the source of the dispute is largely a matter of whether one should, in view of the absence of a whoop, speak of whooping cough, This is an *a priori* issue. But that there is this *a priori* difference . . . is obscured by the fact that the dispute probably also *in part* arises from different expectations as to the course the illness will take and how it will respond to this treatment or that . . . (and) by the fact that . . . 'It is whooping cough', 'It isn't', always can at any stage in the dispute be used to express an empirical dispute, since it is quite true that there always remains some uncarried out test, with the consequence that it is always possible to pretend that it was an empirical issue one had in mind in raising the question' (M25).

Or take, for instance, a debate on the question: 'Can one ever know what is going on in the mind of another in the same sort of way that one knows what is going on in one's own mind?' For part of the time at least in such a debate the discussion may be on whether certain imaginable phenomena, of a sort we should probably call 'telepathic', occur or not, e.g. 'Does it ever happen that Smith by feelings like his normal feelings of jealousy, anger, pain and so on can tell whether or not Jones is having feelings of jealousy, anger and pain?' I may think that one day one might actually come across cases of this sort; you may have no such expectations. This might be the only difference between us, and we might agree that if such phenomena were to be encountered they would prove that the answer to our question was Yes and that if they never happened the answer would be No. If so, our difference would be purely empirical. On the other hand we might agree in expecting or in not expecting ever to find such phenomena, but disagree in that you thought that such phenomena, if they occurred, would prove that the answer was Yes, whereas I thought they would not prove this. If so, our dispute would be purely *a priori*. But in any actual debate we might easily discover that our differences were of both sorts, e.g. You might expect the phenomena but think that they didn't prove the case: I might not expect the phenomena but think that if they were to occur they would prove the case.

The course of such a debate can sometimes be described by saying that the question was at first an empirical one and later turned into an *a priori* one. For a person may start by contending that the answer is No, offering as his reason that the phenomena in question do not occur. If so, it looks as though he is assuming as an *a priori* truth that the occurrence of the phenomena would make it proper to answer Yes, so that the only issue is the empirical one 'Do the phenomena occur or not?' But later, after the alleged phenomena have been carefully described and their bearing on the question critically examined, and especially if it has been meanwhile established that such phenomena do occur, he may still defend the answer No, but now give the *a priori* reason that such phenomena, even if they occur, would not prove the case. Here one is inclined to say that he has shifted his ground. At first he defended the empirical thesis that such phenomena do not occur; now he defends the *a priori* thesis that such phenomena do not make Yes the proper answer. The question under debate has changed from empirical to *a priori*. At first the question meant: 'Assuming that such phenomena would prove the case, do they occur?', and later it came to mean: 'Would any imaginable phenomena prove the case?' But there may, in a given case, also be grounds for saying that, even though he gives reasons in the way described, he has not really changed his ground; that all along he meant the question in the second way. Perhaps he expressed himself carelessly or maybe he wasn't quite clear himself as to what he did mean. In a given case we may be asking a conflict-question if we ask: 'Did he change his ground, or did he all along really mean the same thing, even though perhaps obscurely at first?' (on all this see M126–129).

(c) The man who makes a paradoxical remark like 'Aren't we all mad, really?' is making a notational recommendation. His remark is *a priori* not empirical. But he may (or may not) be prompted to suggest this new way of talking by empirical considerations. He may for instance expect to find more similarities and continuities between the mad and the sane than most people expect to find, and feel that these similarities and continuities he expects to find would make his way of talking an appropriate one. And, indeed, if his expectations are right and those of the rest of us are wrong, his new way of talking would be less inappropriate than if his expectations were wrong and ours right (cf. M29).

Moreover, our actual standard linguistic conventions—the laws of strict logic—are not in every way independent of what the world is like, what sorts of things there are and how they resemble and differ from each other. But the connection is a loose one. Empirical considerations may make it desirable for us to have one standard convention for the use of certain expressions rather than a different standard convention, if we are to have a system of language which is an efficient instrument with which to describe the world. But the nature of things does not force us to have one possible standard convention rather than another, except in the sense that natural selection will see to it that those with the most efficient instrument of communication will survive. A convention is a convention: it might be silly, but it could not properly be described as false or as incorrect. 'There are no doubt some cows which are more like horses than others but upon the whole the animals which we actually come across fall very definitely under one or other of the animal names in our vocabulary and the law 'If it's a cow it can't be a horse' serves us well. But if Nature were to begin to produce beasts as much like cows as horses, as much like dogs as cats, our language would begin to break down again and again and the law 'If it's a cow it can't be a horse', though it would not become false, would become as much a menace as a help' (277 n.).

(3) *Changing views on the nature of philosophy*

Twice in the last half-century or so a new conception of the nature of philosophical problems has come into vogue in advanced circles. Once upon a time (stage one) philosophical problems were thought to be of essentially the same nature as scientific ones, only perhaps more general. (It was not, I think, that people had clearly in mind the distinction between the different types of question explained in section (1), and thought that philosophical questions were best classified along with scientific ones under the heading 'empirical'. It was rather that they had not clearly grasped that there are these different types of question, and so, having only one heading for classification, naturally put into it philosophical problems alongside scientific ones.) Then (stage two) about the beginning of this century, when the distinction between empirical questions and those of strict logic became fully clear, a new conception came in. Philosophical problems came to be regarded as not empirical, like scientific ones, but questions of strict logic. 'As science grew and people saw better how it is based on observation and experiment there grew a suspicion of anyone who professed to have obtained new factual information by anything but empirical methods. There were sneers at the philosophers. . . . To this situation came Moore and Russell . . . they revolutionised philosophy for many of us by reinterpreting the philosophers' "What is an X?" as a request for logical analysis' (59).

The key notion in this era was that of a logical construction. Wisdom explains it thus: 'One of the best ways of saying that a material thing is a logical construction out of its appearances . . . sense-data . . . or what not, is to say that a material thing is to these as the average plumber to plumbers, as a nation to its nationals, as energy to its manifestations, as the representative firm to firms, and *not* as a political representative to those he represents, not as an original to its copies, not as a mechanism beneath a bonnet to its manifestations, not as a sheep to shadows in the grass' (233). This was an advance. 'When Russell said that the realities we speak of are not guessed at from appearances but are logical constructions out of them and therefore follow deductively from them he substituted for an old and muddling model of the connection between realities and appearances a new model' (205). Statements about logical constructions purport to be ones of strict logic. For it is a point of strict logic that 'The height of the average plumber is 5 ft. 6 in.' follows deductively from and entails 'The sum of the heights of all plumbers divided by their number equals 5 ft. 6 in.' And the problem of e.g. material objects was supposed to be that of finding a similar statement of strict logic, connecting e.g. 'There is cheese here' with some complicated statement about sense-data, in the way that the statement about the average plumber is connected with a statement about plumbers. The latter statement was then to be called the 'logical analysis' of the former.

It was an optimistic movement, convinced that it had finally got the key conception which was to solve all philosophical problems, and Wisdom himself, in the early days, participated fully in it. 'Mounted on logical constructions philosophers of the 'twenties were able to cut exhilarating but confusing capers round about their less up-to-date contemporaries. Logical constructions enabled philosophers to ride down the dragons of mythology, to come up with the elusive "beings for thought". No wonder they asked "What price now they'll catch the creatures of noumenal, supersensible world of matter, mind, value, and necessity?" ' (205). Wisdom's series of *Mind* articles on 'Logical Constructions' are not reprinted. But the first two papers reprinted in *Philosophy and Psycho-Analysis* belong roughly to this period. 'To philosophize is to analyze', he there (3) roundly says. 'The philosopher's statement is verbal.'

Then (stage three) in the 'thirties another conception of the nature of philosophical problems came in, different from either of the previous ones, although the conception of stage two was a perhaps indispensable half-way house on the way to the third conception. This new idea was largely due to Wittgenstein, under whom Wisdom studied, and by whom he was converted. The papers on 'Philosophical Perplexity' and 'Metaphysics and Verification' are the first publications of the new convert, and in them Wisdom tries to expound the new view and to argue against the notion of philosophy as strict logic which he previously had. The same is true of 'Philosophy, Anxiety and Novelty', perhaps the best short summary of Wisdom's whole position.

According to this third conception of philosophy philosophical remarks are neither empirical nor ones of strict logic but either (*a*) the answers to conflict questions or (*b*) paradoxical answers to paradoxical questions. Presumably these days, too, they may be remarks designed to elucidate the paradoxical or conflict character of questions.

(*a*) Wisdom had previously said, firmly, 'The philosopher's statement is verbal' (3) as if this were a truth of strict logic. In 'Philosophical Perplexity' he now regards the question 'Are they verbal or not?' as a conflict-question like 'Did the dog go round the cow?' Accordingly he starts his paper with 'Philosophical statements are really verbal' (36), and then starts the second section of the paper with: 'I have said that philosophers' questions and theories are really verbal. But if you like we will not say this or we will say also the contradictory.' In his next article Wisdom considers the question: 'Given such a sentence as "There is cheese here" does this mean the same as any string of sentences about what we should see if we looked, smell if we sniffed, etc.? Is there any sensation-sentence which means the same, expresses the same proposition as, stands for the same fact as the cheese-sentence?' Of this question he says that the proper answer is: 'You are not asking anything about cheeses [i.e. not an empirical question][1] . . . what is more, you are not asking what would be said here nor what the language experts would say [i.e. not a question of strict logic]. What you are asking for is a decision and the reasons for it *in the sense in which reasons can be offered for a decision*—by counsel for the plaintiff and counsel for the defendant' (97).

(*b*) A paradoxical question is one the answer to which, if it is regarded as a question of strict logic, is obvious and known to the questioner, who in asking it is not therefore requesting information on a point of strict logic. Answers to such questions will be from the point of view of strict logic either obvious falsehoods or obvious truisms.

'We are all mad really' is an example of such a strict-logical falsehood, whose point has already been explained. Examples of philosophical remarks that have this character are: 'A proposition is a sentence' (39); 'The laws of mathematics and logic are really rules of grammar' (48). Since in fact the word 'proposition' is not synonymous with 'sentence', and we would violate an established linguistic usage if we called '$326 \times 3 = 988$' a rule 'of grammar' we may if we like call these remarks 'certainly false'. And yet 'to leave one's criticism at that is to attend to the letter and not the spirit of the theory criticised'. Such a procedure would be 'legalistic' (116). For it would miss the point of such a remark, which is not to put forward the false thesis of strict logic but, by

[1] Square brackets indicate my interpolations.

suggesting a reform of language, to underline continuities and similarities that ordinary language conceals. Such a remark may thus be 'metaphysically' illuminating in drawing attention to what is ordinarily overlooked. For instance the strict-logical falsehood about laws of mathematics and logic has the merit of drawing attention to '(1) an unlikeness and (2) a likeness concealed by ordinary language; (1) an unlikeness to the laws of hydraulics and an unlikeness in this unlikeness to the unlikeness between the laws of hydraulics and those of aeronautics; for it is an unlikeness not of subject-matter but of manner of functioning—and (2) a likeness but not an exact likeness to the functioning of rules.'

An answer which, from the point of view of strict logic, is a truism does not have this sort of merit. It may, in certain contexts, do good. When said in opposition to a paradoxical remark it may serve as a timely reminder that such a remark is, after all, a strict-logical falsehood. 'It stops over glibness, it forces us to realize that "there's more to it than that" ' (116), But often remarks that are, from the point of view of strict logic, impeccable may be 'metaphysically' useless or misleading. This is especially likely to be so if the answer is 'made to measure' (50) as an answer to the question. Consider for instance: 'Propositions about numbers, universals or propositions are about what is objective, real and possible, but non-sensible, neither subjective nor palpable and spatial. These objects do not exist but they subsist'. About this Wisdom remarks (84): 'These theories are perfectly correct. They could not be otherwise since they proceed along the lines: The peculiarity of facts about classes, numbers, propositions and characteristics is that they are about *subsistent entities*. What are subsistent entities? Well, they are not chairs and tables. Indeed they are not known by the senses but by the intellect. Characteristics, for example, are subsistent entities, so are propositions, numbers and classes.' To give another example of something 'made to measure', which cannot therefore be faulted in strict logic: 'Suppose the word "sense-datum" has never been used before and that someone says "When Jones sees a rabbit, has an illusion of a rabbit, has an hallucination of a rabbit, dreams of a rabbit, he has a sense-datum of a rabbit". One cannot protest that this is false, since no statement has been made, only a recommendation' (39).

Such made-to-measure answers to questions are often misleading or useless. The 'sense-datum' recommendation is misleading for it 'is liable to suggest that sense-data are a special sort of thing, *extremely* thin coloured pictures, and thus liable to raise puzzles, such as "How are sense-data related to material things"?' (40). And one who, philosophically puzzled about the nature of propositions, numbers, and characteristics, has his question answered by 'They are subsistent entities' is unlikely to be illuminated thereby. For he might well reply: 'All right, then, let me put the question I wanted to ask in different words: What I wanted to know was, what is the nature of subsistent entities?' When one comes to see the general nature of a philosophical statement 'the question "Is it true or not?" vanishes into insignificance . . .' (52). For an obvious falsehood in strict logic may be illuminating and a truism of strict logic may be useless or misleading.

(4) *Style and stuff*

The above account of Wisdom's view of the nature of philosophical statements needs expanding. According to him, philosophical statements are answers to what I have called puzzle questions, that is to paradoxical and conflict questions. But not all answers to puzzle questions are philosophical. How do answers to philosophical puzzle questions differ from answers to ordinary puzzle questions?

Every answer to a puzzle question underlines similarities or differences. But answers to ordinary puzzle questions underline similarities or differences between sorts of thing, person or happening, whereas philosophical answers underline similarities or differences between 'manners in which sentences work'. Thus 'We are all mad, really' emphasises the similarity and continuity between the mad and the sane. And 'The dog did not go round the cow' emphasises the difference between what happened when the dog attacked the cow and other happenings, such as a dog's tracing a circular path about an immobile cow. On the other hand 'Laws of mathematics are really rules of grammar' emphasises a likeness between the manner in which mathematical sentences work and the manner in which rules of grammar work. 'Material things are reducible to sense-data' emphasises the connection between the manner of working of sentences like 'There is cheese here' and the manner of working of sentences reporting how things look, smell, sound, etc., to the speaker at the moment of speaking.

A statement about the mad differs from one about the sane in subject-matter. Similarly a statement about one sort of happening, such as a dog circling a rotating cow, differs in subject-matter from a statement about another sort of happening, such as an explosion, or the circling of a stationary cow. Statements can resemble each other in respect of the similarities of their subject-matter; differ in respect of the unlikeness of their subject-matters. But there is not this sort of similarity and/or difference between mathematical statements and rules, or between thing-statements and sensation-statements. The likeness or difference here 'is not one of subject-matter (stuff) but of a different manner of use (style)' (46). Wisdom has various phrases to express this notion of a difference in 'style'. Thus he sometimes speaks of a difference in the 'manner in which sentences work' (38), sometimes of a difference in 'the manner in which sentences are used' (50). He also describes it as a difference in 'style of functioning' and as a 'difference in general nature' (53). So we could put it: answers to ordinary puzzle questions under-line differences and similarities between different subject-matters of sentences; answers to philosophical questions underline differences and similarities between different styles of functioning of sentences.

Compare the statement that cancer is due to a germ with the statement that it is due to a chemical poison. These are statements of two different theories. But the two statements are of the same general nature—the sentences used in making them work in the same manner. For both are used to express the same sort of scientific theory, namely that sort of theory which causally explains some phenomenon by reference to something which could in principle be detected independently of the phenomenon to be explained. Next compare two remarks, both made in the words: 'The man sitting opposite me in the train yesterday was small and furtive, and there was a bulge in his coat-pocket'. The first remark made in these words is made by someone recounting something that had happened to him. The second is made by someone making up a story to entertain the company. The general nature of these two remarks is different; the sentence works in a different manner on the two occasions. In one case, we could say, it is used factually, in the other case fictionally.

In such a case as this, where the difference in 'style of functioning' is very striking, we are inclined at times, as Wisdom remarks (53) to use the words 'not really a statement' to underline the difference. People are apt to say that 'fictional statements are not really statements', in order to emphasise the difference in style of functioning between sentences used in fictional narratives and those used in reminiscences. Similarly one is inclined to say of a sentence used poetically that it is 'not really a statement' or that ' "1+1=2" does not express a statement but registers a decision'. 'Now there are differences of this sort *within* the range of statements which are on most occasions unhesitatingly called statements and to which it is quite usual to apply the expressions true or false. When this is so, the differences in general nature are apt to be overlooked.' Thus the difference between mathematical statements and those like 'that is made of silver', and the difference between ethical statements and those like 'that is red' are differences in the style of functioning of the sentences, not differences in subject-matter. These statements differ from each other in the same *sort* of way (though not of course in the same way) that fictional statements differ from factual ones, and not in the sort of way that statements about horses differ from statements about cows.

People sometimes describe even the difference between factual and fictional statements as if it were a difference in subject-matter. Thus they may say: 'The difference is that the former are about real people and real happenings, whereas the latter are about imaginary people and imaginary happenings', as if the difference were like that between statements about sane people and statements about mad people. But this would be a most misleading way of describing the difference. And it would be misleading in just the same way, according to Wisdom, to say that the difference between mathematical statements and those like 'This is made of silver' was that the former are about numbers whereas the latter are about material things. It would be similarly misleading to describe the difference between statements like 'This is red' and ethical statements by saying that the former are about natural or physical qualities whereas the latter are about non-natural qualities, or about ethical qualities and relations, or about values.

The view Wisdom is opposing could be put: All statements, of whatever sort—material-object statements, sense-data or sensory statements, mathematical statements, ethical statements and so on —all such statements work in precisely the same 'statement-making' way. (They all attribute a predicate in the same sort of way to a subject.) They differ in being, respectively, about material objects, about sense-data or sensations, about numbers, and about non-natural qualities or values.

(5) Categories of being, translated into the formal mode

Philosophers who take the last-mentioned view would some-times elaborate it somewhat as follows: 'Material objects, sense-data, numbers, values and so on constitute the different categories of being. So the different sorts of statement, though they function in the same way, differ in respect of being about objects belonging to different categories of being. It is the philosopher's task to investigate these different categories of being and their inter-relations.'

This account of the philosopher's task is, in Wisdom's view, confused. But it is also, in a way, dead right. It is confused in so far as it carries the suggestion that different general types of statement differ in what they are *about*—one about objects of one category, another about objects of another—and in suggesting that one has to examine these 'objects' and their interrelations. It is dead right in that, according to Wisdom, the philosopher's job is to investigate the interrelations between different general types of statement—between the chief different manners in which sentences are used. And this is the same investigation that is confusedly thought of as an investigation of the categories of being. 'The point of philosophical statements . . .', says Wisdom (37), 'is the illumination of . . . the relations between different categories of being or (we must be in the mode) the relations between different sub-languages within a language.' 'The philosopher's intention is to bring out relations between categories of being, between spheres of language' (39). 'The philosopher's purpose is to gain a grasp of the relation between different categories of being, between expressions used in *different manners*' (42).

It was the obsession with the subject-matter idea, 'that is, the idea that all sentences in the indicative differ only in the way that sentences about dogs and cats or even wind and water differ' (118), that kept us for so long 'hanging about those impenetrable coverts where universals lurked, facts preyed upon events, and variables

C

with logical constants frolicked for ever down the rides of infinity' (117). But 'at last Wittgenstein gave tongue, and the quarry went away to the notes of "Don't ask for the meaning (analysis), ask for the use", and the transformations of the formal mode—transformations such as . . . "X in saying that S is P is asserting a proposition about mathematical entities" means "X is using the sentence 'S is P' mathematically"; "X in saying . . . there's a dagger in the air is asserting a material thing proposition" means "X is using the sentence . . . 'there's a dagger in the air' materially, i.e., objectively"; "X, in saying there's a dagger in the air, is asserting a proposition about a sense-datum merely" means "X is using 'there's a dagger in the air' subjectively"; "'S is P is an ethical proposition" means " 'S is P' is an ethical sentence", i.e. "The sentence 'S is P' is used ethically".' These new formulations 'leave us with the old questions, though wonderfully transformed.'

(6) *How to philosophize*

The philosopher's task today, then, is the same task as it has always been, namely what used to be described as that of 'getting a grasp of the relations between the different categories of being'. But nowadays we understand better what this task amounts to. We know that it is a matter of getting a grasp of the relations between the different manners in which sentences work. How can we set about trying to get this grasp?

We can try to describe in the fullest possible detail, point by point, what it is like for someone to use a sentence mathematically or ethically or generally. 'If we permit ourselves to imagine vividly the talkers and the occasions when sentences of the sorts in question are used and then describe the talkers by setting down a lot of that about them which makes us say that they are using sentences "generally", "ethically", etc., including all their purposes, and therefore purposes other than preparing their hearers for tigers or no cake, and all their ways of supporting their sentences (not tied down by logic-book models) then we shall have descriptions of all talkers which, though very long and still incomplete, involve nothing but talk, nods, smiles and surprises' (118).

For example, the long story descriptive of the difference between Smith who uses the sentence 'There's a dagger in the air' objectively, and Jones who uses it subjectively, would include such things as: Smith would be prepared to support his statement by reference to other people's reports of what they see, and by his experience prior and subsequent to the moment of speaking; would regard lack of confirmation by other people's reports and certain possible subsequent experiences of his as telling against the truth of what he says. Jones would not be prepared to support his statement in these ways, nor would he count as telling against his statement the things that Smith would count as telling against his. Smith would understand, even if he disputed, the suggestion that he might be mistaken. Jones would not. And so on. (On this see M42-44, also M149-157.) And a full description of mathematical talkers would mention the way children are taught to recite by heart 'One, two, three, four, five, six . . . etc.', and are taught to use this recitation in counting and measuring. It would include a description of the learning of multiplication and addition tables, and of how remarks like 'five and seven is twelve' fit into the carrying out of such activities as making change, working out how many screws will be needed for a certain carpentry job and so on. This would be only the beginning of a very long story.

The trouble with this sort of thing is that we tend to lose ourselves in the mass of detail, and fail to see the wood for the trees. 'The detailed description,' says Wisdom (117), 'doesn't give us *grasp*.' But no single short statement in general terms will adequately give the place of a general type of statement on the language-map. A correct short answer won't do the trick. 'The only *correct* answer to a metaphysical question "What is an X?" is "An X" ' (M53). And that's not much use.

Alternatively we might try uttering metaphysical paradoxes— statements false in strict logic, but illuminating in that they show the familiar in a new light, bring out connections hidden by ordinary language. But 'metaphysical paradoxes, such as "Ethical discussion is propaganda", "Reflective thought is thought about words", are dangerous and need to be balanced by the reassertion of the old truths in their opposites' (263). So 'we may try opposite falsehoods or we may say, "Be careful that this expression . . . does not suggest certain analogies at the expense of others. . . . Do notice how like to . . . etc., and yet, etc." ' (50).

Up to a point this description fits Wisdom's procedure in dealing with specific philosophical problems. He does set alongside each other the opposing falsehoods and the corresponding truisms. He does try to bring out what it is that tempts people into the falsehoods, and thereby shows those resemblances and connections between ways of speaking that, ordinarily concealed, are brought by them into the open. He does this, not for one falsehood about a particular matter, but for many different falsehoods. He also warns us that falsehoods are falsehoods, and warns us against being misled by some of the analogies they suggest. And in the course of explaining what can be said in favour of and against the different views he does, incidentally, give a lot of the detailed point by point description of talkers.

But this description still misses a most important feature of philosophical problems, and of Wisdom's way of dealing with them. People *worry* about philosophical problems. They are harassed by logical conflicts in ways that have some resemblance to the ways in which neurotics are harassed by emotional conflicts. Typically a person in the grip of a philosophical puzzle feels that 'unquestionable premisses have led by unquestionable steps to an entirely questionable conclusion. In these cases the difficulty is not removed by doing any of the three things to be done, namely (1) deny the premiss, (2) protest at a step, (3) accept the conclusion. For, whichever one does, the repressed objectionableness of it leaves a haunting anxiety which in the end leads to rebellion in oneself or others' (132). And, according to Wisdom, the proper way to deal with philosophical worry is to use a technique that has some analogy to the psycho-analytic technique for dealing with emotional conflicts. 'The whole difficulty arises like difficulty in a neurotic; the forces are conflicting but nearly equal. The philosopher remains in a state of confused tension unless he makes the effort necessary to bring them all out by speaking of them and to make them fight it out by speaking of them together. It isn't that people can't resolve philosophical difficulties but that they won't. In philosophy it isn't a matter of making sure that one has got hold of the right theory but of making sure that one has got hold of them all. Like psycho-analysis it is not a matter of selecting from all our inclinations some which are right, but of bringing them all to light . . .' (M115n). In the concluding part of this article something will be said about the sources, according to Wisdom, of philosophical worry.

(7) '*Metaphysical double-vision*'
Wisdom is concerned to emphasize the complexity of philos-

ophy, and to bring out how two puzzles, however similar they are, are never exactly similar, and require slightly different treatment. But he is also concerned to generalize about philosophical problems —to discover and describe those features which are common to large groups of important puzzles. There is one large group of different puzzles that have this in common, that they all give rise to a 'feeling of taking the same reality twice over', to a 'feeling of superfluous entities', to a 'feeling of metaphysical double-vision' (92). In an early paper he refers to it as the 'Reduplication Paradox—*the* kind of paradox in analytic philosophy' (27). How does this metaphysical double-vision arise?

(*a*) We often know one fact (which for the present I shall call the 'supported fact') on the basis of our knowledge of some other fact or set of facts (which I shall call our 'basis' or the 'supporting fact'). Thus we may know that the petrol-tank is empty on the basis that the petrol-indicator has pointed to zero for the last mile or so and the car has now coughed to a stop. We may know that a woman is incapable of prolonged or strenuous exertion on the basis that her complexion is pale, her limbs thin, and so on. And we may know that Smith is angry on the basis that he has just been insulted, his face flushes and his voice trembles.

But the relation of supporting to supported fact is not always the same. Three cases need to be distinguished.

(*b*) Sometimes we can come to know the supported fact not only on the basis of the supporting fact or facts, but also directly. For our knowledge that the petrol-tank is empty we do not have to rely solely on the petrol gauge and so on: we can cut the petrol-tank open and look inside. And for our knowledge that Jane is incapable of prolonged or strenuous exertion we do not have to rely solely on her physical appearance; we can watch her as she tries to tackle the week's washing. In such cases we know that the supporting fact does provide a good basis for the fact supported because facts of the two sorts have both been independently observed, and because such observation has shown that whenever a fact of the supporting kind occurs there is always a corresponding fact of the supported kind. A zero-pointing petrol-indicator provides a good basis for our judgment that the tank is now empty because whenever the pointer is observed at zero we can independently observe, by looking into it, that the tank is empty. A certain physical appearance is a good basis for the judgment that

Jane is incapable of prolonged or strenuous exertion (if it is) only because whenever we can observe such an appearance in a person we can independently observe a failure to be strenuous for long. Supporting facts that are related in this way to the facts they support could be described as 'signs' of them, or as providing an 'inductive basis' for them.

(c) But in a number of cases we seem to have to say that we can know supported facts of certain sorts only on the basis of supporting facts: that there is in such cases nothing at all corresponding to looking into the petrol-tank itself or watching Jane at the wash-tub, which we could call 'directly observing the supported fact itself'. Thus we seem to know that Smith is angry only on the basis of such facts as that he has been insulted, goes red in the face, swears, and so on. There seems to be nothing we could call 'observing Smith's anger in itself', like looking into the tank, but only observing the situation he is in, and observing his bodily behaviour and responses, including what words and other sounds are produced by his mouth and larynx. And yet Smith's feeling of *anger* seems to be something other than these. To distinguish such cases it will be convenient to refer to supporting facts which have this sort of relation to the facts supported as 'manifestations' of them, rather than as 'signs' or 'inductive bases' for them.

(d) There is a third sort of relation between supporting and supported facts which could best be described by saying that the former provide a 'deductive basis' for the latter. For instance I may know that one man went upstairs and come to know that another man went upstairs, and on the basis of this knowledge know that two men went upstairs. I may know that there are five men on a certain committee, aged 67, 72, 62, 59, and 40. On the basis of these facts I know that the average age of a member of that committee is 60. In one respect the relation of such bases to the facts supported resembles the relation between manifestations and the facts manifested. For here, too, there is no such thing as a direct observational check of the facts supported. Having read the petrol-indicator I can look in the tank and see if the reading is true. But having observed Smith's situation and behaviour I cannot look into his mind and see if those bodily indications are true. And here, too, having found out the ages of the committee members and done my sum there is no such thing as locating the average committee-member and asking him his age, thereby checking the reliability of my indirect evidence for it.

But in another respect a deductive basis differs from a manifestation. The facts manifested are further facts, or so it seems, over and above the facts which manifest them, Smith's anger is a further fact over and above the fact that he was insulted, flushes and swears. But we should hardly say that besides the fact that one man went upstairs and then another man did there was a further fact, over and above this, that two men went upstairs. On the contrary, we should be inclined to say that in saying 'two men went upstairs' we were just restating the fact that we had already stated in saying that one man went up and another man did. We do not have a further fact supported by our deductive basis, but a 'redescription' of the facts which provide the basis. Similarly the fact that the average age of the committee is 60 could hardly be said to be a further fact, over and above the facts that are our basis for it. Here, too, we have a redescription. We could, for instance, very naturally express the relation by saying: 'The five committee members were aged 67, 72, 62, 59 and 40, respectively. *In other words* the average age was 60'.

The facts supported by a deductive basis, then, are not further facts, over and above the supporting facts.[1]

(e) There is a number of different classes of fact which we know, or so at least it can plausibly be argued, on the basis of manifestations. Other minds we know only through such manifestations as bodily behaviour. We know about material objects, it seems, only on the basis of our sensations—by how things look, feel, sound, taste and smell to us. We know about past events only on the basis of such present manifestations as memories, reports of others and physical traces such as diary entries, documents, footprints and ruins. We know what will happen in the future and know the truth of omnitemporal laws only on the basis of present and past facts and past regularities.

In two other cases we are inclined to say the same sort of thing.

---

[1] Some may protest against the examples I have chosen, saying that here the supported fact is a further fact over and above the supporting one. If so, I invite them to transfer these examples to section (e) below and substitute cases where they would not wish to speak of a further fact, e.g. perhaps they would not want to claim that 'No Prime Ministers are women' expresses a further fact over and above that expressed by 'No women are Prime Ministers'. Or is the fact that Smith has a wife a further fact over and above the fact that he is a married man?

How do we tell that something is beautiful? We see that it has certain attributes—balance, contrast, and the like—attributes not identical with beauty, but ones in respect of which a thing is beautiful. And we and others, especially art critics, have certain feelings when we look at it. It is only on the basis of these manifestations of beauty that we know a thing is beautiful. There is no such thing as 'looking at the beauty itself', apart from seeing these attributes and having these feelings. Similarly, how do we tell that a state of affairs, a person or an action is good? We can see that something is productive of happiness, is an instance of disinterested inquiry or of fortitude in adversity and so on. And we and others feel approval. And surely it is only on the basis of such things that we call something good. There hardly seems to be, though some would claim there is, something we could call 'observing the quality of goodness itself'—a quality distinct from disinterestedness, fortitude, conduciveness to happiness, and the like, and from feelings of approval.[1]

There are two other cases that seem somewhat less fundamental. Certain technical scientific phrases like 'electric current', 'invisible germ' and the like seem to refer to entities known only through their manifestations—such as glowing lights, deflected magnets, rashes and high body temperatures. And we speak of nations, such as England, France, Russia, but no one has ever seen nations as such. Our only bases for assertions about them are facts about Englishmen, Frenchmen and Russians.

Our list, to date, is as follows:

Facts known only through Manifestations

1. Other minds.   Behaviour, etc.
2. Material things.   Sensations.

---

[1] I am here only giving a rough and very general sketch of a number of tendencies of thought. If one were to try to give more detail one would have to note, for example, that: (a) Some have said that the goodness of something is manifested to us only through our having feelings of approval for it and have sometimes gone on to say that 'x is good' means 'x is approved' and the like; whereas others have thought that goodness was manifested in such characteristics as productiveness of happiness or disinterested enterprise. Similarly with beauty. (b) If one, e.g., starts by saying that other minds are manifested through bodily behaviour, i.e., through facts about material objects, and then also says facts of the latter sort are manifested only through sensations, past, present and future, and then also says that past and future are only known through present manifestations, one is led easily enough to think that all these different types of fact are known only through one's own sensation of the moment. Along this route some people have been pushed towards 'solipsism of the present moment'. But people sometimes say one sort of thing about one class of fact and refuse to say the same sort of thing about others.

3. Past events.	Present memories and traces.
4. Future events and laws.	Present and past facts and regularities.
5. Beauty.	Characteristics other than beauty itself, aesthetic feelings.
6. Goodness (ethical characteristics and relations generally).	Non-ethical facts and feelings of approval.
7. Electric currents, etc.	Deflected magnets, etc.
8. Nations.	Nationals.

(f) All these cases give rise to similar epistemological problems, or, if you like, to the same problem. The problem does not arise with inductive bases. For there we can establish that one fact is a good basis for another by establishing an empirical correlation between the two sorts of fact. We can observe facts of the first sort and also observe facts of the second sort, and so establish that whenever facts of the first sort are observed facts of the second sort can also and independently be observed. Nor does the problem arise in the case of deductive bases. For there, although there is no independent observing of the supported fact, that fact is not a further fact over and above the supporting facts we already know. But in the case of facts known through their manifestations (a) the supported fact is apparently a further fact over and above the known facts which manifest it; (b) since we cannot independently observe the supported fact we cannot establish any empirical correlation between the two sorts of fact, and so cannot in this way establish that the manifestations are a good basis for knowledge of the supported facts. The problem then arises: what right *have* we to say they do provide a good basis?

Impressed by such considerations we may be driven to the sceptical conclusion that we do not really know those facts which we are alleged to know through manifestations of them. If so, our argument will, in outline, be of the following pattern:

Premiss 1: The supported facts are further facts, over and above those facts which are alleged to provide us with a good basis for knowing them.

Premiss 2: But we cannot directly and independently observe facts of the supported kind.

Conclusion: Therefore, since we cannot establish an empirical correlation between facts of the supporting kind and

those of the supported kind, we have no right to regard
any fact of the supporting kind as providing us with a
good basis for knowledge of a fact of the supported kind.

(g) But such a sceptical conclusion, in the case of each of the
sorts of fact we have listed, seems quite absurd. We surely do
sometimes know about what is going on in someone else's mind.
We surely do know facts about material things, about past and
future events, about beauty and goodness, about electric currents
and nations. But if our argument was valid and the conclusion is
false, one at least of the premises must be false. For a false
conclusion cannot be validly deduced from true premises. Then
which premiss is false?

Perhaps the second premiss is false. Perhaps, after all, there is,
in these cases, some way of finding out directly and independently
of their manifestations that facts of the kind in question are the
case. Surely it must be, for after all we do know these facts. So
there must be a direct way of looking into someone else's mind,
some sort of special intuition or telepathy or empathy, whereby
we can tell what another is thinking or feeling without basing ourselves on his bodily behaviour. We must have some direct
intuitive way of knowing about material things other than the
normal way of knowing about them on the basis of our sensations.
There must be a direct retrocognition of the past and precognition
of the future, a special intuitive way of knowing directly the
presence of beauty and of ethical qualities and relations without
basing ourselves on the present, the non-aesthetic and non-ethical
manifestations of these. And so on. Only then could we be
justified in judging of such facts on the basis of their manifestations.
For we could then, with the help of our direct intuitions, establish
an empirical correlation between facts of the supporting kind and
those of the supported kind. And with this established the
supporting facts would constitute a good inductive basis for
knowing the facts supported.

(h) But these 'intuitionist' answers, involving mysterious
special ways of knowing, seem equally wrong. Perhaps, then, it is
the first premiss that is false. In fact, if the argument is valid and
scepticism and intuitionism are both false, the first premiss must
be false. So in these cases the supported facts cannot be further
facts over and above the supporting facts, and the latter must
provide a good deductive basis for the former. The supported

facts must be 'reducible to', 'analysable into', 'logical constructions out of' the supporting facts; must follow deductively from them. Just as for every statement about the average plumber one can give a complicated statement, meaning the same, about plumbers, so every statement about other minds can be translated into a complicated behaviour-statement, every statement about material things can be translated into some complicated sensation-statement, every statement about the past can be translated into some statement about the present, every law-statement and every statement about the future can be translated into a complicated statement about present facts and past regularities, every ethical statement means the same as some statement about approvals and non-ethical features. And so on.

But these 'phenomenalist' or 'reductionist' (in ethics commonly called 'naturalist') solutions seem just as unconvincing and objectionable as the sceptical and intuitionist ones. Surely 'Smith is angry' means something more than any statement, however complicated, on the lines: 'Smith has been insulted, he goes red in the face, his voice trembles, if you are rude to him again he will probably become abusive, and so on'. Obviously it won't do to say a chair *is* a set of sense-data, for one could sit on one but not on the other. But will any more sophisticated version of phenomenalism about material objects do any better? Is there any sensation-statement, however, complicated, that means the same as 'There is a chair'? Can one really say that 'I had an egg for breakfast' just means e.g. 'I now have a memory as of egg for breakfast and if you look in the dust-bin at home you'll find egg-shells, etc.'?

In all these cases we are in the typically worrying philosophical situation in which 'unquestionable premisses have led by unquestionable steps to an entirely questionable conclusion' (132); one where the 'conclusion is as shocking as the denial of the premisses which led to it' (M51). We are driven by the above dialectic from one paradox to another, and cannot rest content anywhere (cf. 255, M56, M58).

(i) In some of the cases, notably in the 'other minds' case, it looks as though there is another sort of solution. It looks as though one could say: 'The step from the supporting to the supported fact is neither deductive nor an ordinary inductive step (like that from petrol-indicator to tank-contents). But we can validly get from one sort of fact to the other, or at least to the probability of the other, by an argument by analogy'. The trouble with this is that just those very features of the situation which incline us to say that the supporting facts cannot be an inductive basis, also, when we come to look into it, make this 'argument by analogy' very different from those other arguments by analogy of whose cogency we are satisfied. 'Call it good evidence if you like, call it argument by analogy proving the existence of things it is beyond our senses to detect, but notice that it is uncommonly like those cases where we say "But it was found that here the analogy breaks down" ' (M66).

(j) There are certain other types or categories of fact which can give rise to puzzles that have some similarity to the puzzles about other minds, material objects, the past, and so on. For example, we sometimes know that a curtain is not red. But, we are inclined to say, when we look at the curtain we do not see the 'notredness', do not apprehend the negative fact about it. What we see is the curtain's blueness or greenness or whatever it is—some positive fact. Thus we are inclined to say that we know the negative fact on the basis (and only on the basis) of some positive fact. Similarly we do not, it seems fair to say, directly apprehend a general fact, such as 'All gases obey Boyle's Law', but come to know this on the basis of singular facts such as 'The mercury rose three millimetres'. And if we know some indeterminate fact like 'Smith is somewhere in the building' it is not through apprehending this indeterminate fact itself, but on the basis of knowing some determinate fact.

Then there is the case of logically necessary truths, such as those of formal logic and mathematics, and statements like 'The same surface cannot at the same time be both red and green all over'. Corresponding to each necessary statement there is a linguistic statement, e.g. corresponding to the necessary statement about red and green there is the linguistic statement 'In English the phrase "red and green all over at the same time" has no descriptive use'. Now there are 'intutionists' about logical necessity, who claim that these are statements about 'necessary connections' between 'universals', and claim to be able to 'see' these universals and their necessary connections by direct inspection, by a special intellectual and non-sensory sort of insight. And there are 'reductionists' about logical necessity who say they do not know what people are talking about when they speak of this intellectual insight. Seeing with the eyes and hearing with the ears they can understand. With their eyes and ears[1] they can observe the facts reported in the linguistic statements corresponding to the necessary statements, and in so doing are checking on the truth of the logically necessary statements which report no further facts over and above the linguistic facts, but are reducible to linguistic statements. Finally there are people who might be called 'sceptics about logical necessity', who claim that we can never know any logically necessary facts—that there are none to know.

'The metaphysically-minded person,' says Wisdom (92), 'feels that the world is made up solely of positive, specific, determinate, concrete, contingent, individual, sensory facts, and that the appearance of a penumbra of fictional, negative, general, indeterminate, abstract, necessary, super-individual, physical facts is somehow only an appearance due to lack of penetration upon our part. And he feels that there are not, in addition to the ways of knowing the non-penumbral facts, additional ways of knowing . . . the penumbral facts. At the same time the penumbral do not seem to be identical with the non-penumbral and thus *do* seem to call for extra ways of knowing.'

(*k*) We are concerned with different types of fact: physical facts, sensory facts, psychological facts, facts about the present, the past, the future, ethical and aesthetic facts, contingent and necessary facts, and so on. In traditional terminology we are concerned with facts about different categories of being. From Wisdom's point of view the different types of fact are not distinguished by what they are about, but by being expressed in sentences with different styles of functioning, different manners of use. So, to put it in other words, we are concerned with different categories of statement, i.e. statements expressed by sentences with different styles of functioning.

Between one physical fact and another (and perhaps between one psychological fact and another) inductive relations may hold, e.g. the petrol-indicator may be a good inductive basis for the empty tank. Between two facts of any one type deductive relations may hold; a physical fact an entail a physical, a sensory fact entail a sensory fact, an ethical fact entail an ethical one, and so on, e.g.

---

[1] Cf. Norman Malcolm, 'Are Necessary Propositions Really Verbal?', *Mind*, 1940, p. 195.

'this is scarlet' entails 'this is red'; 'this looks scarlet to me now' entails 'this looks red to me now', etc. But between facts of different types neither inductive nor deductive relations, it seems, hold. Strict logic applies within a category of facts; it does not apply to inferences from one category to another. And yet in some cases facts of one type are a good basis upon which we can know facts of another. If we study such relations between facts of different types 'not tied down by logic-book models' we could be described as studying logic in the wide sense.

In traditional terminology: deductive, and in the case of some categories inductive, relations hold between facts about objects belonging to one category of being and other facts about objects belonging to the same category of being. They do not hold between facts about objects belonging to different categories of being. But in some cases there are 'logical' relations, though not of the sort normally treated of in logic-books, between facts about objects of different categories of being. And it is the philosopher's task to study these relations between different categories of being.

Expressed in the 'formal mode': deductive, and in some cases inductive, relations may hold between statements expressed by sentences with the same style of functioning. They do not hold between statements expressed by sentences with different styles of functioning. But in some cases a statement expressed by a sentence with one style of functioning may support one expressed by a sentence with a different style of functioning, though neither deductively nor inductively. It is the philosopher's task to investigate the different styles of functioning of sentences and the ways one statement may support another, even though the sentences used in expressing them have different styles of functioning (cf. M106n).

(8) *Ratiocination in Philosophy*

'Grey, your faith in ratiocination is pathetic,' says White in *Other Minds* (M86). Wisdom holds that no controversial question in philosophy can ever be decided by a demonstrative argument.

(*a*) A deductive proof will never settle a controversial question in philosophy. For 'in the course of a good proof the level of certainty for the conclusion rises to that of the premises and the level of certainty of the falsity of the premises rises to the level of certainty of the falsity of the conclusion. When the level of the independent certainty of the premises is great and there is nothing against the conclusion, as in mathematical calculations, then we speak of proving the truth of the conclusion from the truth of the premises. When the independent certainty of the falsity of the conclusion is great, whereas the premises are weak, then we speak of the falsity of the conclusion proving the falsity of the premises. . . . Proof is like putting a pipe between two tubs of water' (130).

When we establish that r follows from p and q jointly two things happen. Any grounds we already independently have in favour of p and q then become for us also just as much grounds in favour of r. And any grounds we already independently have for rejecting r become for us also just as much grounds for rejecting either p or q or both. For if r is false the premises from which it is validly deducible cannot both be true: true premises cannot validly lead to a false conclusion.

There are two cases in which we would regard a demonstrative argument as a proof of something. (1) We start by having good grounds for asserting both p and q, but no ground for either asserting or denying r. When the deductive connection is established our grounds for asserting p and q are now seen to be just as much grounds for asserting r too. Before the deductive connection is established we have grounds in favour of p and q but no ground either way for r; after it is established we have grounds for asserting p, q and r. (2) We start by having good grounds for denying r, and no grounds for either asserting or denying either p or q. When the deductive connection is established our grounds for denying r are seen to be just as much grounds for denying the conjunction of p and q as well. Before the deductive connection is established we have grounds for denying r but no grounds either way for p and q; after it is established we have grounds for denying r and at least one of p and q.

But the typically puzzling philosophical case is one where 'unquestionable premises lead by unquestionable steps to an entirely questionable conclusion', i.e. where we have, independently of the argument, good grounds for accepting both p and q and also good grounds for *rejecting* r. So when the deductive connection is established our good grounds for accepting both p and q become for us also just as much good grounds for accepting r, a proposition which independently we have good grounds for rejecting. So before the connection is established we merely have good grounds for rejecting r; after it is established we both have good grounds for rejecting r and also good grounds for accepting r. Likewise when the connection is established the good grounds we independently had for rejecting r become for us just as much good grounds for rejecting one at least of p and q. Before the connection is established we merely have good grounds for accepting both p and q; after it is established we both have good grounds for accepting both p and q and also have good grounds for rejecting at least one of them.

Thus before being presented with the proof—before seeing that p and q together entail r—we are reasonably sure one way or the other about the truth or falsity of all three propositions. At least we are not, in respect of any one of them, pulled both ways by conflicting considerations. But after seeing the proof we see that in respect of all three propositions there are considerations pulling us both ways. We had hoped to settle our doubts about one proposition. Instead the logical conflict is intensified and extended to all three propositions.

This, however, is its philosophical merit. 'A demonstrative proof decides nothing. The old difficulties about the conclusion will be there still. And the better the proof the more they will reflect on the premises. But demonstrative proof is not therefore futile. It musters for us those things which tend to make us accept the conclusion and forces us to bring out those things which tend to make us refuse the conclusion and therefore the premises' (M155).

When we have on our hands one or more propositions such that there seems to be good reason to say it is true and also good reason to say it is false, we are inclined to ask the question 'Is it true?', and to feel that there must be a correct answer. What one then has to do is to give a 'description of (1) those features of the use of the expressions involved . . . which incline one to answer "Yes" and of (2) those features of their use which incline one to answer "No" ' (100). In doing so one will give a pretty full and detailed account of the use of those expressions. If, after all this, someone still wants to ask 'Is it true?', his question will be like that of one who, knowing exactly and in full detail what the cow and the dog did, still asks 'Did he go round her?'. To such a one we may say: 'With great patience we drew a pretty detailed picture of the animal you and I met in the wood last night. You recognize the picture but at once you tear it up and ask, "Was what we saw a man or a horse"?' (M142).

(b) Another way of describing the fix we are often in, in philosophy, is to say that we often seem to have good grounds for accepting each of three propositions which constitute an inconsistent triad or 'antilogism'—a set of three propositions which are inconsistent and cannot all of them be true. Now if three propositions, p, q and r, cannot *all* be true we can validly argue from the truth of any two of them to the falsity of the third, and we can do so in any of three ways. We can argue from p and q to the contradictory of r, from p and r to the contradictory of q, or from q and r to the contradictory of p. To each antilogism there correspond three different demonstrative arguments. The typical arguments of the Sceptic, the Intuitionist and the Reductionist are interrelated in this way: they are all based on the same antilogism, the same three propositions which, though we seem to have grounds for asserting each of them, cannot, it seems, be all three of them true.

The antilogism in question is:
A: The supported facts are further facts over and above the supporting facts.
B: We cannot independently observe facts of the supported kind.
C: Facts of the supporting kind provide us with a good basis for knowledge of facts of the supported kind.

In the case of each of the 'categories of being' mentioned, we seem to have good grounds for asserting each of these propositions. Yet they seem to be inconsistent. Accordingly the sceptic argues from A and B to the unpalatable conclusion that C is false. The Intuitionist argues from A and C to the contradictory of B, escaping the paradox of scepticism at the cost of accepting the mythology of new modes of knowing (cf. M106). The Phenomenalist argues from B and C to the falsity of A, escaping the sceptic's paradox and the mythology, but only at the cost of embracing such paradoxes as that 'Smith is angry' means 'Smith's body is angry-behaving'.

This sort of situation, in which we seem to have good grounds for assenting to each of three propositions, which nevertheless seem to constitute an antilogism, with the result that people tend to put forward one or other of the three unconvincing proofs of

D

paradoxes, based on that antilogism, is not uncommon. As a further example, consider the following antilogism-pattern (cf. M84-88):

> A: If there is no conceivable way of finding out whether or not it is the case that p, then the question 'Is it the case that p?' makes no sense.
>
> B: There is no conceivable way of finding out whether or not it is the case that p.
>
> C: The question 'Is it the case that p?' makes sense.

For instance one particular antilogism that is of this pattern results from substituting for p the proposition: 'God exists.' Another results from substituting: 'All the physical evidence at time t_1 (bodily state, behaviour, the words framed by his lips, etc.) points to Smith being in pain at t_1, and never in the future will such evidence point to his not having been in pain at t_1, but Smith is not in pain at t_1'.

With many antilogisms of the above pattern, including for most people the two suggested, there seem to be good grounds for asserting all three propositions. And so you will get the sceptic-about-meaning, the adherent of the verification-principle, 'proving' his paradox by the argument 'A and B, therefore not C'. You will have the Intuitionist arguing 'A and C, therefore not B'. And you will have 'proofs' of the anti-verificationist paradox that run 'B and C, therefore not A'.

Here is yet another antilogism-pattern:

> A: If to know that p is the same as to know that q, then 'p' means the same as 'q'.
>
> B: To know that p is the same as to know that q.
>
> C: 'p' does not mean the same as 'q'.

One instance of an antilogism of this pattern is got by substituting for 'p' the sentence 'sensations will consistently bear out that this is cheese', and for 'q' the sentence 'This is cheese'. Another is got by putting for 'p' the sentence 'Physical manifestations will consistently bear out that Smith is angry', and for 'q' the sentence 'Smith is angry'.

With such substitutions people are often inclined to think there are good grounds for asserting all three propositions. And so you will tend to get 'proofs' of the paradoxical contradictories of each of them. The Phenomenalist will argue from A and B to the contradictory of C. The Intuitionist will argue from A and C to the contradictory of B. And some will argue 'B and C, therefore not A', and thus embrace a paradox about the relation of meaning and knowledge.

(9) The consistency procedure: obliteration of a contrast

Another source of paradoxical statements is what Wisdom calls the 'consistency procedure'—that of 'counting as fatal in any degree what in a high degree we already count as fatal' (M185). This is the source (or *an* important source) of such paradoxes as 'Perfect love is impossible', 'Inductive conclusions are never really justified', 'We never know what we see is real and not a dream', 'Nothing is really the same from moment to moment', 'All words are vague' (cf. 54).

If the affaire between Albert and Amelia lasts only a week or so we tend to say 'So it wasn't really love, only a passing infatuation'. On the other hand we don't normally say 'It wasn't really love' just because the relationship fails to last more than ten years; we say 'Finally, love cooled'. We count a high degree of transience as fatal to the claim 'It was love,' but do not normally count as fatal any degree of transience. Similarly with nearly all descriptive words there is, in respect of their application, a 'fringe', i.e. a range of 'borderline cases' where most would hesitate between applying and withholding the word, and perhaps some do one thing and some another. Where the fringe is very extensive, as with 'warm' or 'bald' we say the word is 'vague'; but with a small fringe we do not say 'vague'. We do not count as fatal to the claim that a word is not vague the presence of any fringe however small, only the presence of a big fringe. (As a matter of fact, I do not think it correct to say that *all* words have a fringe: e.g. in chess terminology the phrase 'a winning position' certainly has a considerable fringe, but 'in check' is an expression with a different sort of use, and a fringe doesn't come into the picture at all. But it is easy to overlook such cases.)

If now we apply the consistency procedure and refuse to count it as love unless it lasts forever, or count as vague an expression having any fringe at all, we shall be led to say 'Perfect love is impossible' or (overlooking cases like 'in check') 'All words are vague'. This would be like saying 'Everyone is bald'. This new usage of 'love' and of 'vague' we should thereby be insisting on would not be arbitrary. 'Maybe it caricatures our actual usage but it comes naturally out of our actual usage' (M185).

What is the result of applying the consistency procedure? There exists a certain range of cases that could be arranged in a series or 'slide', in such a way that cases near the two extreme ends would differ markedly from each other (as e.g. 'bald' differs in width of fringe from 'temperature 97.6 degrees Fahrenheit') but such that any two neighbouring cases in the series differed from each other only very slightly if at all (as perhaps 'viscous' and 'springy'). We have in our ordinary language a pair of expressions (e.g. 'vague'—'not vague'; 'love'—'passing infactuation') by which we distinguish cases near one end of the series from cases near the other end of the series. In the middle of the series there will, of course, be a fringe more or less extensive where we should not feel quite happy about applying either expression. Roughly speaking: one expression covers the left half of the whole range of cases, the other expression covers the right half. As the result of the consistency procedure we have a new usage according to which one of the two expressions now covers the whole range of cases that was previously shared by the two expressions, and the other of the pair of expressions is now without a use. As a result, a distinction—a contrast—that is marked in our ordinary language (by two expressions for the contrasted sorts of case) is now not marked at all in the revised notation, for there is just one word to cover all the cases. 'Vague' now comes to mean what was previously meant by 'vague or precise', 'infatuation' now comes to mean what was previously meant by 'infatuation or love', and the words 'precise' and 'love' are now unemployed. 'Vague' previously meant 'vague as contrasted with precise' and 'infatuation' previously meant 'infatuation as contrasted with love', but now these words do not mark a contrast at all.

By introducing the new notation we have abolished an existing linguistic device for marking a distinction. But we may nevertheless at times still want to express this old distinction. If so, since we have abolished the old device for doing this we shall have to devise a new one 'to do the work the old one did' (44). We now describe as 'vague' both 'bald' and 'at a temperature of 97.6 degrees Fahrenheit', since both have *some* fringe, whether extensive or narrow. If we want now to contrast the former expression, as having a wide fringe, with the latter as having a narrow one, we cannot now do so by calling one 'vague' and the other 'precise'. So we may very likely do so by calling the former 'very vague' and the latter 'slightly vague'. And then, in our new notation 'very vague' will mean what was previously meant by 'vague' and 'slightly vague' will mean what was previously meant by 'precise'. Our new linguistic device does the work the old one did. Similarly, when 'infatuation' comes to cover both 'infatuation' and 'love', we shall very likely distinguish 'passing infatuation' (i.e. the old 'infatuation') from 'enduring infatuation' (i.e. the old 'love').

Propositions we might assent to may be divided into (*a*) those concerning which we have some grounds, though not very strong grounds, for supposing that we shall not find ourselves to have been mistaken, (*b*) those about which we have pretty strong grounds for supposing that we shall not find ourselves to have been mistaken, and (*c*) those concerning which the supposition that we should subsequently find ourselves to have been mistaken makes no sense. Propositions of type (*a*) are distinguished from the rest by the fact that it would not be reasonable to put our shirt on them; the others we could reasonably risk anything on. This distinction is marked in ordinary speech by our using 'p is probable' and 'I am of the opinion that p' of type (*a*) propositions and 'p is certain' and 'I know p' of the rest, whether type (*b*) or type (*c*). We normally count as fatal to the claim of knowledge and certainty any considerable weakness in our grounds for them. If, by the consistency procedure, we come to count as fatal any weakness in the grounds, we shall describe as 'probable' and speak of 'opinion' only in connection with propositions of type (*b*) as well as type (*a*), reserving 'certain' and 'know' for type (*c*). When we want to mark the old distinction between types (*a*) and (*b*) we are likely to do so by speaking of (*a*) 'probable' propositions concerning which we have an 'opinion' and of (*b*) 'very probable' propositions concerning which we have a 'very well-grounded opinion'.

The new notation, which obliterates the old distinction, will now mark a new one, namely the distinction between propositions of types (*a*) and (*b*) on the one hand, where the supposition makes sense that we might find ourselves to be mistaken, and propositions of type (*c*), where this supposition makes no sense. Since this distinction is not marked by our ordinary terminology the recommendation of this new notation may well be also a sign of linguistic penetration. So the paradoxes that 'We can never know there's a chair there' or that 'It is not certain there's a chair there' could also be regarded as 'penetrating suggestions as to how (language) might be used so as to reveal what, by the actual use of language, is hidden' (100).

(10) *The philosopher's mirage: special ways of knowing*

For the sort of reason that has been explained philosophers sometimes dream of new direct ways of knowing things that can (we ordinarily think) only be known through their manifestations. People imagine a sort of direct telepathy which would check the reliability of the behavioural indications we normally go by; retrocognitive vision to assure us that what is attested by surviving documents and so on really did happen; even a direct access to the noumenal world which would assure us that our sensations do not consistently lie. But all such notions, promising though they may seem at first, turn out on closer examination either to be self-contradictory or not to do what they were supposed to do.

(*a*) No new instrument would do the trick. One might imagine a 'psychoscope', with clamps to put over Smith's skull and a screen on which to see his visual sensations, or an 'historiscope' with a screen on which to see what happened in history. What is wrong with this can be seen if one remembers what would happen if someone invented a new sort of thermometer, with a prod to apply to the object and a pointer moving over a dial. The new instrument would have to be calibrated. Thus one would have to apply the new instrument to an object that was at 0 degrees according to ordinary thermometers and write '0' on the dial where the new machine's pointer came to rest; then apply the new instrument to something that ordinary thermometers said was at 100 degrees and mark '100' on the dial, and so on. And if the new machine came with a dial ready marked one would still have to check the calibration: make sure that its readings corresponded to those of ordinary thermometers. So, with one reservation to be mentioned shortly, the new machine could not supply you with any reading that was at variance with the readings of ordinary thermometers, for if it did it would be rejected as wrongly calibrated.

The one reservation is that, although the new instrument must agree with the old instruments over the latter's range of discrimination, outside that range the new instruments, if they all agree with each other, will be regarded as giving new information not given us by the old instruments. If the new instruments show a difference whenever the old instruments do, but sometimes show very small differences when the old instruments do not, all the new instruments agreeing with each other in such cases, they will be regarded as an improved model. Similarly a new style microscope will be rejected unless what it shows agrees with what the old microscopes agree in showing, but if the new microscopes sometimes all agree in showing something (and the same thing) where old microscopes show nothing, they will be accepted as an improved model. But new instruments will not be accepted as accurate unless they agree with old instruments over the latter's range of discrimination. They can thus, if they agree with the old instruments whenever the latter speak, give new information, but only in cases where the old instruments are silent.

These considerations apply equally to any imagined psychoscope or historiscope or whatnot. These must be calibrated or their calibration checked. A pretended historiscope will be laughed out of court unless it almost always agrees with what all competent historians say, although if it had been definitely shown to do so we should no doubt take some notice of what it showed about episodes concerning which history is silent. We should not accept a psychoscope unless nearly always when our ordinary evidence (e.g. what Smith says) shows Smith to be seeing red the psychoscope shows this too.

This point could be summed up: any new instrument for knowing 'directly' what we ordinarily know through its manifestations must be calibrated against these manifestations. It could not therefore be used as a direct check on the reliability of those manifestations in general (cf. M95–96, M110–111).

(b) A reliable historiscope will not give us a direct vision of ancient Babylon, but will give us advance information of what we shall find on the site of Babylon when we dig. If it does not, it will not be accounted reliable. Similarly a psychoscope, in so far as it is reliable, will not show us Smith's sensations themselves but will give us advance information about Smith's answers to our questions concerning his sensations (cf. M96). What we shall have, in fact, will be a new set of manifestations to set alongside the old ones. Besides archaeological manifestations of what Babylon was like there will be historiscopic ones: besides behavioural manifestations of Smith's mind there will be psychoscopic ones (cf. M111).

(c) The readings of the X-scope are public: anyone can look at the screen or the pointer and see what is there. But suppose someone had a private sensory X-scope, so to speak. Suppose you could, at will, say by saying to yourself 'Smith's sensation' or 'Babylon 4000 B.C.', get private mental pictures or images like those we have imagined being publicly visible on the screen of the X-scope. Nothing is altered, except that the sensory X-scope is private to you. It still has to be calibrated. We should not accept you as having genuine clairvoyant powers unless what your private images told you corresponded with what the normally accepted manifestations told us about history or other minds or whatnot. So, for the same reasons as before, your images would not be direct knowledge of X, but another manifestation of X. If you were a properly accredited clairvoyant you would, from your image, have advance information of what you would find on the site of Babylon or of how Smith would answer your question. And these latter things you would know, if you did, through their sensory manifestations. Thus there might be a new private way of knowing about X's. 'But this other way consists still in having feelings and sensations of my own and from these expecting other sensations of my own. And to talk of any other kind of knowing of anything lacks a sense. . . .' (M97).

(d) Such imagined new 'direct' ways of knowing turn out, on examination, to be not in principle different from the old ways. We are still confined to manifestations; we just have a new one. When the new way of knowing is first described people 'may, at first, staggered by the novelty and value of the imagined gift, waver. But when they look into its cash value they will see that it doesn't differ in principle from what they have already rejected, that it buys still only the same sort of goods' (M118).

But couldn't one, it might be suggested, some day come to know other minds, the past, the future, etc., in the same sort of way that one knows one's own sensations at the moment one is having them? This, surely, would be direct infallible knowledge! This supposition hides a contradiction. If one knew something in the way one knows one's own sensation of the moment it would be one's sensation of the moment that one knew (cf. M157–8). For (1) one supposes oneself to know the truth of some statement which is not about one's sensations of the moment, that is not subjective but objective. But 'objectivity is nothing short of infinite corrigibility, infinite liability to correction from experiment' (M145). Any objective statement 'makes a claim about the future in spite of its present tense' (M148). 'What makes the statement objective also makes it predictive' (M151). If I say 'A lake and palm-trees over there', meaning this as an ordinary objective statement, I shall have to withdraw it as mistaken if when we get there neither you nor I can see, nor our cameras record, anything but sand. Therefore my objective statement implicitly predicts that this will not happen when we get there. On the other hand (2) one supposes oneself to know the truth of the statement in the way that one knows about one's sensations of the moment, i.e. in such a way that it could not be falsified by any future sensations, i.e. in such a way as not to contain any implicit prediction. And a person's statement 'involves nothing about the future only if it is used to describe only . . . his own sensation at the moment' (M151). If I mean my statement about the lake and palm-trees to express a truth known in such a way as not to be open to correction in the future, then I mean it as a report of how things look to me at the moment of speaking.

(e) People sometimes dream of an infallible knowledge of the future to be obtained, not in the way one knows one's own sensations of the moment, and not in the way one knows logically necessary truths, but by a combination of these methods. The method would consist in making a deduction about the future from two infallible premisses: (1) a minor premiss purely about the present, involving no prediction and infallible in the way a purely subjective statement is; (2) a major premiss, infallible in the way a logically necessary statement is. But this notion, too, hides a contradiction. All inferences to the future are either problematic or from premisses that covertly involve prediction and so are problematic.

Suppose I argue:
Every X in the past has been followed shortly by a Y,
This is an X,
Therefore there will be a Y shortly,
and mean the minor premiss 'This is an X' as a non-predictive subjective statement. Then neither of my premisses will contain any reference to the future. But my inference will be problematical,

for there is nothing self-contradictory about the supposition that some future X will not be followed by a Y, even though this has not happened before.

If I replace the major premiss by

Every X is followed shortly by a Y

then my argument is demonstrative. But my major premiss, being an empirical law-statement, is open to correction in the light of future experience and thus is implicitly predictive.

If I replace the major by the (logically necessary) statement:

Every X is necessarily followed by a Y

then my minor premiss can no longer be purely subjective and non-predictive. Previously if something seemed to me to be an X then it was an X, and nothing in the future could ever show me to have been wrong. But the new logically necessary major premiss entails that the statement 'This is an X' is corrigible and implicitly predictive. For, if something seems to me to be X and it is not followed by a Y, I must, in virtue of the logically necessary major, deny that it was really an X. Hence there cannot be a non-problematic inference to the future from premisses all of them non-problematic (cf. M137).

(11) *Some further points*

Finally I should like to draw attention to, without trying to expound, a number of points which seem to me especially helpful or illuminating:

(*a*) People sometimes answer a puzzle question with 'In a sense Yes; in a sense No'. On the philosophical uselessness of this move and the confusions involved see M38n, 96, and M108.

(*b*) For a very clear account of some puzzles about infinite numbers, see 198–200.

(*c*) On the question 'Are sensation-statements *verbally* corrigible?', see 241 and M162–4.

(*d*) On the relation between sensation-statements and material-thing sentences, see M250 and M169–170, also M42–44.

(*e*) On what knowledge is and why it is misleading to speak of knowledge of one's own sensations, see M159 and M161.

(*f*) For an account of what it is for someone to use a sentence to express a necessary truth, see M180, and notice in this connection what Wisdom says about a 'contingent copy' (76, 81).

(*g*) On the difference between verbal statements and logically necessary statements, see 38 and 62. Wisdom's remarks here constitute a helpful sketch towards an account, but this is one of the places where one would like to see a much more detailed working out of the problem.

(h) At 157 Wisdom issues a warning against confusion that can arise from a very natural but unusual use of the word' probable'. Some purely *a priori* reasoning, in which the premisses support the conclusion 'like the legs of a chair, not the links of a chain' 'lends itself to description in terms of conflicting probabilities'. Misled by 'probable' here we tend to think of the reasoning as empirical.

(i) See the example of the 'Taj Mahal hat' on 248, and the illustrations on 264–266 to bring out how something can be a discovery, 'although neither a scientific discovery by observation and experiment nor a deductive discovery in strict accordance with well-recognized customs of presentation'.

(j) See 80–81 and M104–107 for an elucidation of the following point:

Suppose there is a set of phenomena such that (a) always in any given case either all the members of the set are absent or else all or *nearly* all are present; (b) every single member of the set is on *some* occasions absent when all the rest are present; (c) the presence of all or of nearly all the members of the set constitutes a good basis for our saying that a certain fact, F, is the case.

In such a case we cannot say of any one of the phenomena that it is a necessary condition for F. For by (b) it may be absent when the rest are present, and by (c) the presence of the rest is a good basis for F. And so we are inclined to suppose that the single phenomenon must be a more or less reliable inductive sign of the presence of F. (Indeed, it will by (a) be a more or less reliable inductive sign of the rest of the phenomena of the set.) This in turn leads us to fancy that F must be a further fact, over and above the presence of the phenomena, or to think that somehow we ought to be able to apprehend F directly. In this we may well be wrong. The presence of most (though not necessarily all) of the phenomena may be a non-inductive basis for our saying that F is the case.

II

MOORE'S TECHNIQUE REVISITED[1]

JUDITH JARVIS THOMSON

> Remember how the translation of sentences about the average man seems to make him vanish.—JOHN WISDOM.[2]

1. The sentence

> (1) G. E. Moore has two hands; therefore there are hands

does not appear anywhere in Moore's 'Proof of an External World'. But a great many people would, I think, say that if Moore had written it in 1939 (when he wrote 'Proof') he would have been giving a proof of the existence of hands, and thereby of material objects—for Moore did at that time have two hands, and it follows from the fact that Moore has two hands at a certain time that there are hands, and therefore material objects, at that time.

But now what of

> (2) The word 'bank' has two meanings; therefore there are meanings.

Does one who writes (2) similarly prove the existence of meanings, and thereby of abstract entities? For the word 'bank' *does* have two meanings. And is there better reason to say that an assertion of (1) is valid than there is to say that an assertion of (2) is valid?

We might call (2) a descendant of (1). Indeed, Moore's proof of an external world might be said to have many descendants: a way of doing philosophy was born of it. We needn't after all have started with (1). We could have looked instead at

> (3) The hand G. E. Moore is holding up before you now is the same as the hand he held up before you a minute ago; therefore there are hands.

An assertion of this in the right sort of circumstances would be a proof, wouldn't it? And so why not the same for

---

[1] I am grateful to James Thomson for discussion, criticism, and suggestions about the material discussed here.

[2] From 'Moore's Technique', reprinted in *Philosophy and Psycho-Analysis*.

(4) The meaning of the English word 'red' is the same as the meaning of the French word 'rouge'; therefore there are meanings.

And why stop at meanings? Compare

(5) The thing G. E. Moore is holding up before you now is a hand; therefore there are hands

with

(6) That Hubert Humphrey will run in '72 is a possibility; therefore there are possibilities

and

(7) That L.B.J. will not run in '72 is a fact; therefore there are facts.

What could be better proof of the existence of X's than giving an example of an X? Or again, compare

(8) There is a hand which G. E. Moore is holding up before you now; therefore there are hands,

with

(9) There is a possibility that Hubert Humphrey will run in '72; therefore there are possibilities

and

(10) There is a fact which is plain to one and all, namely the fact that L.B.J. will not run in '72; therefore there are facts.

Many philosophers seem to regard arguments such as these for the existence of abstract entities as valid in the same straightforward way as Moore's argument for the existence of material objects. They may call them trivial; they may say that they don't take us very far, that we still stand in need of an analysis of their conclusions, or of their premises and their conclusions. But valid, obviously yes. For how could there be a possibility that someone will run, without there being *any* possibilities? a fact that someone won't run, without there being at least one fact? a word which has two meanings, and there be *no* meanings?

But other philosophers regard meanings, possibilities, and facts as queer, dubious, obscure, not to be 'countenanced'. Some amongst them may say these arguments for their existence may be valid, but we needn't worry: their premises are false. Or that their premises aren't 'strictly speaking' true, or that they are true only in a 'loose and popular way of speaking'. But this seems an unappealing stand to take. It would be an exaggeration to say the Party loves Hubert Humphrey; something which was not, strictly speaking, true. But it seems a plain undecorated truth, strictly speaking a truth, a truth thought to be so by the most tiresomely careful commentators, that there is a *possibility* he will run.

Others of those who regard these entities as dubious may instead say that while the premises of these arguments are true, the arguments are not valid. It is this claim that I want to concentrate on.

2. A fairly common defence of the claim runs as follows: 'The sentences asserted in putting forward the premises of these arguments are translatable into sentences which neither quantify over nor refer to any of the odd entities. Thus sentences (2) and (4) are translatable into

> (2*)   The word 'bank' is ambiguous; therefore there are meanings,

> (4*)   The English word 'red' and the French word 'rouge' are synonymous; therefore there are meanings

respectively; (6) and (9) are both translatable into

> (6–9*)   It is possible that Hubert Humphrey will run in '72; therefore there are possibilities;

(7) is translatable into

> (7*)   L.B.J. will not run in '72; therefore there are facts,

and (10) into

> (10*)   It is plain to one and all that L.B.J. will not run in '72; therefore there are facts.

Since assertions of the starred sentences are not valid arguments, assertions of their unstarred correlates are not valid either.'[1]

---

[1] Some philosophers appear to have been under the impression that assertions of such sentences as 'There is a possibility that Hubert . . .' entail that there are possibilities, but that assertions of what they say are their translations do not. That they cannot have it both ways is brought out by W. P. Alston, in 'Ontological Commitments', reprinted in *Meaning and Knowledge*, eds. E. Nagel and R. B. Brandt.

But what is supposed to show that the starred arguments[1] are not valid? It seems a fair proposal that (1) is translatable into

(1*) G. E. Moore is two-handed; therefore there are hands.

Presumably (1*) had better be valid if (1) is; and we need to be given reason to say that while (1*) is valid, the other starred arguments are not. It plainly won't do just to say that (1*) is valid because (1) is, and because for a person to be two-handed *is* for him to have two hands; for it could equally well be said that (2*) is valid because (2) is, and because for a word to be ambiguous *is* for it to have two meanings.

It might be argued that (1*) and (1) are both valid because their premises—better, their premise, since they are translations of each other—must be construed as an assertion not merely about Moore, but about hands as well: that we must so construe it if we are to preserve the validity of arguments such as 'G. E. Moore has two clean hands; therefore he has two hands'. In other words, we must say that the sentences 'G. E. Moore has two hands' and 'G. E. Moore is two-handed' are of the form shown by 'There are two hands which are G. E. Moore's'; and thus that (1) and (1*) are of the form shown by

(1**) There are two hands which are G. E. Moore's; therefore there are hands,

which is plainly valid. But (the argument goes on) there is no argument to preserve the validity of which we need to construe an assertion of 'The word "bank" has two meanings' as an assertion about meanings as well as about the word 'bank'. So there is no reason to say that the sentences 'The word "bank" has two meanings' and 'The word "bank" is ambiguous' are of the form shown by 'There are two meanings which are the word "bank"'s', and so no reason to say that (2) and (2*) are of the form shown by

(2**) There are two meanings which are the word 'bank's; therefore there are meanings.

Unfortunately this argument simply presupposes that (2) and (2*) are invalid. For if they are valid, there is excellent reason to say they are of the form shown by (2**).

---

[1] To avoid clutter, I shall sometimes speak of the indented sentences as if they were themselves the arguments put forward in asserting them.

3. I shall come back to this talk of translations again below. Meanwhile, however, I should like to draw attention to an argument very like (2) and (4), which Quine thinks is invalid. He says

> it is argued that if we can speak of a sentence as meaningful, or as having meaning, then there must be a meaning that it has, and this meaning will be identical with or distinct from the meaning that another sentence has.[1]

And he says that this argument 'involves the fallacy of subtraction'. I take it he would say the same of (2) and (4)—and perhaps also of the other arguments we are concerned with.

Quine does not explain what this fallacy is, but he says about arguments which involve it that 'we could as well justify the hypostasis of sakes and unicorns on the basis of the idioms "for the sake of" and "is hunting unicorns".'[2]

I take it he means that

> (A) I did it for the sake of peace and quiet in the house; therefore there are sakes

and

> (B) Ernest is hunting unicorns; therefore there are unicorns,

for example, are bad in the same way as the argument about meanings he had pointed to, and involve the same fallacy.

Is there some one fallacy that both (A) and (B) commit? They plainly are bad arguments, but it is not plain that they are bad in the same way, or precisely how their badness is supposed to shed light on arguments such as (2) and (4).

Nevertheless they are exceedingly suggestive. (B) may remind us that we often talk of creatures of myth, legend, fiction, and speak truly when we do, without its following that those creatures exist. Consider, for example,

> (C) Cheiron was a centaur; therefore there are centaurs,

and

> (D) There is at least one centaur in Greek mythology; therefore there are centaurs.

[1] *Word and Object*, p. 206.
[2] *Ibid.*, p. 207.

Surely it would be unreasonable to say that the premises of (C) and (D) are false; a child would get a poor grade who denied that Cheiron was a centaur or that there is at least one centaur in Greek mythology. Yet there plainly are no centaurs; so there being centaurs does not follow from the premises, and the arguments are simply invalid.

Now I suppose that some of those who regard meanings, possibilities, and facts as queer, obscure, dubious, would be prepared to say flatly that there are no such things—just as flatly as we should all say that there are no centaurs or unicorns. (They may even be heard to say that meanings, possibilities, and facts are creatures of [philosophers'] myths.) In their view, to be taken in by our proofs for the existence of these entities would be very like being taken in by (B), (C), and (D)—(C) and (D) in particular, for doesn't (C) proceed by giving an example, just as (6) and (7) did? doesn't (D) call (9) and (10) to mind?

But others of those who regard these entities as queer, obscure, dubious, would not be prepared to say flatly that there are no such things. In *their* view, these entities are in a worse state than unicorns and centaurs: we at least know what centaurs and unicorns are, or would be if there were any, whereas we do not know this about meanings, possibilities, and facts. Quine, for example, does not himself really seem to think he knows what they would be if there were any; it does not seem as if he thinks they are, like unicorns and centaurs, creatures whose outlines would be plain enough if they had existed, but which in fact do not. In the view of these philosophers, it is no clearer what it comes to to say 'There aren't any such things' than it is to say 'There are'. In their view, then, there is an important disanalogy between (B), (C), and (D) on the one hand, and our purported proofs of the existence of meanings, possibilities, and facts on the other.

But then it is perhaps (A) which these philosophers would say the more clearly illustrates what is wrong with our purported existence proofs. For if a man says 'There are sakes', what can he be claiming existence for? And if anyone says 'There aren't any sakes', it is no clearer what he claims *non*-existence for. This seems to me the interest and importance of (A). Indeed, I shall suggest that in the light of what I think many of these philosophers believe about meanings, possibilities, and facts, they would be

E

right to say that our purported existence proofs of these entities are bad arguments in the same way as (A) is.

4. But we have first to see what precisely is wrong with (A). One's first reaction is perhaps to wonder if 'There are sakes' is so much as a sentence of English. It certainly sounds odd, or, as is said in some quarters, 'deviant', 'anomalous'. The point isn't just that it would be odd, puzzling, peculiar for a man to say, suddenly, out of the blue, 'There are sakes' ('we would *stare* at him', as people used to say in *Mind*); it would be equally odd for a man to say, suddenly, out of the blue, 'There are men', and yet there really are men, and if it's odd or dull to say so, it's all the same true. Nor is it obvious that anything is wrong with the grammar of 'There are sakes'. 'There are if' is plainly ungrammatical; 'there are' seems to have to be followed by a plural noun phrase, which 'if' is not. But 'sakes' does seem to be a plural noun phrase. No doubt it is more common to say 'I did it for the children's sake'; but one does hear, and it surely can be said, that someone did it for 'the children's sakes'.

But surely there is something wrong with 'There are sakes'. I implied above that if a man says 'There are sakes', then it is not at all clear what he claims existence for. Perhaps we can say something stronger than this: that there is nothing at all he claims existence for. For what on earth (or off it) could a sake *be*?

We might be told that a sake is just precisely that thing which a man does a thing for if and only if he does it for someone's or something's sake. Here, for example, is a man who bought an air conditioner for his wife's sake; the thing he bought it for is a sake, in fact a quite particular sake, namely his wife's.

But what shall we say if it turns out that although he bought it for his wife's sake, he also bought it for the kitchen, and he also bought it for $150? Here there does not seem to be any such thing as '*the* thing he bought it for'.

The account might be revised, to run: a sake is just precisely that thing, or anyway one of those things if there are more than one, which a man does a thing for if and only if he does it for someone's or something's sake. But which is the sake, when there are more than one? Could the kitchen turn out to be the sake in the case I described? No doubt our man's wife's sake is the sake; but perhaps the kitchen *is* his wife's sake—we have not been told anything which would rule this out.

Consider the following argument: 'John kissed Mary; therefore there are kisses.' Well, why not? If John kissed Mary, then he gave her a kiss, and surely you can't give someone a kiss unless there are kisses to give. If John kicked Mary, then he gave her a kick, and surely you can't give someone a kick unless there are kicks to give. And we all know what kisses and kicks are, don't we? A kiss is just precisely that thing which x gives y if and only if x kisses y; a kick is just precisely that thing which x gives y if and only if x kicks y. But suppose on some occasion when John kicks or kisses Mary, he gives her a bunch of flowers and a box of chocolates. Then on that occasion there isn't any such thing as '*the* thing he gives her'; and if the account is revised, so as to allow for his giving her several things, which thing is the kiss or kick?

Fascinated by this game, someone might say: 'The words "kick" and "kiss" are both verbs and nouns in English. The word "eat" is just a verb. But isn't this a mere accident? Let's give it a use as a noun by the same procedure. We'll say that an *eat* (noun) is just precisely that thing which x gives y when x eats y. And then we'll be able to argue validly as follows: John ate a steak; therefore there are eats. For if John ate a steak there was a unique thing he gave it, which, as I said, is an eat. And you surely can't give a thing an eat unless there are eats to give.' But does a man who eats something give it anything at all? We can say he does, but should we? Would it be true? Perhaps sometimes it is. Perhaps sometimes when a man eats a steak, he gives it a greedy look (therefore there are looks?). But always?

This procedure for explaining what sakes, kisses, kicks, and the new entities eats are is plainly not a success. And it is worth noting that the same procedure will be in the same way, and for the same reason, an unsuccess in the case of meanings. That is, we might have been inclined to say this: a meaning is just precisely that thing which a word has if and only if it is meaningful. Or, in light of ambiguity: meanings are just precisely those things which a word has one or more of if and only if it is meaningful. This of course simply assumes the point at issue, namely that if a word is meaningful, there is an entity which it *has*, which is a meaning. And just as we asked whether or not a man who eats something always gives it something, so we should ask whether or not a word which is meaningful always has something. But even if we grant that all meaningful words have something, which of the things a meaningful word has is a meaning? For of course a word may have many things—for example, it may have a pleasant sound, a long history, and three occurrences in the writings of Chaucer.

If somebody has constructed a mapping of words on to numbers in such a way that every meaningful word has a number—two or more, if the word is ambiguous —then every meaningful word does have something, viz. a number. Are the numbers, perhaps, meanings?

No doubt it doesn't *follow* from the fact that a man buys something for his wife's sake that he buys it for the kitchen. It doesn't follow from the fact that someone kisses or kicks someone that he gives that person flowers. It doesn't follow from the fact that a word is meaningful that it has a pleasant sound. So it might be thought that we can improve our accounts of the nature of these entities by taking this up into them, perhaps as follows: meanings are just precisely those things such that it follows from the fact that a word is meaningful that it has one or more of them, and such that it follows from the fact that a word is not meaningful that it has none of them. But it can be seen that this still leaves it open that a word's pleasant sound, or its long history, should be a meaning; and thus that it is no improvement on the earlier account. True enough, it doesn't follow from the fact that a word W is meaningful that it has a pleasant sound; and it doesn't follow from the fact that W is not meaningful that it doesn't have a pleasant sound. But it is consistent with this that W's pleasant sound *is* a meaning. Compare the following account of what a child is: children are just precisely those things such that it follows from the fact that a person is a parent that that person has one or more of them, and such that it follows from the fact that a person is not a parent that that person has none of them. Now suppose that John Smith has an admirer. It doesn't follow from the fact that he is a parent that he has an admirer; and it doesn't follow from the fact that he is not a parent that he doesn't have an admirer. But it is consistent with this that John Smith's admirer is a child, and indeed that it is his own child.

It may be said that the sense in which a word has a meaning is different from the sense in which it has a pleasant sound. But then that special sense of 'has' would call for explanation—'has' cannot be used without explanation to explain 'meaning'.

Someone may object that I should not have fastened attention so closely on 'has a meaning'. He may say we should, instead, give an account of 'meaning' by appeal to *all* the contexts in which it occurs. However it is not plain how this is to be done. 'Meanings are just those entities which all true statements about meanings are true of' obviously won't do—John, for example, is one of the things which 'John and Mary know the meaning of the word "red" ' is true of, and he presumably is no meaning.

5. It might be asked how we can suppose ourselves to know what a man is saying who says 'I did it for the sake of peace and quiet in the house' or 'The word "bank" has two meanings' if we do not know what sakes and meanings are. If a word occurs in *both* the premise-sentence and the conclusion-sentence, then if we are in the dark as to what the conclusion is, shouldn't we be equally in the dark about what the premise is?

It is important to note that this is a mistake. Suppose a man says

(E) G. E. Moore has two boggles; therefore there are boggles.

We might know perfectly well what he is saying in saying 'G. E. Moore has two boggles'. He might just have told us that he wishes for us to use the following new code: we are to regard the sentence 'G. E. Moore has two boggles' as meaning the same as the English sentence 'If it doesn't rain this afternoon, the neighbours will probably go for a walk'. So that is the premise of his argument. But what is its conclusion? Goodness knows. Nothing he has so far said, either in explaining his code, or in uttering (E), makes it at all clear what boggles are, and so nothing makes it at all clear what it is he is saying there are in saying 'There are boggles'.

Of course it might be that there is more to his code than he told us of, and that 'There are boggles' does have a sense in it. If it seems to us that it does, then what we should say is, not that his argument is invalid, but rather that we don't know if it is. We know what the premise of his argument is, but we don't know what its conclusion is, and so of course are in no position to assess its validity.

But suppose when we ask, he replies 'Look, what I told you was the whole of the code. There is no more. Nevertheless my argument is valid anyway. For if G. E. Moore has two boggles, then there must be boggles for him to have—just as if he has two hands, or a word has two meanings, there must be hands, or meanings, available for the having. Indeed, my argument is not merely valid, it is a proof: for G. E. Moore has two boggles, since if it doesn't rain this afternoon, the neighbours probably *will* go for a walk.' This obviously won't do. To have given a meaning to 'G. E. Moore has two boggles is not thereby to have given a meaning to 'There are boggles'. But then it is not as if he here puts forward an argument, our trouble being that although we know what its premise is, we do not know what its conclusion is. What he puts forward is not an argument at all, for it has no conclusion. He merely pretends to argue from premise to conclusion.

It is just worth stressing that this would have been so even if the sentence he had assigned the meaning 'If it doesn't rain this afternoon, the neighbours will probably go for a walk' was, not 'G. E. Moore has two boggles', but 'There is a boggle which is G. E. Moore's'. And thus that, if this had been the whole of his code, he would not have been putting forward an argument in saying

   (F) There is a boggle which is G. E. Moore's; therefore there
       are boggles.

6.[1] In the preceding section we talked about sentences introduced via a code book. By contrast, I suppose that none of us learned the meaning of, for example, 'I did it for the sake of peace and quiet in the house' via a code book. Well, what does that sentence mean? I think we can say it means 'I did it for peace and quiet in the house'. It would be neat and tidy if we could say that the phrase 'the sake of' is always eliminable: that a sentence of the form 'A did X for the sake of Y' means exactly the same as what you get if you simply take 'the sake of' out of it. But we can't. 'John went to the doctor for the sake of his wife' doesn't mean exactly the same as 'John went to the doctor for his wife'. The latter sentence is ambiguous. One possible reading of it is, of course, that he went to the doctor for the sake of his wife (she had been so worried about his health). But there are others: a second is that he went to the doctor to fetch his wife, and a third is that he

---

[1] I am grateful to Gareth Matthews and Vere Chappell for showing me that a proposal I had made in an earlier version of this section was false; and to John Guiniven for suggesting a way of side-stepping the trouble.

went to the doctor in place of his wife, in order to substitute for her (what was in question was giving blood). And we plainly cannot say that S means exactly the same as T if T is ambiguous, and the meaning of S is only one of the meanings of T.

The situation, then, *seems* to be this. Sometimes the result of eliminating 'the sake of' from 'A did X for the sake of Y' is a sentence which means the same as the original: e.g., 'I did it for peace and quiet in the house' means the same as 'I did it for the sake of peace and quiet in the house'. In such a case, 'the sake of' makes no contribution at all to the meaning of the sentence it appears in. In other cases, however, the result of eliminating 'the sake of' from 'A did X for the sake of Y' does not mean the same as the original: e.g., 'John went to the doctor for his wife' is ambiguous, and meaning of 'John went to the doctor for the sake of his wife' is only one of its meanings. In the latter sort of case, 'the sake of' does make a contribution to the meaning of the sentence it appears in. The contribution it makes to the meaning of the sentence it appears in is analogous to the contribution which a subscript attached to an ambiguous word makes to the complex consisting of word and subscript.

If this is right, and if, moreover, it were all there was to be said about the matter—i.e., if 'the sake of' makes at most this, and never any other, contribution to the meaning of the sentence it appears in—then I think the point would be plain enough. Suppose, for example, that we decided to adopt the following convention: where you mean by 'bank', place for depositing and withdrawing money, and someone might think you instead mean side of a river or canal, and you wish to prevent confusion, say 'bank with a boggle' instead of just 'bank'—'bank with a boggle', then, means place for depositing and withdrawing money, which is a possible reading of 'bank'; and 'with a boggle' has the role of a subscript. And now suppose a man who agrees to the convention I just described says 'Aha, a new existence proof:

(G) John went to the bank with a boggle; therefore there are boggles.

(You can't go to the bank with a ten dollar bill if there are no ten dollar bills, can you?)'. This is merely a bad joke. 'There are boggles' has been given no sense.

I am sure there is more to be said about the locutions 'the sake of Y' and 'Y's sake'. But I am inclined to think that none of it will make plain what is the sense of 'There are sakes', or even that it has one. And thus that what is wrong with 'argument' (A) is that it lacks a conclusion: that it is not a valid argument because it is not an argument at all.

7. I don't wish to claim anything nearly so strong as that our purported proofs of the existence of meanings, possibilities, and facts have no conclusions. I do think that those who regard these proofs with suspicion are right to do so. I think that the difficulty about meanings I drew attention to—namely the fact that the account one might initially be inclined to give of what they are is an unsuccess, and the fact that no other account is ready to hand—is ground for suspicion of the proofs of the existence of meanings; and that analogous trouble faces possibilities and facts, and therefore that there is ground for suspicion of quick proofs of their existence too. No doubt those who say these proofs really are proofs (have true premises, and are valid) are prepared to say we don't know the analysis of their conclusions, or of their premises and their conclusions. But I think they ought to wonder how, if we don't 'know the analysis', they can be in a position so straightforwardly to say they *are* proofs.

One thing which I think can be brought out is this: that many of those who regard meanings, possibilities, and facts as queer, dubious, not to be 'countenanced', hold certain views of these entities such that *if* those views are true, then purported proofs of the existence of meanings, possibilities, and facts do lack conclusions, and so are not proofs of their existence. I shall concentrate on meanings alone of the three kinds of entity; and my account will be rough and over-simple—partly because there are differences amongst the philosophers I am concerned with, partly because the views themselves are not very clear.

Some of the philosophers I have in mind, the really devoted enemies of meanings, believe that *no* talk of meanings makes sense. In their view, therefore, to say 'There are meanings' is to say something which has no sense; and so of course in their view arguments (2) and (4) have no conclusions. Of course they have no premises either.

But others of them think that some talk about meanings does make sense, and this is of more interest. They may grant that it makes sense to say that, for example, the meaning of one word is the same as the meaning of a second, and even that to say such things is often to speak truly. But if so, this is because they think that sentences such as 'The meaning of the English word "red" is the same as the meaning of the French word "rouge" ' are translatable into sentences which themselves makes sense, and which are such that to assert *them* is *not* to be talking about meanings, but is instead to be talking about other things, perhaps words or people or word-inscriptions, or nerve-endings, or classes of these or other things, or what you will. It must be stressed that in their view, to assert these 'favoured' sentences is to be talking about entities, no one of which is a meaning. If you think that meanings are entities of kind K, and you regard meanings as dubious, you can hardly fail to regard K's as dubious. And then you can hardly suppose that talk about meanings makes sense only in so far as and because it is translatable into talk about K's.

This kind of view used to be widely held in respect of a great many different kinds of entities. We may remember a time at which it was said that talk about nations makes sense only in so far as and because it is translatable into talk which is not about nations, but instead about their nationals. It was said that talk about events makes sense only in so far as and because it is translatable into talk which is not about events, but instead about the participants in events. It was even said that talk about material objects makes sense only in so far as and because it is translatable into talk which is not about material objects, but instead about sense-contents or sense-data.[1] The model these philosophers had in mind was The Average Man. Talk about the average man, they said, makes sense only in so far as and because it is translatable into talk which is not about the average man, but instead about individual men. They said that 'The average man is five foot ten' is translatable into 'The sum of the heights of men, divided by their number, is five foot ten'; 'The average man lives in the surburbs, and washes his own car' is translatable into 'Most men live in the suburbs, and wash their own cars'; and that these sentences make sense only because they are so translatable. Of

---

[1] Did Russell think that talk about numbers, points, and instants is translatable into talk which is not about these entities? It depends on whether or not he thought that the classes out of which he 'constructed' them were to be identified with them. If he meant to say that points, for example, *are* classes, then his translation of talk about points into talk about those classes is *not* translation of it into talk which is not about points.

course it never did come across just precisely what their view was. There were difficulties which never got entirely cleared away.[1] For what precisely is 'talk about the average man'? And if in asserting a sentence you do talk about the average man, how could you fail to be talking about him in asserting some translation of that sentence? It can be seen that the same difficulties arise for the view about meanings which I set out above. Which talk is talk about meanings? And if to assert (as it might be) the sentence 'The meaning of the English word "red" is the same as the meaning of the French word "rouge" ' is to talk about meanings, then how can the 'favoured' sentence into which it is translated fail to be about meanings as well? But I think we can just side-step these difficulties. I think we do have a (perhaps only very rough) sense of what the view is; and in any case, I am not concerned to defend that view, but only to draw attention to a consequence of adopting it.

What I have in mind comes out when we ask what sense a man will attach to the sentence 'There are X's' if he thinks that talk about X's makes sense only in so far as and because it is translatable into talk which is not about X's, but instead about Y's.

In the case of the average man, the answer seems plain enough: none. The translation-procedures by means of which sentences in the asserting of which we talk about the average man are translated into sentences in the asserting of which we do not talk about the average man, but instead about individual men, just seem to yield no translation whatever for 'The average man exists'. John Wisdom said that 'the translation of sentences about the average man seems to make him vanish'. Not because it shows he doesn't exist; rather because it assigns no sense to his existing or not existing. And if you suppose that if *it* assigns these no sense, nothing assigns them a sense, you will suppose they haven't any.

Now I suppose that some of the philosophers, perhaps most of them, who take this view of meanings would say the same: that the translation-procedures which make sense of *some* talk of meanings simply assign no translation at all to 'There are meanings', and thus that 'There are meanings' has no sense. Thinking this, they would of course be right to say that though arguments (2) and (4) may have premises, they have no conclusions.

---

[1] For the most serious and sustained survey of, and attempt to eliminate, the difficulties, see John Wisdom, *Logical Constructions*.

But I think it is worth bringing out that they needn't take so abrupt a stand about the sentence 'There are meanings'. They can allow that the translation-procedures might assign it a translation. Of course there is nothing which seems, *prima facie*, a likely candidate. Friends of meanings would probably object to the proposal that 'There are meanings' is translatable into 'There are meaningful words'—they may be expected to say that there would be meanings even if there were no words, and hence *a fortiori*, no meaningful ones. But whether there is a likely candidate or not, the philosophers I am concerned with need not dogmatically claim that nothing at all translates 'There are meanings', and thus need not dogmatically claim that it has no sense. They can leave it open. Yet all the same, they would be right to say that purported proofs of the existence of meanings have no conclusions.

Let's take a simple case. We might well imagine someone to say that talk about kisses makes sense only in so far as and because it is translatable into talk which is not about kisses, but instead about people and occasions. Thus, for example, that the sentence 'John gave Mary two kisses' does make sense, but only because it is translatable into 'John kissed Mary twice', neither John nor Mary, of course, being a kiss. Someone who took this view might insist that 'There are kisses' has no such translation, and therefore no sense; but he might instead be prepared to assign it a translation, indeed an explicitly existential translation, perhaps 'There are occasions on which someone kisses someone or something'. No doubt his theory would commit him to saying that no such occasion *is* a kiss; but presumably he would be entirely happy to say so.

The situation is rather more complicated in the case of material objects. Perhaps some of those philosophers who said that talk about material objects makes sense only in so far as and because it is translatable into talk which is not about material objects, but instead about sense-data, thought that the translation-procedures would not, and did not need to, assign a translation to the sentence 'There are material objects'.[1] That is, they may have thought that

---

[1] For a discussion of the difference in their attitudes towards 'There are material objects' and 'There are hands', see John Wisdom, 'Moore's Technique', *op. cit.* This article contains easily the best discussion of Moore's 'Proof' in the literature; and those who are familiar with it will recognize that it is in the background of my own discussion of arguments which descend from Moore's 'Proof'.

this sentence really doesn't have a sense. But on the other hand, those who took this view of material objects generally, took it about the different kinds of material objects, and so in particular about *hands*—talk about hands, they thought, makes sense only in so far as and because it is translatable into talk which is not about hands, but instead about sense-data; and most of them, presumably, if not all of them, thought that 'There are hands' had to be allowed a sense, and therefore assigned a translation. Of course it is hard to say just what sort of translation they thought it would receive, in that none of them ever did succeed in producing translations of any talk about even the smallest material object. But perhaps they would have thought 'There are hands' would turn out to be translatable into something like this: 'Certain (handish and handishly related) sense-data are now had by me or would have been had by me if I had had sense-data as of doing certain (hand-hunting) things'. Or perhaps into something explicitly existential, like this: 'There are classes of actual and possible (handish and handishly related) sense-data'. No doubt their theory would commit them to saying that no such class of actual and possible sense-data itself *is* a hand. But they may not only be presumed to be willing to say this, they all did say it, over and over again.

Yet the translations of sentences about kisses and hands seems to make them vanish just as surely as the translations of sentences about the average man seems to make him vanish—even if 'There are kisses' and 'There are hands', unlike 'The average man exists', *are* assigned translations, and thereby given sense. For if 'There are kisses' means (as it might be) 'There are occasions on which someone kisses someone or something', *and* no such occasion is a kiss, then to say 'There are kisses' is to say there are things no one of which is a kiss; kisses seem to be lost if one can't say there are such things, if, that is, try as hard as you will, the only way of saying there are such things is to say there are things which admittedly *aren't* kisses. So a man who thought that talk about kisses made sense only in so far as and because it is translatable into talk which is not about kisses might well be expected to regard kisses as dubious, obscure, not to be 'countenanced'— anyway, not to be countenanced 'over and above' people, and occasions on which people kiss people and things—even if he thought that 'There are kisses' does have a translation and thereby a sense.

And so for hands too: if you think that to say 'There are hands' is to say there are things no one of which is a hand, then hands seem to be lost, to be dubious, not to be 'countenanced', anyway, not to be countenanced 'over and above' sense-data.

And you would begin to feel that something peculiar had happened to argument (1), with which we began. Of course if both 'G. E. Moore has two hands' and 'There are hands' are assigned translations into sentences about sense-data, and if, moreover, they are translations such that an assertion of the first entails an assertion of the second—and presumably the translations they are assigned had better have this relation to each other —then an assertion of (1) is a valid argument. But is it any longer an argument for the existence of *hands*? For its conclusion is a claim to the effect that there are things, no one of which *is* a hand.

I suppose that nobody, nowadays, is inclined to take this view of material objects generally, and hands in particular; and nobody, nowadays, regards hands as queer, dubious, not to be 'countenanced'. So nobody, nowadays, worries about argument (1).

But the view is held by many people nowadays in respect of meanings. If you think that talk about meanings makes sense only in so far as and because it is translatable into talk which is not about meanings, then you may be prepared to assign, or to allow for the possibility of assigning, a translation to 'There are meanings' as well as to 'The word "bank" has two meanings' and 'The meaning of the English word "red" is the same as the meaning of the French word "rouge" '; and you may even be prepared to assign them translations such that assertions of (2) and (4) thereby become valid arguments. But even if you are prepared to do this they will not then be proofs of the existence of *meanings*: for their conclusion, if it is an existential assertion at all, is an assertion to the effect that there are things, no one of which *is* a meaning.

And if anyone asserts (2) or (4), insisting that what *he* deduces from his premise is an assertion to the effect that there are meanings; if, that is, he says he does not mean by 'There are meanings' that there are things, no one of which is a meaning, or indeed anything else which is *not* about meanings, then he does not attach to 'There are meanings' any sense which the translation-procedures might assign to it. And if you think that 'There are meanings' only has such a sense as these procedures do assign to it, you will think, and in light of your theory be right to think, that his argument has no conclusion.

8. Why should anyone think that talk about meanings makes sense only in so far as and because it is translatable into talk which is not about meanings? And, assuming the view could be got stated clearly, would it be right to opt for it? This is matter for another paper. I want only to suggest that at least part of the inclination to opt for it arises from the difficulty I drew attention to, namely the difficulty that confronts one who tries to say what meanings *are*. It is often said that the trouble with meanings (and possibilities and facts too) is that we lack identity conditions for them. But I cannot think that this is anyway the whole of what inclines people to opt for this view. For there are those who regard classes as fully as dubious as meanings, and who suppose that talk about classes makes sense only in so far as and because it is translatable into talk which is not about classes. Yet they are quite content to say that (as it might be) the class of men is identical with the class of featherless bipeds if and only if the members of the class of men are identical with the members of the class of featherless bipeds. Of course this is because they think that to say these things is to say what makes sense only because 'The class of men is identical with the class of featherless bipeds' *and* 'The members of the class of men are identical with the members of the class of featherless bipeds' are both translatable into 'Everything which is a man is a featherless biped and everything which is a featherless biped is a man'. I am inclined to think that these views about meanings and classes have anyway in part a common source: the fact that there seems to be nothing which counts as saying what the entities *are*.

Perhaps it connects with what issued in the theory that talk about material objects makes sense only in so far as and because it is translatable into talk which is not about material objects. The actual grounds they put forward are plain enough. On the one hand, they took the view that, as Ayer put it, 'we know that it must be possible to define material things in terms of sense-contents, because it is only by the occurrence of certain sense-contents that the existence of any material thing can ever be in the least degree verified.'[1] And on the other hand, they took the view that no sense-content or class of sense-contents itself *is* a material

---

[1] A. J. Ayer, *Language, Truth and Logic*, p. 53.

object—they thought it would be an absurdity to say that to shake someone's hand is to shake a class of sense-contents. But perhaps only someone who was worried about what a material thing *is* would have been inclined to think we had better concentrate on that by which we verify claims about material things, and define such claims about material things as we are prepared to opt for in terms of it.

THE VIRGINIA LECTURES

D. C. YALDEN-THOMSON

IN THE spring of 1957 Professor Wisdom, while a Visiting Professor at the University of Virginia, gave a series of lectures under the title 'Proof and Explanation'.[1] The lectures included discussion of a large number of philosophical topics: recognition, universals, paradoxes, metaphysics, the analytic-synthetic distinction, scepticism, mistakes, statements, border-line cases, induction were all considered in some detail. The central theme linking them to each other and to the title was what he called 'case-by-case procedure' or 'reasoning by parallels'.

The importance Professor Wisdom attributed to the role of case-by-case procedure in all reasoning can be demonstrated by some of his general remarks; 'deduction itself is a case-by-case procedure'; 'all reflection comes in the end to a case-by-case procedure'; '. . . one might well say that the difference between deduction and argument by parallels is merely a matter of form'.

A distinction was drawn between case-by-case procedure (or reasoning by parallels) and reasoning by analogy, in that analogy is confined to actual instances while case-by-case procedure encompasses imaginary or conceivable instances as well. It was pointed out that imaginary instances can be just as cogent in, say, moral or legal discussions as actual cases—as exemplified, one might add, by Hume in the *Treatise*, e.g., in the section 'of love and hatred'. Presumably the distinction was intended to be

---

[1] A version of these lectures was prepared by Professor S. F. Barker, now of The Johns Hopkins University, from tape recordings and notes and Professor Wisdom kindly permitted the distribution of a limited number of copies to interested persons. This article is based upon this version together with my own notes and recollections.

The lectures, to an audience of twenty-five or so graduate students and faculty members, were given once a week and lasted for about two and a half hours each. Each meeting opened with a lecture of about one hour; then there was an interval of fifteen minutes and the meeting was resumed with a discussion period of questions, some of startling irrelevance, raised by the audience. The lecture was then continued until the end of the meeting.

How deeply I am indebted to Professor Barker for composing his version of the lectures is obvious.

stipulative, since analogy is sometimes used with reference to imaginary cases in ordinary discussions.

Wisdom's view that so-called 'inductive' argument is reasoning by parallels or analogy does not need to be laboured, nor, perhaps, his claim that all reflection comes in the end to case-by-case procedure. When we are wondering whether the object before us is a spade, whether the right legal decision was reached, whether the firm of Baker and Sons is bankrupt, whether it is true that love is always, in part, hate, we look to parallels, noticing affinities and dissimilarities between the objects or cases before us and the similar instances we can see or conceive: in particular, one notices that in discussions as to whether an action was or would be right or wrong, obligatory or otherwise, people so often argue by pointing to comparable actions whether they have in mind general moral principles or not.

But Wisdom's remarks on the relation of case-by-case procedure to deduction are more likely to evoke surprise. The contention that all reasoning comes in the end to case-by-case procedure must include formal deduction, and formal deduction does not appear to be argument by parallels. I propose, then, to describe in detail some of the reasons he advanced.

Taking first the claim '. . . when someone offers a deductive form of justification for a statement ("This has twelve edges because it is a cube"), then the support, reason, and justification which he thus gives in a deductive form are no stronger than that which might be given by that sort of case-by-case procedure which is apt to be regarded with contempt.' (Professors Blanshard and Broad had been cited as evincing this attitude). For the conclusion 'This has twelve edges' can be equally well justified by asking with regard to every conceivable cube, other than the one before us, isn't this a case of having twelve edges? 'One who offers a deductive proof for his conclusions offers as much as one who offers a case-by-case proof . . . but he doesn't offer more.'

The use of syllogistic proofs, he urged, leads to the same result. Consider an argument such as this: 'this is an argument in the fourth figure of the syllogism which obeys the general rules of the syllogism and the special rules of the fourth figure; all arguments which answer to these conditions are valid; therefore this argument is valid'. Here Wisdom makes the familiar point, 'Do you or don't you include this argument under your principle? If

F

you do, your argument is circular; if not, it's invalid.' And this result he claimed to be perfectly general. Since the only answer to the challenge is to display paradigm cases of, say, arguments in the fourth figure which are valid and then to show that the argument in question parallels the paradigm cases—such a procedure is, of course, the case-by-case procedure. (In reply to a question, Wisdom agreed that we are misled by the way in which we are taught logic. Because we are taught the rules governing validity first, we lose sight of the fact that the rules were obtained by looking at instances which are patently valid and generalizing from them.) Putting the matter somewhat differently: 'The deductive proof of C from P is no more than a case-by-case proof of C. . . . for to prove a conclusion C from P is valid only when every investigation and every comparison required for the establishment of C is also required for the establishment of P,' and this holds equally whether one is considering general statements of fact or a principle of logic or mathematics. 'There does,' he then remarked, 'dawn on us the shocking affinity in kind between the procedures of respectable reflection (deduction) and those which we regard as disreputable.'

To say that deduction of a conclusion from a premiss 'comes to no more than' a case-by-case proof of the conclusion is not, of course, to deny that they are different processes. Moreover, the deductive process is most useful, convenient, though sometimes less vivid than reasoning by parallels: nor, again, is it anything but absolutely conclusive, whereas case-by-case procedure is, e.g., when used to try to settle a border-line dispute, often anything but conclusive. But, it was urged, we shall not see deduction correctly in its relation to all other forms of thinking unless we recognize that whether a piece of reasoning is good or bad is not decided by whether it is a formally deductive or a case-by-case procedure. And deductive argument may present, for all its admirable brevity, only part of the whole scope of the justification which could be provided by a complete case-by-case procedure, e.g., 'when the premiss is related to the conclusion in such a way that though the premiss entails the conclusion the conclusion does not entail the premiss'. What one may assume Wisdom to have had in mind here might be an argument of this kind: 'If a thing is a square, then it is a rectangle.' Presumably a full case-by-case procedure here would, *en principe*, involve considering every actual and conceivable instance of a rectangle and noticing that all squares were also rectangles, whereas the justification of the premiss would involve considering every actual and conceivable instance of a square.

No claim to novelty is made here, in the sense that all accept that in deduction any statement C is deducible from P when and only when 'every investigative measure and every reflective measure, every comparative act for the justification of C, is also required for the justification of P. It may be the case that P requires more justification than C, but it cannot require less. So it's no wonder that in a deductive proof we don't present better justification than we do when we use a direct procedure for establishing C'.

A reader may guess that even such a very abbreviated account as has been given above of Wisdom's remarks about deduction and the case-by-case procedure provoked some objections. One, inevitably, was that no justification of 'self-evident' propositions about cubes having twelve edges, squares being rectangles and the principles governing the validity of syllogisms was called for. If 'self-evidence' was an unwelcome term then they could be called 'rules of grammar', 'stipulative rules' and so on. Wisdom's reply here was to point out that 'Not both P and not P' is not something which one knows to be true simply by looking at the symbols. We come to understand them by being given cases: 'A thing couldn't be a tree and not a tree, could it?' And the same sort of response is appropriate in regard to the meaning of formation rules and transformation rules. They are taught by instances in the first place, and then we say 'and so on'. The process of proving, he repeatedly stated, was the process of learning in reverse.

This summary account of Wisdom's views on the case-by-case procedure in relation to deduction omits, necessarily, a wealth of illustrations which he offered. When speaking in very general terms about the procedure, he described it as not being 'a process of reasoning' in the sense of a process of deduction or induction, 'but it is a process in which reason is operative' and he re-iterated the claim that 'in cases of deductive reasoning the conclusion is no better established . . . than it is by this process of the direct case-by-case procedure.'

One was left with the impression that he saw our neglect of the primary role of the case-by-case procedure in learning and in reflection as having led to cramped notions, among philosophers and others, of explanation and proof. Specifically, he viewed our inadequate grasp of the procedure as having led to one widespread mistake. So many philosophical enquiries arrived at the position that if a problem was not amenable to further empirical investigation and if no deductive reasoning was of avail, then the question at issue *must* be just a matter of words. He provided a plethora of examples.

One type of illustration was from the law. Taking hypothetical cases of bankruptcy and negligence, one could suppose situations in which all the law was in, the facts agreed upon, the counsel on each side having pointed to the closest parallels among precedents (on the one hand to cases very like this one under adjudication which had been found to be cases of negligence: on the other side, cases very like this one in which the accused was judged innocent) and then the judge is asked for a verdict. No further deductive reasoning is relevant: no further investigations would reveal relevant facts. What is called for here, in Wisdom's view, is not a shrug of the shoulders, a flip of the coin, the consoling thought that it is just a matter of words, but more reflection. Indeed, one would not much care to appear before a judge on a negligent driving charge in which, perhaps, one's assets and liberty were at stake, who took the view, because of clear, if superficial, philosophical *dicta*, that it was not his duty to reflect (since it must be fruitless to do so), the issue being a 'matter of words'. He saw this kind of mistake as stemming, also, in part, from the misleading remark that 'all matters of fact are settled by observation', which could be an expression of one premiss of the verbalist's argument, but at the same time he noted that 'no form of words puts a question of fact unless at *some* stage in the proceeding of answering it a person, as one might say, looks about him.' However, that at a stage after observations further questions may yield a better apprehension he described as a most fundamental and far-reaching point.

Another cluster of examples was drawn from claims about the unconscious in literature and in the writings of Freud. He quoted from Dostoievsky's *Eternal Husband* the remark by Velchaninov about Pabel Pabelovitch: 'All along he intended to murder me, although the idea never entered his head. . . . It's nonsense, but it's the truth'. Such explanations of behaviour in terms of unconscious desires and intentions produce responses of standard varieties: (i) the explanation is an unverifiable hypothesis; (ii) it's not an explanation at all, but a description involving a stretched word; (iii) it is a case in which no further evidence is available and there is no room for further investigation, so it's a matter of words.

He sometimes referred to advocates of 'It's a matter of words' as the 'verbalists', but more often as 'the clever chaps'. He pointed out that they could defend their view by claiming that matters of words were very important: a new symbolism may entail enormous convenience and may affect attitudes (as in legal cases—and here he quoted Professor Glanville Williams as an exponent of this view). But the clever chaps' stance misleads us because, for one thing, it suggests that there is no conflict between one who advances the explanatory theory of the unconscious and one who says the theory is false: it may mislead us equally into thinking that in a dispute in which neither party can *prove* he is right, then there is no point in continuing with it.

It may well be, of course, that in a particular dispute the question may be a matter of words: it may be the case that one accountant in bankruptcy proceedings may be using the word 'solvent' more strictly than another: such questions as 'Do people call this a tallboy?' are plainly questions of words, in the sense of being questions as to what people will say about such words. And border-line case disagreements may arise whether the word is definite (as in bankruptcy cases) or relatively indefinite (as in claims and counter-claims about the unconscious)—though he held that where the meaning of the word is more definite, the range of cases in which such arguments arise will be smaller. And, also, that the temptation to say 'It's a matter of words' will be greater the vaguer the word and the more indefinite the procedure. (And this mistake, again, is connected with 'the habit of thinking that one doesn't understand a word unless one can define it . . .' —a habit which ties our hands). What is called for is more reflection, a further searching for similarities and dissimilarities. Wisdom did not, however (and in this he was consistent in adhering to the case-by-case procedure) offer any formula or criterion for distinguishing verbal from non-verbal questions. But he drew attention to the fact that, while verbal disputes differ from dis-agreements about border-line cases and paradoxical assertions, the same form of words, e.g., 'we are all dishonest' may generate an argument which is purely verbal, but it may lead to a discussion in which one party really grasps another's conception of dishonesty for the first time and one could not then say that this was a purely verbal accomplishment. Philosophical questions could properly be said to be about words but not of words.

He reviewed a number of examples of the mistake of claiming that a dispute was 'a matter of words', some general and some specific. One (unnamed) philosopher had written of Sartre's view that in love one party devours another as a purely verbal matter—this he (Wisdom) described as 'soothing prattle'. He criticized Ryle in *Dilemmas* for the way in which he described conflicts between scientists and their commonsense opponents on such issues as whether tables and chairs were solid. He objected in more general terms to the way in which some linguistic philosophers tended to call metaphysical questions 'questions of words'. And he commented, in regard to William James[1] and the squirrel, '. . . if I had been with James at this picnic party and had come back and found these people . . . had thrashed out very fully their conceptions of "going round", at that stage . . . I think it might indeed have been a waste of time to continue that dispute. It would, however, even here be misleading to call this a case of a purely verbal misunderstanding'.

Wisdom's vehement attack on the line of argument 'No further deductive reasoning can help; no further investigation would reveal facts; therefore, the issue is a matter of words' (or, as he sometimes put it, 'when sense and reason fail us, it must be a matter of words'), was extended by pointing to other consequences. In instances of chronic hesitancy over questions, the clever chaps' response, 'It isn't a real question', tended to stop reflection when further reflection might be fruitful, for a question is so often a question of fact when it calls *only* for reflection. And this school of thought obscured the role of reflection in revealing facts of a most elementary kind, often described as determined by mere observation, such as 'is this a piece of chalk?' or 'is this the Stars and Stripes?'. Yet another type of error into which we can be led by such a line of thought is to suppose that a question is merely verbal because no different expectations or predictions would result whichever view is adopted.

One suspected that he saw the general position as one which he

---

[1] William James, *Pragmatism*.

regretted having shared[1] when he opened one lecture by saying 'I'd like to describe in a rather egocentric way the object I'm concerned with in these lectures: I'm devoting the second part of my philosophical life to remedying the mischief I helped to make in the first'.

Having exhibited the relation of case-by-case procedure to deduction and the neglect of that procedure as the genesis of the verbalist error—an error of which the long history derives in English philosophy from Hume's exclusive and exhaustive disjunction of propositions into matters of fact and relations of ideas —in later lectures he explored the relation of induction and case-by-case procedure.

Induction, on any account, involves recognition. And recognition is clearly a necessary part of case-by-case procedure, whether the procedure in a given instance is good or bad. On this topic— 'This is the situation which makes one feel that the more you look at thought the more it disappears into nothing at all'—it was contended by Wisdom that at least one contemporary view was wrong. Wittgenstein, and Ryle following Wittgenstein, used such expressions as 'There is not *another* process which is an action of the understanding', 'There isn't another process which is *different* from the seeing process'. This he held to be inaccurate, because the process of seeing is not identical with the process of recognizing. The parrot may see the Stars and Stripes, and even say 'Stars and Stripes' in the most appropriate way when we produce the flag, but this does not tell us that he recognizes it. He criticized two other accounts: the account which tells 'psychological lies suggesting that this process . . . never occurs unless a sort of penumbra of images appear in the mind'; and the dangers of the account offered in terms of universals.[2] He himself offered no positive explanation of recognition, but seemed to suggest that the form of the question, 'What is it that *happens* when someone recognizes a thing as of a certain kind?' was unhappy: '. . . while they put the question in this form, this trouble . . . will persist— this trouble in which one is tempted to make up another process which is happening at the same time, of the same type as the seeing of the object, and the temptation to invent more and equally

[1] e.g., in *Mind and Matter*, perhaps.
[2] Professor Wisdom's opinions on this topic were recorded in a talk, reviewing Professor H. H. Price's *Thinking and Experience*, on the B.B.C.

unenlightening descriptions of the situation'. He said, instead of offering an account, that here one saw an instance of the principle that the meaning of a statement is the method of its verification, because the only proof that a person recognizes an object depends on 'how he can go on'; whether the person (or the parrot) can produce the right word on the right occasion.

Ordinary inductive argument Wisdom described as 'a kind of case-by-case procedure', but, he implied, it is narrower because it is concerned with actual cases and does not refer to cases which are merely conceivable. Further, in the typical inductive conclusions of the scientist, prediction and further investigation are involved. He took up, at some length, Russell's argument[1] about the farmer's wife and the chicken and pointed out that Russell did not allow room for any distinction to be made between the 'inferences' of the chicken and the inferences of Rutherford. And this Wisdom took to be, on Russell's part, an instance of bad case-by-case procedure. He noted that Russell's chicken should not be regarded with contempt; certainly it was a more intelligent chicken than one which expected a human being who approached it to feed it, although no one had done so before. While Russell's contention had the value of reviving before the mind the difference between the 'therefore' in inductive argument and in demonstrative argument, it is associated with the sneer that all scientific reasoning is of the *post hoc ergo propter hoc* variety and with the contention that when one looks out of the window and sees everything dripping and says 'Must have been raining very hard', one is committing the fallacy of affirming the consequent. A listener was left with the impression that the Humean-Russellian stance had been of value but that it had also been most misleading in that it suggested, not only that all inductive argument was of equal value or of no value, but an absolutely fundamental dichotomy between induction and deduction which was false since induction was a form of the case-by-case procedure and that 'absolutely all deductive argument comes in the end to case-by-case procedure; that it is a form of presenting the argument which might have been presented in a case-by-case piece of reasoning'.

One particular piece of reasoning, Moore's argument[2] that he

[1] *The Problems of Philosophy*, Chapter VI.
[2] G. E. Moore, 'Proof of an External World', Proceedings the British of Academy, Vol. XXV.

knew there were two objects in the external world, i.e., two hands, before him when he addressed the British Academy, was examined separately and at length. Wisdom first drew attention to the curious character of Moore's statement that, while in the case of his hand, a sceptic might touch it and examine it —thus *'establishing'* that it really was a human hand—he did 'not believe that any proof is possible in nearly all cases'. Next he said that 'Moore seems to go rather far in speaking extremely confidently when he says that such statements ("Here are two hands") cannot be proved', although, of course, Moore made it clear that it did not follow from the fact that such statements could not be *proved* that they cannot be *known*. And he criticized Moore for not emphasizing the distinction between cases where a person sees, feels and tastes, say, a piece of cheese, and cases where some creature comes to a correct conclusion without, as we say, 'having any reason for it', e.g., the antelope's instinctive fear of the first lion that he meets. And, along the same lines, he said that Moore's claim that he had *conclusive* evidence that he was awake but could not prove it, suggested that Moore's examples were like those of the doctor who has *conclusive* evidence that a patient is suffering from an enlarged liver although that was very different from having *proof* of it. Finally, Wisdom said it was misleading of Moore to step from 'I cannot tell you what all my evidence is', in the claim 'here are two hands', to the words 'I cannot *prove* what I assert in this case'. Wisdom concluded this section by saying, 'The expression "I cannot *prove*" does suggest . . . either that there are no reasons at all or that these reasons are inconclusive.'[1]

Wisdom did not give explicit reasons for considering Moore's argument in the context of his thesis of the case-by-case procedure, but one might suppose that, in any attempt to prove the existence of objects in the external world, he would point to the necessity of exemplification, whether the instances were Moore's two hands or the stone which Dr. Johnson kicked. But there are, it seems to me, aspects of Moore's argument which deserve attention in addition to those which Wisdom selected in this particular lecture. Wisdom is correct in following Moore when he says that it is all right to say 'I know X, but I cannot prove it', as, for instance, when Moore said he knew he was awake but could not prove it. But it is still an unusual thing to say and in some circum-

---

[1] The italics are mine.

stances evokes suspicion as to the knowledge claim, e.g., 'I know he was lying but I cannot prove it'. And, also, it is sometimes used misleadingly. A witness to a crime may say that it was committed because he saw it done, but cannot prove it. Here, however, one might plausibly urge that two different propositions are being elided: the witness has proof that the crime was committed because he saw the act: what he cannot prove is something else, namely, he lacks proof of the proposition that he saw the crime committed.

But what I find strange are Moore's statements that, on the one hand he is offering a 'perfectly rigorous proof' and, on the other, that he cannot prove his premises. One may say, of course, that an argument is 'perfectly valid' and the premises unproven or false: one might say, of a deductive proof, 'this is a proof, but the premises are false' (though even that, and granted that the expression is sometimes used, seems rather odd—it would seem more natural to say 'this is a valid argument with false premises'). To use one of Wisdom's expressions, Moore does seem to be 'stretching a word'. Further, in two ways, Moore had proof: there were his hands before his audience (could a better 'proof' of an empirical fact be offered?) and additional 'proof' was available— they could be touched and so forth—though to speak of 'additional proof' rather than 'additional evidence', if 'proof' in the first instance has been used strictly, is itself faintly paradoxical. And, although Moore considered his proof deductive, this again seems to be stretching a word, for the feature of his argument which makes it so interesting in the history of philosophy is that the essence of it lay in his displaying two physical objects—his hands. Had he not done that, he was offering no proof, deductive or otherwise: in presenting his proof he may have been unable to *say* what all his evidence was, but he was *showing* it.

Wisdom noted the curiousness of Moore's saying that a sceptic, by touching, might 'establish' that it was a human hand before him, and yet say that he could not 'prove it'; he could also have justifiably remarked, I think, that it was odd too of Moore to claim he had 'conclusive evidence' for P and could not prove P. Surely, if the word 'conclusive' is used properly, as applied to an argument, then its use signifies that the author takes it, rightly or wrongly, that the proposition which terminates the argument has been 'proved'. And similarly with claims about 'conclusive' evidence, reasons, grounds and demonstrations; whether the claims are correct or not, to say 'conclusive' is final.[1] For 'conclusive' falls in that narrow range of words of which, in one restricted sense, there are no border-line cases. Two persons may disagree about whether an argument is conclusive or not: a person may be hesitant as to whether a particular argument is conclusive or not; but the issue—is or is not this a conclusive argument?—is not one about which it would ever seem reasonable to say 'it's a matter of words: say what you please'. And if this is correct, then it follows that one of Wisdom's remarks was itself misleading when he said:

> And although Moore says that I have no doubt conclusive reasons for asserting that I'm not now dreaming, conclusive evidence that I'm awake, but that this is very different from being able to prove it—this phrase is apt to convey the impression that Moore is in the position of one who has conclusive evidence that a patient is suffering from an enlarged liver although that is a very different point from having proof of it. I'm sure that Moore if this point were put to him would be anxious to allow at once that there are big differences between these cases and his instances when he holds up two hands or holds in his hands chalk.

For while certainly there are big differences, the physician who claims that he has 'conclusive evidence' of an enlarged liver is making no lesser claim, logically or epistemologically, than if he makes it after the autopsy, when the liver is in front of his eyes.[2]

Wisdom drew attention to the fact that the exponent of scepticism about our knowledge of the external world also founds his position upon the case-by-case procedure: he reminds us of hallucinations, mirages, illusions and delusions. He refers to cases in which, in spite of the fact that to all appearances a thing of kind K was present, it nevertheless turned out in the light of experience that there was not. The sceptic then usually takes one of two lines: (i) 'in every case that which gives a man the right to make a statement as to the external world is never such as to be incompatible with subsequent happenings giving him grounds to hesitate as to whether that statement which he made was altogether

---

[1] We do speak of people jumping to conclusions: would that they did.
[2] Wisdom himself at a later point remarked, in another context, '. . . these reasons lend some probability to these statements we make, but are far from *conclusive* reasons and cannot be counted as *proofs*'. (My italics).

correct'; or, (ii) 'whatever ground a man has to date for making an assertion about the external world, it's still conceivable that subsequent happenings should be fatal to the claim that he has made'. Line (ii) he described as 'unduly violent', as unnecessary in that extreme form. (No allusion was made *apropos* of (i) to J. L. Austin's view[1] about a 'goldfinch' which subsequently exploded.) And from such reasonings the inference is made that 'no one at any time knows to be true any statement about the external world'.

This result is often re-inforced by another piece of case-by-case reasoning. Sceptics will try to press the similarity between a claim to know that there is a dog barking (in the days of gramophone records and radios) because a noise as of a dog barking is heard and a claim to know that we have a piece of chalk in our hands. This type of reasoning he referred to as the 'You might as well say' form: 'You might as well say that a man who hears a dog bark has proof that a dog is there'; in Russell it occurs too: 'You might as well say that a chicken has proof that he's going to be fed.' Wisdom also noticed the similar procedure adopted by those who, while ashamed to say that one never knows anything about an external world, claim, as Wittgenstein did in the *Tractatus*, that all such statements are hypotheses. Some argue that we can never prove conclusions about the general course of nature or what is going to happen because the reasons are always inductive and no inductive reasons are really reasons. 'This whole family of talk,' he put it, 'is a labyrinth.'

The novelty of Wisdom's claim that not only all proof but all knowledge rests upon case-by-case procedure ('Every statement calls for reflection—every statement is challengeable': ' "It's a spade" involves reflection as well as verification of enormous complexity, running over the whole of time and space') led to a number of questions being addressed to him upon the criteria for distinguishing good and bad case-by-case procedure.

Consistently with his own contention about case-by-case procedure, argument by parallels or (as he once put it) reasoning by comparison, Wisdom's reply was that only a case-by-case procedure could illuminate the difference between good and bad case-by-case procedure. He appeared to think that to put such a tempting general question is, in itself, to fail to recognize the

[1] J. L. Austin, *Philosophical Papers*, first ed., p. 56.

fundamental role of the procedure in all reasoning. (Analogously, having in a lecture stressed the value in Wittgenstein's technique of the use of case-by-case procedure, he had once been quickly asked 'And how do you distinguish between philosophical and non-philosophical questions?'). But, while there was, of course, no general formula, this did not mean that it was worthless to examine instances of good and bad procedure, and in some areas one could offer definite rules for good procedure. The question 'When are arguments in the fourth figure of the syllogism good and when bad?' could be answered satisfactorily, even though these responses, when challenged, had ultimately to be supported (as was described earlier in this essay), in terms of examples. (At one point he had said enigmatically, 'The whole of logic is contained in the lines:

> "So tell your papa where the yak can be got,
>   And if he is awfully rich
> He will buy you the creature or else he will not,
>   I cannot be positive which." '

Again, with regard to such rules, it was perhaps a token of his sense that philosophers have tended to overemphasize the importance, respectability and distinctiveness of deductive reasoning in relation to reflection in general that he said at one point, 'We fasten on the excellence of the deductive step from premisses to conclusion, neglecting the steps required for establishing the premisses themselves'. But while we had good rules for deductive reasoning, it was notorious that attempts to give an account in general terms of when scientific or inductive reasoning was good or bad had been a failure 'not only compared with the attempt to give such an account of deductive reasoning but also as compared with what we may achieve when asked about reasoning concerning probabilities.'

When, in discussions and disputes, the issue was the applicability of a term K, it was often possible to state the necessary and sufficient conditions, but sometimes it was not possible—and this *could* be the case because there were no terms in the language to do so. (Wisdom gave no instances here). He mentioned William James and Wittgenstein as philosophers who have emphasized that it is 'perfectly possible to know what is meant by a term, to explain what is meant by a term, without giving a definition'. He named Quine as an example of a philosopher who made a mistake in this connection. 'Quine reviews the various things that philosophers have said in trying to characterize the difference between analytic and synthetic statements, and he points out that all these characterizations are vague . . . that (they) do not prevent there being many border-line cases in which we should hesitate over a statement, not knowing whether to call it analytic or synthetic. And he says, "a boundary between analytic and synthetic statements simply has not been drawn"[1] . . . this will hardly do. One might hesitate over the case of satyrs, not knowing whether to call them goats or men: but this doesn't mean that there's no difference between a goat and a man'. It was necessary, he urged, to combat the view that unless one had a criterion that a thing was of a certain kind or that a term was applicable, then one had no rational ground for claims of such kinds and this applied, *inter alia*, to disputes about whether we had before us a chair, a goat or a case of schizophrenia.

In the event, Wisdom, in using the case-by-case procedure to illustrate differences between good and bad procedures, gave many more examples of bad than good. He cited, as a notorious instance of malpractice, the argument that there can never be a crowd, because, if you start with one person and then intermittently add one person, the continuity of this process would preclude a person from ever saying that a crowd was assembled. It is, however, hard to imagine that such an argument was ever seriously advanced. He also instanced the argument that all actions are selfish, whether supported by cases or by a deductive proof from the premiss that in all voluntary actions agents are acting as they wish. Other examples he gave included further references to Russell and the chicken (he pointed out that a Russellian might say to a mother whose child was, after having been burned, afraid of fire that the child had 'no good reason' for being afraid) and to McTaggart's arguments for scepticism about the external world. 'McTaggart and Russell seem to have no grasp of the fact that "know" or "have real reason" have been so modified in (their) use that the sceptical statement they make is necessarily true. . . . The fact is that (they) bring it out as true without bringing it out as something which couldn't have been false'. And, among many other examples, he reminded one again

---

[1] W. V. Quine, *From a Logical Point of View*, p. 37.

of the 'you might as well say' argument about the piece of chalk and the noise heard as of a dog barking.

He suggested that one symptom of poor case-by-case procedure was that it evoked the response 'That's different': this sort of reply was appropriate to the contention that shooting an enemy soldier in wartime was murder: that Rutherford had no more reason for his views than the chicken, and so forth. But, he explained elsewhere, 'If you think that this (the response "This is different") provides a criterion for whether this sort of argumentation is good or not, you'd be quite wrong. Because, when a case quoted in support is different from a case concluded to, then to say that the argumentation therefore is not good, this would be as good as to say that no such argumentation is good; since you can't have argument by parallels unless the case referred to is other than the case in question'. In conclusion, he said that it was profitless to talk in terms of general formulae about relevant differences and relevant affinities between the examples, for this was question-begging. On the other hand he seemed to think it worth characterizing fruitful case-by-case procedure with the remark that it is a matter of 'not missing an affinity . . . (one) is *aiming to mark*; not missing a difference . . . (one) is aiming to mark'. 'You might be tempted to say that a person's grasp of a manifold is complete when he's caught every affinity and every difference—but of course this doesn't happen. . . .'

In conclusion, I should like to note that this essay is a summary of only one theme among many in Professor Wisdom's lectures at Virginia: that while I hope it does not distort his views either by abbreviation or misunderstanding (and I have not consulted him on any point), if it does so the hoped for remedy will lie in the publication in full of the lectures.

IV

PARADOXES AND DISCOVERIES*

ILHAM DILMAN

I

IN 1939 G. E. Moore gave a lecture to the British Academy in which he aimed to refute the philosopher who claims that there are no material things. He lifted up his hands saying 'Here is one hand and here is another'. How absurd it would be (he said) for anyone in the audience to doubt this. Since hands are material things it follows, he asserted, that there are at least two material things whose existence it would be absurd for him and his audience to doubt or deny. Hence, he concluded, he had shown clearly and conclusively that philosophers who deny the existence of material things *must be wrong*.

Moore thought that at least some philosophers who said that material things do not exist were saying something that is an affront to common sense, denying something which anyone who has not taken leave of his senses believes to be true. He, therefore, regarded himself as a spokesman for plain common sense and a defender of its tenets.

He was, of course, right to insist that it would be *absurd*, in the circumstances, for anyone in the audience to claim that Moore did not know that he had a hand, but only believed or thought it extremely likely that he had one. He thought that we are all constantly confronted with similar situations in which we have a right to be confident about the truth of a great many material object propositions which we would not so much as find the need to assert. Wittgenstein who gave much thought to what Moore was saying[1] pointed out that the fact that there are a great many occasions on which we trust our senses, act without hesitation or doubt, underlies the working of any part of our language which, in one way or another, involves a reference to physical reality. The

---

* The figures given in parentheses in this essay refer to items in the bibliography at the end of the chapter.
[1] See *On Certainty* (Basil Blackwell, 1969).

very intelligibility of any doubt we may feel in other situations rests on there being occasions on which most of us find a doubt unintelligible: 'If there is a making sure *here* then there is no making sure at all' (Wittgenstein).

In a reply to his critics Moore said: 'I have sometimes distinguished between two different propositions, each of which has been made by some philosophers, namely, (1) the proposition "There are no material things" and (2) the proposition "Nobody knows for certain that there are any material things". And in my British Academy Lecture I implied with regard to the first of these propositions that it could be *proved* to be false. . . . But with regard to the second of these two propositions I do not think that I have ever implied that *it* could be *proved* to be false in any such simple way.'[1]

Moore thought that he had at least proved the proposition that there are no material things to be false. Was this not a rash assumption? Had he really succeeded in silencing those philosophers who want to deny the existence of material things? Had he shown that if we grant that there are two human hands we *must* also grant that matter exists? Berkeley, it seems, did not think so: 'That the things I see with mine eyes (he said) and touch with my hands do exist, really exist, I make not the least question' (*Princ.*, sec. 35). Yet he did not hesitate to deny the existence of material things. Was this a logical blunder? Not according to Wittgenstein: 'Those philosophers (he said) who have denied the existence of matter have not wished to deny that under my trousers I wear pants.'

Still one can agree with Moore, as Professor Wisdom does, that this is an oversimplification. In his paper 'Moore's Technique' Wisdom says that 'Moore's claim that philosophers, when saying that Matter does not exist, have been discussing a negative existential hypothesis like "There are no unicorns" has plenty of excuses. As Moore pointed out to me, McTaggart said: "So matter is in the same position as the gorgons and the harpies". And, undoubtedly, people who say that Beauty and Goodness do not exist expect to shock us" ' (*PPA*, p. 137). Wisdom went on to say that there are many small differences between one who says that matter does not exist and one who says that matter is nothing over and above our sense impressions

---

[1] *G. E. Moore*, edited by Paul Schilpp, p. 668.

G

(p. 139). The approach of one who says that matter does not exist to his conclusion and the air with which he brings it out are like those of the man who brings out the conclusion that though there are lights on the ship in the distance and its sails are well set, there is no one aboard (p. 138). He appears both to himself and others to advance a negative hypothesis. Besides he feels very differently as he speaks from one who is putting forward an analysis of the concept of matter, and he differs in his reactions to the implications of what he says from the conceptual analyst: 'The former doesn't look at you as if you are mad if you infer that he denies that there are cherries on a tree' (pp. 139–40).

Does it follow from this that the two philosophers do not mean the same thing by what they say? Wisdom's answer is that the only thing that follows from these considerations is that it would be an oversimplification to say that they do mean the same thing. He does not deny that there are good reasons for saying that the philosopher who denies the existence of material things is not denying the truth of an existential hypothesis: 'In order to learn what a man means (he writes) we cannot rely on the form of words he uses, nor even on what he says he means' (*PD*, p. 96). If we look at the considerations that lead philosophers to deny the existence of material things we shall see that unlike someone who puts forward an hypothesis, positive or negative, they do not 'at any point rely upon some premiss which though true could conceivably have been false' (p. 75).

Wisdom reminds us of occasions outside philosophy where words to the effect that 'such-and-such a thing does not exist' are used to make a conceptual point, to prevent a logical misunderstanding. For instance, with the words 'The average man does not exist' one may combat the idea that the relation between the average man and individual men is like the relation between a member of Parliament and his constituency (see *PPA*, pp. 137–8). He says that although this way of putting the point may muddle people into suspecting the familiar remarks we make about people's tastes, incomes, and abilities with the help of such expressions as 'the average man', 'the average taxpayer', 'the average plumber', it is nevertheless a natural way of speaking.

More strongly still, no one can coherently deny the existence of material things *in the way* that a traveller in the desert may deny that there is water in the distance when it looks as if there is.

Therefore insofar as one who denies the existence of matter thinks he is denying the truth of an hypothesis he must be confused.

Moore was not, then, altogether wrong in thinking that *some* philosophers who said that material things do not exist *thought* they were asserting a negative existential hypothesis, *meant* their words in that way, and *expected* to shock us. But he was wrong in thinking that their words *can* express a general hypothesis. In his 'Proof of an External World' he assumed that such a proposition as 'Here is a hand and here is another' *entails* the proposition that there are material things. He thought that one cannot consistently accept his premiss and deny that there are material things. But whether this is true or not depends on how the words 'There are no material things' are used. If a philosopher means these words as one who says that the average man does not exist means his words, if what he means is that material things are not anything over and above sense impressions, then he can consistently accept Moore's premiss and continue to deny his conclusion. Therefore what Moore's proof shows is not that one cannot deny the existence of material things without absurdity, but that one cannot deny it *in the way* that one can deny the existence of unicorns. Thus Moore's proof will force one who denies the existence of material things without being clear about this 'to become unmuddled, to gain a grasp of what he wishes to do with his words, what he wishes to understand by them' (*PPA*, p. 140). It will force him to reformulate what he is trying to say: 'Material things are not anything over and above our sense impressions'. This is not an existential hypothesis and, whatever one thinks of it, it is at least free of the confusion Moore's proof helped to clear.

Berkeley, who is known to have denied the existence of matter, cannot be justly accused of this confusion. When he said that matter does not exist he meant that the idea of matter as something over and above our sense impressions involves a contradiction. Yet he was in two minds about whether he was opposing our everyday conception of matter or only a philosophical account of what it comes to. On the one hand he said that 'the philosophical notion of matter involves a contradiction' (*Princ.*, sec. 9) and denied he was finding fault with our everyday notion of matter: 'No sort of writings which use those and like words (e.g. timber and stone, etc.), in the *vulgar acceptation* are in danger of having their truth called in question by our doctrine' (sec. 82). He denied that when we speak of timber and stone we mean something over and above our sense impressions: 'Whether others mean anything by the term *reality* different from what I do (*i.e.* matter is nothing but idea), I entreat them to look into their own thoughts and see' (sec. 36). On the other hand he also said that the vulgar opinion itself involves a contradiction: 'It is indeed an opinion *strangely* prevailing amongst men, that all sensible objects have an existence natural or real, distinct from their being perceived by the understanding. . . . Yet whoever shall find in his heart to call it in question, may, if I mistake not, perceive it to involve a manifest contradiction' (sec. 4).

Thus while he was concerned to combat views that could be attributed to philosophers such as Locke, he did not think that these views were confined to the philosopher's study. The 'prejudice' that matter is something distinct and independent of our sense impressions (he said) 'is riveted so deeply in our thoughts, that we can scarce tell how to part with it' (sec. 74; also see sec. 75). Did this mean that our everyday talk and thought is vitiated by philosophical misconceptions? Berkeley was not clear on this question. He was divided in his reactions over the question 'Has the sentence "Here is a human hand" a correct use?'—as are many philosophers who deny the existence of material things over the question 'Are there no cherries on the tree?' (see *PPA*, p. 140).

Professor Malcolm has said that a philosopher who holds that the notion of a material thing involves a contradiction finds fault with everyday language. It is therefore sufficient, he thought, to remind him that the notion of a material thing has a perfectly good use, that such sentences as 'There is water in the glass', for instance, 'do have a correct use in ordinary discourse, which they could not have if they were self-contradictory' (*Mind*, Jan. 1960). But this is by no means clear, and it could not be said, without oversimplifica-tion, that such a philosopher must be setting his face against the language in which we successfully communicate with each other. He may not be clear that his words cannot be coherently meant in the way that Malcolm takes them, and insofar as Malcolm reminds him of this his contribution will have been invaluable. But there is more in Berkeley's words than meets the eye and Malcolm is repeating Moore's naïvety in failing to appreciate this.

To see what Berkeley was trying to say one has to take his

words in their proper setting—that is in the context of the questions
with which he was concerned. He was concerned to combat
scepticism and to understand how any question about material
things is in the end answered, how we can even form a conception
of matter if it is logically independent of our sense impressions.

It was this feature of the grammar of material things that
troubled him most. He recognized it as being an essential part of
what we all mean by matter and not merely a philosopher's
invention. Yet it seemed to him that it has the consequence that if
we know the existence of material things at all we can only know it
indirectly, that is in the way we know from the images we see in
our driving mirror that the car behind is getting ready to pull out.
But we can in this way know something about the car behind us
only because we can look away from the mirror to the car itself,
and because others on other occasions have done so and seen
besides the reflection the thing itself. Berkeley recognized this
and, because he thought that if matter exists independently of our
sense impressions those impressions can at best give us inductive
reasons for what we claim about material things, he said that the
notion of matter involves a contradiction. On this point he was
wrong. But this is not a mistake about language. If matter exists
independently of our sense impressions does it follow that we can
at best have inductive reasons for what we say about material
things? The answer to this question is not to be found in our
language in the way that the answer to a straightforward logical
question is to be found there: If John and Tom are brothers, and
Mary and Jane are their daughters, does it follow that Mary and
Jane are cousins?

The philosopher who denies that matter exists or that it is
anything over and above our sense impressions means to reject an
idea that seems inextricably tied up with what is an essential part
of our notion of matter. The idea he wishes to reject is one that is
not alien to our own thoughts and it does really involve a contradiction. Hence there is overwhelming reason for accepting what
he says. However because he cannot separate what he wishes to
reject from what is of the very essence of a material thing, there
are equally overwhelming reasons for rejecting what he says. His
words bring these conflicting reasons into play. That is why
Wisdom calls them *paradoxical*: 'It cannot be that matter is not
something that exists independently of our sense impressions, and

it cannot be that it is. Yet it must be one or the other.' Berkeley thus found himself 'insensibly drawn into an uncouth paradox'.

It is this sort of predicament that Wittgenstein likens to that of the fly in the fly bottle. The point is that the way out does not lie in any of the obvious alternatives; it lies in an unsuspected direction. The problem, in Berkeley's case, was to know how to reject a picture of the logic of matter which he saw to be defective without distorting that logic—without accepting another defective picture. There is no recipe for solving the problem, and neither does the solution consist in finding an alternative picture of the logic of matter. No simile, no simple formula will capture what the philosopher is trying to get an overall view of here, though it may have the virtue of correcting an error we are prone to make.

II

Consider, for a moment, the philosophical sceptic who says that no one can know the thoughts and feelings of another. He may put this by saying that our notion of the knowledge we have of other people's minds involves a contradiction. Surely he does not wish to imply that this man who says he knows that Mary is fond of her mother does not stand to other men making similar claims about friends and acquaintances as his words suggest. He is trying to say that the kind of knowledge this man claims to have does not stand to other kinds of knowledge as his words suggest. He does not wish to deny, in other words, that this man may have very good reasons for what he claims relative to other people making similar claims. He does not mean to doubt what this or any other man claims about Mary's feelings; he is interested to understand what it means to make such a claim.

When we say of a man that he knows something, or when the man says this of himself, these words are meant to indicate how he is placed relative to other men talking and thinking about the same kind of thing. Whether or not the use of the word 'know' is justified in a particular case depends on whether he is in fact so placed. If he is not placed as his words suggest we would say that he should not say he knows, but perhaps only that he believes. The sceptical philosopher who says that we cannot or should not speak of knowledge in any of these parallel cases does not wish to deny that we constantly need to know of men thinking and talking about other people how they stand relative to each other. He does not wish to deny that the word 'know' used here adequately meets the need to say something about this relation—the relation between cases of men concerned with other people's feelings. He would gladly agree with Berkeley that 'we ought to speak with the vulgar' (sec. 51).

Yet he would also agree that 'we ought to think with the learned'. Why? What would be lost if the philosopher thought with the vulgar? Not an appreciation of how the particular case of any man concerned with other people's thoughts and feelings stands in the manifold of similar cases, but an appreciation of how the whole manifold stands in relation to other such manifolds—cases of people who claim knowledge of other things. The former is a question of fact, the latter a matter of grammar. The philosopher who finds a contradiction in our conception of the knowledge we have of other people's thoughts and feelings is concerned with the grammar of this knowledge; he is concerned to reject a particular model of it: 'We cannot know the minds of other people *in the way* we know our own.' But, like the philosopher who claims that the notion of matter involves a contradiction, he cannot see his way to rejecting it without taking away from the knowledge in question something without which it cannot be what it is. His words are thus paradoxical. In them he opposes our use of the word 'know' in connection with other people's thoughts and feelings because he fears that in using it both here and in other contexts we shall obscure the differences between them. This doesn't mean, however, that our language is defective for not marking these differences. They are of no interest to us when we use the word 'know' in connection with other poeple's thoughts and feelings. They are of interest, however, to the philosopher who is concerned with what it means to have such knowledge, and a philosophy which ignores them would be defective.

Malcolm wrote that when Moore said such things as 'I am not afraid to say I do now perceive that this is a door', 'Both of us know for certain that there are several chairs in this room', he was reminding his audience that such sentences as 'I see a door over there', 'We know for certain that there are several chairs in this room' can be correctly used to make true statements. So he characterized Moore's 'defence of common sense' as being in reality 'a defence of ordinary language' (*Mind*, January, 1960). That is he thought that the philosophers whom Moore was

opposing either made mistakes about the language they spoke
('philosophical reasoning has a peculiar power to blind one to the
obvious', KC, p. 180) or they wanted to reform it. Unlike Moore
he did acknowledge that the statements which Moore opposed
contained some truth: 'The truth is, not that the phrase "I know
for certain" has no proper application to empirical statements, but
that the sense which it has in its application to empirical statements
is *different* from the sense which it has in its application to *a priori*
statements.'[1] But he thought of them too much as mistakes, even
if he acknowledged something of the good in them: 'Many first-
rate contributions to philosophy have been made by thinkers who
developed their ideas in disregard of absurd consequences' (KC,
p. 182, fn. 38).

If Malcolm is guarded about the value of those extravagant
remarks in which philosophers 'use familiar words not with a
disregard of established usage but not in bondage to it' (PPA,
p. 271) this is at least partly because he fears that those who depart
from the everyday use of words are finding fault with language.
Can we blame him altogether in view of the number of philosophers
who have complained about the actual state of our language?
There are indeed deep-going misconceptions here both about the
nature of language and about the nature of philosophy. Perhaps
the most persistent one is the idea that our philosophical difficulties
are accidental to the language we speak and that altering that
language, devising an ideal language, will remove them. This is
connected with the idea that the language we speak may be
defective, that its concepts may distort the reality we use it to
speak about, that they are therefore in need of a justification, and
that it is the philosopher's business to see if it can be found.

Wittgenstein opposed these misconceptions. He denied that
our language is defective. He denied that it makes sense to speak
of language as being defective. Language does not describe or say
anything; rather we use language to say or describe things. What
we *say* may be defective in different ways; but the standards of
comparison we employ when we find a description inadequate, an
expression unsatisfactory, themselves come from language. If,
therefore, our ways of speaking are 'in order' philosophy may not

---

[1] 'Moore and Ordinary Language', *G. E. Moore*, ed. Schilpp, p. 355. He
developed this point in another article published in the same year—'Certainty
and Empirical Statements', *Mind*, 1942.

interfere with them. If 'the actual use of language' cannot be unfounded, in the way that what a man claims may be, then philosophy 'cannot give it any foundation either' (*Inv.*, sec. 124). To oppose these misconceptions is not to defend orthodoxy. Wittgenstein did not do so. When he said that 'every sentence in our language is in order as it is' (sec. 98) he was not taking a stand against the inventive use of language. He was impressed by how often philosophers get into tangles because they ignore the actual use of words. So he urged them to seek to obtain a clear view of the actual use of words. But this is not to urge them to say what the plain man would say in answer to *their* questions. He was urging them to consider what the plain man would say in the course of his everyday reasonings, not to treat it with contempt. *They could then please themselves in describing those reasonings.* ('Say what you choose', *Inv.*, sec. 79, *BB*, p. 62). Here they may give 'prominence to distinctions which our ordinary forms of language easily makes us overlook' (sec. 132). He even said that a reform of language 'for particular practical purposes is perfectly possible' (*ibid*).

There is no common sense answer to a philosophical problem. One can defend common sense against the attacks of philosophers only by solving their puzzles . . . not by restating the views of common sense (*BB*, pp. 58–9).

When Moore or Malcolm reminds the philosophical sceptic that 'it is a proper way of speaking to say that we know for certain that there are several chairs in this room', when in reply to the sceptic who asks, 'How *can* previous experience be a ground for assuming that such-and-such will occur later on?', Wittgenstein replies that 'this sort of statement about the past is simply what we *call* a ground for assuming that this will happen in the future' (*Inv.*, sec. 480), they are not defending our everyday ways of speaking. They are inviting the sceptic to consider them. These reminders have their point in connection with the philosophical misconceptions combated. The first inclination of the philosophical sceptic may be to protest: 'No doubt we do in fact speak of certainty in these connections. But is this not a loose way of speaking? I want to know whether we have any justification for speaking in this way.' Or again: 'No doubt we call this sort of statement about the past a ground for such predictions. But I want it explained to me why we do. Is what we have here anything more than a human convention?'. Some philosophers who remember remarks that Wittgenstein made in these connections remain dissatisfied. 'What has to be accepted, the given, is—so one could say—*forms of life*' (p. 226). 'Our mistake is to look for an explanation where we ought to look at what happens as a 'proto-phenomenon'. The question is not one of explaining a language-game by means of our experiences, but of noting a language-game' (secs. 654–5). These are not isolated remarks and there is a great deal in what Wittgenstein wrote that should help us to understand them. Nevertheless misunderstandings persist: 'The adherents of the later Wittgenstein (Russell wrote) do not bother with any kind of justification, and thus secure for language an untrammelled freedom which it has never hitherto enjoyed' (*My Philosophical Development*, p. 218).

What Wittgenstein says we ought to accept without justification, what it makes no sense to ask for a justification of, is a whole language-game and the way of living in which it is embedded. That we speak of certainty in such-and-such connections—for instance, that I can be as certain of someone else's sensations as of any fact (*Inv.*, p. 224)—is a feature of the language-game in which we say things like 'He is in pain'. To say that I can be certain of someone else's sensations is not to make a statement in which the concept of certainty is *used*, as in 'I am certain that he is in pain', 'I can reach certainty in this matter: I have the competence, the intelligence, and the courage'. Here I *use* the concept of certainty to say something about how I am placed with regard to what is in question. It may turn out that I was over-confident, that I had no right to be certain, that I did not have sufficient justification for what I claimed. But when Wittgenstein says that I can be certain of someone else's sensations he is not using the concept of certainty; he is commenting on the language-game in which we speak of other people's sensations, saying that it has this feature.

He is saying that the concept of certainty has a proper use here, that its use in these cases serves to compare and contrast them with one another. What justification could there be for such a remark except that it does in fact serve this purpose? If we consider the actual use of the concept here we shall see what it achieves for us. We may see that it helps us to compare and contrast in certain ways occasions on which we note or report that people feel this or that sensation. Are we justified in comparing and contrasting them in these ways? What could this question mean? The fact is we do. We are interested in these similarities and differences; they are important for us—but they might not have been. Their importance is surely bound up with the way we live—for instance, with what we consider important elsewhere.

A philosopher may say that *only* mathematical propositions are certain and think that the truth of mathematical propositions is *more* certain than the truth of any empirical proposition, however well supported. He is trying to say that the truth of mathematical propositions is fixed independently of experience, that there is no distinction between understanding a mathematical proposition and seeing it to be true. But it does not follow that one cannot doubt a mathematical proposition or that there is no room for verification in mathematics. Perhaps he thinks that mathematical propositions being necessarily true, their falsity being out of the question, they are immune to doubt. For to be able to doubt a proposition one would have to be able to suppose its falsity. But what is it one cannot suppose here? That a mathematical proposition should be false and significant. However, as long as one can suppose that it should be false and senseless one can doubt its truth. If, therefore, a mathematical proposition may *seem* to be true and significant when in *reality* it is false and senseless, it is possible for someone considering it to be unsure which it is.

The truth behind the paradox is that 'sense', 'truth', 'verification', 'doubt' and 'certainty' do not mean the same thing in connection with mathematical propositions as they do in connection with empirical propositions, though what they mean is by no means unconnected. The difference between a mathematician who is certain of the conclusion he has reached and one who isn't is not the same as the difference between a scientist who is certain about the result of an experiment and one who isn't. The scientist may be uncertain, perhaps, because he has not sufficient evidence. He may therefore repeat the experiment. He is unsure about how things will turn out. The mathematician is uncertain about whether he has made a mistake. He may therefore go over his calculations, repeat the proof. Thus the words 'it is certain' assure us of different things in the two connections.

What is in question, then, is what 'being certain' and 'making sure' *mean* in mathematics and how this differs from what they mean in science. When Wittgenstein urges the philosopher to ask how the certainty that something is the case is manifested in human action (*Inv.*, p. 225) he is urging him to consider language-games in which facts are stated. For the actions and reactions into which the use of the word 'certain' is woven are part of these language-games (see sec. 7) and the identity of the concept of certainty in question cannot be grasped in separation from them. So he says: 'The kind of certainty is the kind of language-game' (p. 224).

Wittgenstein knows very well what the philosopher who says that only mathematical propositions are certain is trying to draw attention to,[1] and he has himself done more than draw attention to the difference between mathematical and empirical certainty. He has discussed at length how repeating a proof in mathematics differs from repeating an experiment. But he also opposes the philosopher who draws attention to this difference in words that are paradoxical and he insists that there is no common measure in terms of which a mathematical and an empirical proposition can be compared in respect of their certainty: 'Am I less certain that this man is in pain than that twice two is four?' (p. 224).

We see that if Wittgenstein and Malcolm on occasions remind philosophers of platitudes these reminders are anything but trivial. They are means of bringing out and ways of rejecting the confusion hidden in philosophical paradoxes. They do not, however, represent a censure on paradox. Malcolm does not seem to be always clear on this. He seems to be divided in his reactions to the implications of these reminders just as much as the philosophers he opposes are divided in their reactions to the implications of the paradoxes they assert. He does not always recognize the paradoxical character of the philosophical claims opposed; he is half inclined to regard them as simply absurd. Or, when more indulgent, he thinks of the disagreement between those who assert and those who deny them as merely verbal (see 'Moore and Ordinary Language', 1942). The idea is that what we have here is nothing more than a disagreement between those who want to extend the use of a word and those who are averse to it. It does not involve truth and error, seeing something we have missed or turning away from it.

[1] He had himself said something very similar in the *Tractatus* without falling into the confusion which he later combated; see 4.464.

III

'It is absurd.' 'It is beyond the reach of reason.' 'It is merely a matter of words.' These three reactions to a paradox have a common source, namely the idea that when there is a conflict of reasons for the truth of what someone says then, if he is speaking sense, there are only two possibilities: Either what he says has not been fully confirmed, there are still some facts relevant to its truth of which we are ignorant, or the logical connections between the descriptions in appropriate terms of the relevant facts that have come to light and what is said are too complicated to be at once apparent. If there is no scope for further empirical confirmation and it is clear that the description of the relevant facts does not entail the statement in question then the statement will appear 'senseless' or 'absurd'. If one is reluctant to think of it as absurd then it may seem that its confirmation has not been exhausted, in which case it will strike one as 'chronically speculative'. If one is reluctant to agree with these two alternatives then the only other possible alternative will be to say that if the statement is not entailed by the description of the relevant facts that is only because in it words are used in a new and unorthodox way. In other words, the statement will appear as merely a new way of stating an old and familiar truth, *'une façon de parler'*. It should be clear that behind these three reactions, which Wisdom once referred to as 'the three-headed syndrome', is the idea that there are only two ways in which we can answer questions, check the truth of our answers, increase our grasp of a situation: we can do so by discovering further facts about it, in which case the steps from these to the answer or conclusion we reach are inductive; or we can employ a step-by-step deductive procedure which starts from the record of a complicated set of facts and culminates in a concise summary or formula which definitely answers the question which these facts raised for us—for instance, 'Is the firm solvent?' asked by the accountant who has kept the books for the firm.

Wisdom has done much to loosen the grip of this dichotomy on our thoughts and to expose the harm it does both within and outside philosophy. He showed, to begin with, how it is that a purely deductive procedure can guide us in our apprehension of complex but familiar facts. Few people would deny this. Yet it is not always easy to see that a conclusion which has been deductively obtained from a set of premisses can tell a man who already knows the premisses something he doesn't know or hasn't seen. The question 'Can a man fail to see something that is open to view?', or 'Can he fail to take in a pattern when no part of it is hidden from him?', which Wisdom has discussed at great length is, of course, closely connected with the question of whether a purely *a priori*, reflective procedure can increase our apprehension of familiar facts. Wisdom is particularly concerned to show that a step-by-step, deductive procedure is not the only kind of reflection that can thus increase our apprehension of what is already familiar to us. The procedure in law courts whereby, for instance, counsel tries to establish whether there was negligence, *after* witnesses have been questioned and all the relevant facts have come to light, is one of the many examples Wisdom has discussed in this connection. Here if reflection shows us that given the facts of the situation there was negligence, the connection between the statement of these facts and our conclusion is *not* deductive. Yet, of course, neither is negligence a *further* feature of the situation, something over and above the facts from which the reflection took its start.

Whether everyone reflecting on these facts agrees or not, there need be nothing extravagant or unorthodox about the statement that here there was negligence. It is otherwise with paradoxical statements. For these are statements in which 'the ordinary usage of words is followed and yet left behind, in which words are used so that we cannot say that they are not being used in their old sense nor yet that they are' (*PPA*, p. 227). In his unpublished lectures on 'Proof and Explanation', delivered in the University of Virginia in the spring of 1957, as well as in his published writings, Wisdom has compared the reflection called for by paradoxical statements with the kind of reflection elicited by such questions as 'Was there negligence?' asked after the relevant facts have been established. He further compared both with the reasoning that would be relevant to someone's calling a spade a spade when every part of the spade is visible to him. He insisted that in all these cases the reasoning or reflection takes the form of, or in the end rests on, the comparison of parallel cases. His point, to put it tersely, is that one who says that the accused was negligent, or one who (like Hilaire Belloc) calls a llama 'a hairy sort of woolly fleecy goat with an indolent expression and an undulating throat, like an unsuccessful literary man', is not doing something widely different from one who says that the firm is solvent, or even one who calls a spade a spade. If I had put this by saying that a man who calls a cat a well-behaved little tiger is doing the same thing as one who calls a spade a spade I would have spoken paradoxically.

'With every name we apply (Wisdom wrote) we compare one thing with another, with many others' (*PPA*, p. 274). In thus comparing one thing with another, with many others, he argued, we see what sort of thing it is. For what sort of thing it is, what kind of features it has, how these features are related to one another, is a matter of how that thing stands with regard to other things. This is directly related to Wittgenstein's view that what makes a thing a thing of a certain kind, for instance, a game, a shade of blue, a number, what justifies our use of the word in a given instance, is 'a complicated network of similarities overlapping and criss-crossing: sometimes overall similarities, sometimes similarities of detail' between that thing or occasion and others— a great many others (*Inv.*, sec. 66).

In an interesting paper, 'On the Principle of Comparison in Physics', the Austrian scientist and philosopher Ernst Mach said that 'physics lives and grows by comparison'. He pointed out how what draws the physicist's attention to 'a great system of resemblances' changes his apprehension of the facts and phenomena he is studying (*Popular Scientific Lectures*). Einstein, whose philosophical position differs from Mach's, spoke in similar terms when considering how the field theory came to replace the mechanical view. He spoke of the two views as different modes of description, as different methods for co-ordinating the phenomena being studied, and pointed out the advantages of describing the phenomena in question 'in the new language of fields'. This language was developed as a result of reflections which revealed certain analogies, and, once developed, it brought into focus further resemblances— between electrical, magnetic, and then optical phenomena (see *The Evolution of Physics*, written in collaboration with Dr. Infeld, p. 157). Later on he speculated about the analogy between the relation of an electrical charge to its field and the relation of a physical body to its gravitational field, and the prospects which such a comparison could open up (*ibid.*, pp. 257–8).

It is important to notice that such comparisons are highly theoretical. They are only possible within a theoretical framework which itself derives its existence from many other comparisons.

Similarly for other comparisons elsewhere. Wisdom once said: 'A
person's understanding grows only as his ability to carry out
comparisons grows.' The framework in which these comparisons
are carried out comes from the language we speak; they are
embedded in our way of living. The very possibility of any
comparison requires an enormous amount of 'stage-setting'. For
when a comparison brings out the respect in which one thing
resembles another thing or things it does so by virtue of the
surroundings in which the comparison is made. These may be
taken for granted, but they lie in the background when the comparison is made and its point seen. In separation from these
surroundings to say that one thing is like another thing is quite
empty. What gives the comparison content, what determines the
respect in which the things in question are being compared, are
the reactions, actions and activities in the weave of which the
comparison is carried out.

These constitute the 'stage-setting' in the language that is
presupposed if a comparison that we make is to have a point, if it
is to bring into focus the particular respect in which things are
being compared—their colour, length, density, strength, vivacity,
imaginativeness, courage, or wisdom. What is presupposed is the
grammar within which the comparison is made, the post at which
is stationed the word that characterizes the respect in which things
are said to be alike or different (see *Inv.* sec. 257). It is only when
two people share certain reactions and convictions, when they can
jointly take part in certain activities, in short when they share a
common understanding, that one of them can show the other, by
means of a new comparison, something he had not seen before.
This underlies the possibility of learning from a new comparison.
Hence there cannot be any deep understanding of the connection
between a person's understanding and his ability to carry out
comparisons if we leave out his relation to a way of living, to the
various practices, customs, traditions and institutions that constitute that way of living.

A way of speaking about things, a tradition of inquiry, a way of
understanding them: these things go together. Therefore any
modification in our ways of speaking about certain things will
necessarily go with a change in our ways of understanding them.
What enables us to speak of a *gain* or *loss* of understanding here,
even if only in restrospect, is the continuity in the tradition within

which the innovation has taken place. It is this continuity that provides a common measure which makes it possible to compare the modes of understanding before and after they have been modified. An innovation, a discovery, can only take place in a discipline, with its peculiar criteria of reality, relevance, depth, adequacy, and excellence. It is these that enable us to refer our changing conceptions to the same reality.

Freud modified our way of talking about the human mind and innovated our ways of thinking about human behaviour. At a time when he was concerned to understand the disjointed behaviour of hysterical patients he had come in contact with Charcot and Bernheim A spectator of their experiments, he was struck by two things: People who wake up from an hypnotic trance will carry out orders given to them under hypnosis, act in accordance with suggestions made to them earlier, without realizing that they are obeying orders or complying with suggestions. Under hypnosis they will sometimes remember things they don't normally remember. He says that from these he received 'the profoundest impression of the possibility that there could be powerful mental processes which remained hidden from the consciousness of men' (*An Autobiographical Study*). This is no ordinary inference and it reminds us of the way Galileo is said to have received a similarly profound impression from watching the swinging of an oil-lamp and Newton from seeing the fall of an apple.

What Freud found startling was the analogy that struck him between these facts of hypnosis and the phenomena he met in his consulting room. Concerned as he was to make sense of hysterical behaviour it occurred to him that perhaps here too something like hypnotic suggestion may be at work, in other words fears and intentions, rooted in past circumstances, of which the hysterics are ignorant. Perhaps, he thought, they can be made to recall these circumstances, the fears and desires in them thus becoming conscious. It may be that they can be made to recognize resolutions to which they unknowingly cling, that they can be made to own them and so to assume responsibility for them. In this way the analogy he perceived between the aetiology of hysteria and post-hypnotic suggestion opened his mind to the possibility of distinguishing between appearance and reality in the mental world. Freud exploited this distinction. He spoke of love and hate, anxiety and depression, bondage and responsibility, in new

H

connections—where we don't normally speak of these things, or speak of their opposites. He thus sophisticated our conception of what constitutes a man's freedom or responsibility, of what makes for the presence of love or depression in a man's heart. He sometimes narrowed the use of a word and sometimes stretched it, hoping to free us from the power of connections marked by words whose use he narrowed, and to bring to our attention connections which are not marked by those whose use he stretched. He was thus able to offer a new co-ordination of the facts we use these words to talk about and so to change our apprehension of them. As Wisdom puts it: 'To gain a new apprehension of any part of reality, we have to shake off old habits of apprehension crystallized in a well-known mode of presentation' (*PPA*, p. 263).

A paradox is one way in which this is done; in it 'the ordinary usage of words is followed and yet left behind'. Does this mean that one who speaks paradoxically alters the meanings of the words he is using? Certainly the use and the meaning of a word are internally related. One cannot identify the meaning of the word in separation from its use. Hence it seems that if one uses the word in a new way one will inevitably alter its meaning. But the connection between meaning and use is not so tight and rigid that every time a word is used in an instance which is at some distance from the paradigms which illustrate its meaning we have altered that meaning. This, I believe, is directly connected with Wittgenstein's insistence that the application of our everyday concepts is not sharply bounded, that these concepts do not have sharp contours. If so, then not in all cases where a word is used in a new connection shall we be able to say definitely that it is being used in a new sense. To think otherwise is to assume that a word's application must be sharply bounded. The point of applying an old world in new cases, I suggest, is to draw attention to connections and affinities between them and the cases where we were taught to use the word in the first place,[1] and thus to see the new cases in the light of the old, and also the old ones in the light of the new. To say that in these new cases we are not using the word in the same sense as we use it in the old ones is to deny that the cases are connected; it is to divest the word of its power to draw

---

[1] It may be misleading to talk of paradigms here at all, since there may be nothing paradigmatic about the instances in connection with which we first learn to use most words.

attention to new similarities, new connections. So when Janet said that to speak of unconscious feelings and wishes is simply '*une manière de parler*' he implied that all Freud had done was to use a new word to speak about what was 'old hat' to psychiatrists who were his contemporaries. In this way he denied that Freud had discovered anything new.

Take any case where the use of a word is modified, where the boundaries of its application are widened. Wherever this is done the word is given a greater power to mark certain connections, affinities and continuities to which its previous use may have made us insensitive. This is a *gain*. However, it will acquire this power at the expense of its power to mark differences and discontinuities which it previously marked, and in doing so served us well. This will be a *loss*. So long as one does not forget these differences, so long as one does not so widen the use of a word as altogether to remove its boundaries, one will have gained something and lost nothing. If in speaking paradoxically a person is increasing his apprehension of what he is considering and also obscuring it, he can surely increase his apprehension without at the same time obscuring it. He may have something interesting and important to tell us and he may not be confused at all. The paradox represents an attempt to say something which is not usually appreciated. As for the kind of reflection it calls for, this resembles the reasoning that is carried out in law courts, except that the comparisons in terms of which it is carried out do not follow well trodden lines and even conflict with our established habits of thinking. Yet, of all forms of reflection, this is the one which is best suited to reveal what is furthest from our apprehension. It is (as Wisdom puts it) what 'we need most when most we need to think' (*PD*, p. 7).

IV

Wisdom's interest in paradox goes together with an early disappointment in the changes that were taking place in British philosophy during his formative years—changes which he welcomed and contributed to. In his study of these changes he shed light not only on what was gained but also on what was lost. (See especially his question 'Was this all a mistake?' in 'The Metamorphosis of Metaphysics', *PD*, p. 71). It goes with his concern with what philosophy can offer, his preoccupation with what impedes its progress as well as what makes us think that our efforts have been a waste when we have learnt something. If we do not recognize the paradoxical character of a philosophical statement our discussion of it will tend to go on without reaching a satisfactory conclusion and our lingering reservations will obscure how much we have achieved. If we reject it as simply wrong or mistaken we shall reject the insight it embodies and perhaps turn away from the problems it brings into focus. Moore and Malcolm did not do this, but each missed something of what philosophy can give us.

If philosophy is an *a priori* study, if it is concerned with what is already familiar to us, how can it increase our understanding? If it is concerned with removing the muddle and confusion into which we fall in the course of our reflections on the nature of mind, matter, time, space, love, freedom, knowledge, and necessity, how can it do more than return us 'just where we were?' Wisdom's study of these questions led him to study philosophical reasoning and other forms of reasoning which are like and unlike it, and so took him straight to questions in the *philosophy of logic* where he has made a substantial contribution. His reflections on what philosophy can give us and how it differs from logic brought him to see first how it resembles literature and secondly how much philosophy there is in literature.

One who asks whether there can be knowledge of another person's thoughts and feelings is, as we have seen, concerned with the *grammar* of a whole dimension of discourse. One who asks whether there can be love, real love, of another human being is equally concerned with a *conceptual issue*. I have pointed out elsewhere[1] how the paradox 'Nothing that is not both earthly and saintly can be love and yet nothing can be both: love is impossible' comes from reflection on many cases of love, love of all sorts, including its fake varieties, and how it both sets them and their relations to one another in a new light, and tells us something interesting about our idea of love—what it requires and how its requirements conflict. The better view of things which such a paradox can give us if we engage in the reflections which led to it may also be found in works of literature (see *PD*, p. 144). For some literature manages to make us see something familiar, something we live with, in a new light. In presenting to us the concrete detail of the lives of particular people, for instance, their

[1] 'Review Article: Paradox and Discovery,' *Philosophy*, April, 1967.

relationships, situations, or something that these people see, not only does it bring these to life and make us see them in a new way, but it also illuminates innumerable other lives, relations, situations, things, which at first do not seem connected with the ones it presents.

Elstir's water-colours, for instance, had contributed to transform Marcel's apprehension of such ordinary things as a table before it has been cleared after a meal:

> Since I had seen such things depicted in water-colours by Elstir, I sought to find again in reality, I cherished, as though for their poetic beauty, the broken gestures of the knives still lying across one another, the swollen convexity of a discarded napkin upon which the sun would patch a scrap of yellow velvet, the half-empty glass which then showed to greater advantage the noble sweep of its curved sides, and, in the heart of its translucent crystal, clear as frozen daylight, a dreg of wine, dusky but sparkling with reflected lights, the displacement of solid objects, the transmutation of liquids by the effects of light and shade, the shifting colour of the plums which passed from green to blue and from blue to golden yellow, in the half-plundered dish, the chairs, like a group of old ladies, that came twice daily to take their places around the white cloth spread on the table as an altar at which were celebrated the rites of the palate, where in the hollows of oyster-shells a few drops of lustral wine had gathered as in tiny holy water stoups of stone; I tried to find beauty there where I had never imagined before it could exist, in the most ordinary things, in the profundities of still life (*In Remembrance of Things Past*, vol. IV, p. 128).

Proust, in turn, contributes to our apprehension of water colours and of the perfectly ordinary scenes and subjects depicted in them. 'When we read Proust (André Gide wrote) we begin suddenly to perceive detail where before we saw an undifferentiated mass. Since the things which he looks at are the most common things, it seems to us constantly, as we read him, that it is with our own eyes that he makes us see.'

Such presentation alters our apprehension of the particular things it studies, and this in itself may be exciting and exhilarating or disturbing. But often what is well presented and well chosen also brings home similarities between what we have always regarded as poles apart. In this way literature can and often, does illuminate the general through its study of the particular. It is thus reflective, concerned to give us a better view of things, to purify our vision, to liven our sensibility. It is also sometimes concerned to combat misapprehensions we share with others, and common prejudices, doing this sometimes without doing anything more than just telling a story. What it is thus concerned to shed light on is *life*—I mean people and their struggles and relationships, the forces of good and evil that shape their destiny, their responsibility for what happens to them as well as their helplessness in the face of it, love, hate, destruction, and madness, and also death, and the meaning that can be found in life. In all this, and more, which is a concern with life, a concern which is directed to both the particular and the general, it aims to show us what is merely appearance and what is reality.

Proust was concerned to show us the people he wrote about, people he had known in his own life, to tell us about their experiences and the society in which they lived, to present these things to us as he saw and remembered them in the person of his narrator Marcel. In the minute descriptions he gave of every detail he enriched our vision not only of the particular but also of the general. In the last volume of his big novel he said: '*Là où je cherchais les grandes lois, on m'appelait feuilleur de détails*'—Where I looked for general laws people thought I was merely searching for detail. His novel is, in fact, full of penetrating remarks and observations about a great many subjects: human intercourse, the arts, old age, vice, love and jealousy, living and dreaming, the continuity of personal experience, guilt, grief, self-deception. These hang together and unmistakably come from a unity of vision, thought and experience. In fact, Proust's vision of the world has something of the consistency and character of a metaphysician's view of the world.

In his general remarks Proust guides us in our understanding of the things he writes about much in the way that a metaphysical philosopher guides us in our apprehension of the logical features and conceptual relations he reflects on. Like him Proust too has to work against forces that oppose the understanding sought. He said that an artist is concerned to undo the work which self-regard, passion, our inclination to imitate, our abstract intelligence and our habits have accomplished. He had, himself, to work against habit and prejudice and *cliché* and also what Wittgenstein called 'a one-sided diet' (sec. 593). In fact, Proust works very much by altering our regular diet and by reconstructing intermediate cases. Marcel's love of Albertine, Swann's of Odette, Charlus' of Morel —are these not intermediate cases that link the normal and the abnormal and help us to modify our conception of the common-place in the light of the extreme?

His central theme is the inaccessibility of everything outside of us that we crave to possess or savour—the affections of another person, the beauty of a natural scene. His famous phrase 'the sensation of being always enveloped in, surrounded by our own soul' is well known even to those who have not read his novel. He speaks there of a perpetual struggle 'to break out into the world' and of 'a perpetual discouragement as we hear endlessly, all around us, the unvarying sound which is no echo from without, but the resonance of a vibration from within' (Vol. I, p. 115). He says: 'When I saw any external object, my consciousness that I was seeing it would remain between me and it, enclosing it in a slender, incorporeal outline which prevented me from ever coming directly in contact with the material form' (p. 111). Proust is not, like the solipsist, trying to remark on something that could not have been otherwise. Yet there is an interesting link between what he says and solipsism: 'On the road to solipsism (writes Wisdom) there blows the same wind of loneliness which blows on the road to the house with walls of glass which none can break' (*PPA*, p. 282). So Wisdom spoke of 'non-linguistic and much more hidden' sources besides the latent linguistic ones 'which subtly co-operate with features of language to produce philosophies' (p. 181). He suggested that the forces at work in scepticism and solipsism are 'in part the same as those at work in those other struggles in which something is forever sought and never found, struggles which in their turn are connected with an earlier time when there was something, namely the world of grown-ups, knowledge of which we desperately desired and equally desperately dreaded' (p. 281). Proust certainly gives us a detailed study of these latter struggles and their connection with that earlier time and, interestingly, very much like Schopenhauer and Freud, he speaks of their repetitive character.

Wittgenstein once said that what the solipsist is *trying* to say is true, though the words he comes up with are nonsensical (*Tractatus* 5.62). What he is trying to put into words relates to the form of such first-person expressions as 'I see', 'I am sorry', 'I am in pain', *in anybody's mouth*, and the way these differ from their third-person counterparts. Whereas when Proust speaks of the sensation of being surrounded by one's own soul he is referring to a feature of Marcel's experience. What is in question is true of Marcel, and others like him, in contrast with other people. Marcel, the narrator, is a dreamer, fated, as he says, to pursue phantoms, and for whom everything for which he wants to reach out proves inaccessible. Yet what makes him '*un esprit porté au rêve*', a dreamer, is the very thing that enables him to illuminate our experience for us, to make us see in the most ordinary things a great deal that we constantly miss. One of these is how often our desire to know, capture or possess a thing or a person is riddled with conflict. This gives our desire a quality of feverishness and desperation. The restless imagination with which Marcel approaches everything that he wishes to have and savour seems to stand in the way of any direct contact with it—'just as an incandescent body which is moved towards something wet never touches moisture, since it is always preceded, itself, by a zone of evaporation.'

Proust illuminates this special yet familiar quality; he shows us its presence in what we call 'being in love'. When he says that since the bonds that tie people together are only in their thoughts we are alone, or that our love is not something real since it is never inspired by the woman we love ('my love was less of a love *for* her than a love *in* me'), or that one loves only what one does not completely possess, he is speaking about something that could have been and still could be otherwise. As Wisdom puts it: 'In his words we feel still the air of an old regret, regret for what might have been' (*PD*, p. 97). For Proust, in the person of his narrator, had come to realize that what he dreamed and longed to find in love as a child, what he had caught a glimpse of in his mother's kiss, turned out to have been impossible—impossible in this world, impossible to people who longed for it like himself. If he were otherwise and if the women he longed to possess and be completely open with did not have the qualities of Gilberte, Odette and Albertine, the very qualities that made them so haunting, things might have been otherwise. And yet, if this were so, would we still have that special variety of love, so special that it deserves separate study and yet so common that few people would not have heard of it? Thus Proust had put his finger on something that is an inseparable part of what we mean by 'being in love'—something that is perhaps transfigured in adult love, but often lost, taking away with it not tenderness but something that enables lover and beloved to renew themselves in each other.

In what Proust shows us we find the inclination to say what is paradoxical, namely that what we most deperately want in love is unattainable. Thus his remarks on the actual constantly tend to shift towards the conceptual. For, like many other novelists and poets, he is constantly trying to establish new connections, to remodel our outlook on life, to alter our 'geometry' of the human heart. The metaphysical philosopher may tell us that the scientist can never attain absolute certainty in his inquiries, that probability is all that he ought to seek (*vide* Russell). Proust tells us that the lover can never attain perfect union with the beloved. It could be said that what the metaphysical philosopher says is absolutely, inevitably true, but that he is confused about what the scientist seeks. Proust, however, is not confused about what the lover seeks. It is rather the lover who is often confused in his desires, as Proust shows us, and so in his conception of what he wants. He has to become different in himself, his love has to change, his longings have to be transformed, if he is to find the union which Marcel could never find. It is the possibility of such transformation that Proust could not see. On the other hand, he had no time for lying remedies, and he was able to transfigure in his art the bitter-sweets of life as he had experienced them.

V

The question of what philosophy has to offer is one which Wisdom has always felt deeply about. This question is particularly pertinent in connection with philosophy. First because of its abstract and remote character. Secondly, because of those sources which not only lead to scepticism about its reality as a form of inquiry as well as about its value, but which also often lead those who engage in it to trivialise it. Thirdly, because it is so easy for philosophy to fail to meet the deep needs which make people ask philosophical questions. As Wisdom puts it: 'We may hurry away and drown the cries that follow from those silent places—

drown them in endless talk. . . . Or, more effective, we may quiet those phantasmal voices by doing something for people real and alive' (*PPA*, p. 282). In endless talk, so characteristic of the philosopher, we evade those questions. We can quiet those voices by doing something for people; but this isn't doing philosophy. Wisdom wants to know whether we can meet those needs and do something for people real and alive without turning away from philosophy. He thinks we can: 'There are those who will go with us and, however terrifying the way, not desert us.'

The aridness and triviality of much that is said and written in philosophy has to do with the difficulty of carrying philosophical investigation to any depth. It is not endemic to philosophy. Where there is depth philosophy is never confined to the commonplace and trivial—Plato, for instance, Kierkegaard or Wittgenstein. I believe that in all three writers there is a concern with questions about life. In Wittgenstein's discussions even of questions which are very remote from life there is a breath of life. But more than this, in his work we find a preoccupation not only with fundamental questions about logic and mathematics, but also with questions about good and evil, life and death, sanity and madness. He had thought at first that here philosophy can do no more than put a stop to trivialities:

> My book (the *Tractatus*) consists of two parts (he wrote to Ficker): the one presented here plus all that I have *not* written. And it is precisely this second part that is the important one. . . . I believe that where *many* others today are just *gassing*, I have managed in my book to put everything firmly into place by being silent about it. (*Letters from Ludwig Wittgenstein, with a Memoir*, Paul Engelmann, p. 143).

This line of thinking runs through his 'Lecture on Ethics', though there he manages to say more on problems of life and ethics than he does either in the *Tractatus* or in his *Note Books 1914–16*. Still more is to be found in his 'Lectures on Religious Belief' and his 'Remarks on Frazer'; and more still elsewhere in his writings, even if it takes some reading between the lines to see it. In fact, Wittgenstein's interest in logic and mathematics and his interest in men and in human life and culture interpenetrate one another. When one sees the kind of interest he had in logic one will not find this surprising.

The desire to bring philosophical reflection to bear on 'problems of life' has never been absent from Wisdom's work in philosophy. He has always fought against the narrow specialism that has invaded British philosophy since the early days in which Logical Positivism influenced it. He has enlarged our conception of philosophy, and without shifting its centre of gravity from questions concerning the relation between language, thought and reality. I have tried to show how much his interest in paradoxical pronouncements is connected with these concerns. As early as 1936 he wrote: 'Moore can rapidly reduce any metaphysical theory to a ridiculous story. For he is right, they are false—only there *is* good in them, poor things' (*PPA*, p. 41). In much of what he has written he has explained and developed this remark: even the most blatant falsehood can hide a truth, and if we can tolerate it we shall grow wiser. Is this not the same elsewhere? It was so with Dostoyevsky, Freud, and 'many other explorers of the spiritual world' who had 'the courage to refuse to deny the evil and also the further courage not then to deny the good' (*PPA*, p. 261). This tolerance, courage and sympathy, I find, is one of the steady lights in Wisdom's whole work.

BIBLIOGRAPHY

1. George Berkeley, *A Treatise Concerning the Principles of Human Knowledge*, Everyman's Library, 1950. *Princ.*

2. Ilham Dilman, 'Review Article: Paradox and Discovery', *Philosophy*, April 1967.

3. Albert Einstein and Leopold Infeld, *The Evolution of Physics*, Cambridge 1947.

4. Paul Engelmann, *Letters from Ludwig Wittgenstein, with a Memoir*, trans. by L. Furtmüller, Basil Blackwell 1967.

5. Sigmund Freud, 'An Autobiography,' *Complete Works*, vol. XX.

6. Ernst Mach, 'On the Principles of Comparison in Physics', *Popular Scientific Lectures*, trans. by Thomas J. McCormack, Chicago, Open Court 1898.

7. Norman Malcolm, *Knowledge and Certainty*, Prentice-Hall, 1963. *KC.*

8. Norman Malcolm, 'Moore and Ordinary Language', *G. E. Moore*, ed. by Paul Schilpp.

9. Norman Malcolm, 'Certainty and Empirical Statements', *Mind* 1942.

10. Norman Malcolm, 'White on Moore', *Mind*, January 1960.

11. G. E. Moore, 'Proof of an External World', *Philosophical Papers*, Allen and Unwin 1963.

12. G. E. Moore, 'A Defence of Common Sense', *Philosophical Papers*, Allen and Unwin 1963.

13. G. E. Moore, 'Reply to my Critics', *The Philosophy of G. E. Moore*, ed. by P. A. Schilpp.

14. Marcel Proust, *In Remembrance of Things Past*, trans. by C. K. Scott Moncrieff, London, 1952.

15. Bertrand Russell, *My Philosophical Development*, Allen and Unwin 1959.

16. John Wisdom, *Philosophy and Psycho-Analysis*, Basil Blackwell 1953. *PPA*.

17. John Wisdom, *Paradox and Discovery*, Basil Blackwell 1965. *PD*.

18. John Wisdom, Lectures on Proof and Explanation, delivered in the University of Virginia, Spring 1957; unpublished.

19. Ludwig Wittgenstein. *Note Books 1914–16*, Basil Blackwell 1961.

20. Ludwig Wittgenstein. *Tractatus Logico-Philosophicus*, trans. by D. F. Pears and B. F. McGuinness, Routledge 1961.

21. Ludwig Wittgenstein. 'Lecture on Ethics', *The Philosophical Review*, January 1965.

22. Ludwig Wittgenstein, *The Blue and Brown Books*, Basil Blackwell 1958. *BB*.

23. Ludwig Wittgenstein, *Lectures and Conversations on Aesthetics, Psychology and Religious Belief*, ed. by Cyril Barrett, Basil Blackwell 1966.

24. Ludwig Wittgenstein, *Philosophical Investigations*, Basil Blackwell 1963. *Inv*.

25. Ludwig Wittgenstein, *Remarks on the Foundations of Mathematics*, Basil Blackwell 1956.

26. Ludwig Wittgenstein, *On Certainty*, Basil Blackwell 1969.

27. Ludwig Wittgenstein, 'Remarks on Frazer's *Golden Bough*', *The Human World*, May 1971.

REASON AND PSYCHOLINGUISTICS

M. R. AYERS

PHILOSOPHERS once assumed that there is a unitary faculty of reason which yields all knowledge or, at least, all scientific knowledge, knowledge with understanding. It could be seen at work in Theology, Metaphysics, Mathematics, Logic, Natural Science and Ethics. It seemed to be a primary task of psychology to give an account of the principles that govern its operations. Such a conception now looks antiquated. Some psychologists find 'intelligence' worth studying, but the concept can appear delicate and liable to fragmentation.

It would be a major task in the history of ideas to chart the downfall of 'Reason', but some factors seem fairly evident. For example, the consideration that the proposed laws of thought were discernible *a priori* was objectionable *a priori* to those who wanted to make psychology experimental. Biology made the alleged gulf between men and beasts implausible, and man came to be thought of as a more advanced and complex animal, not as one containing a quite different mechanism.

More fundamentally, from the point of view of epistemology, Hume's Empiricism split the functions of Reason by taking 'causal reasoning' right out of the sphere of *a priori* intuition and understanding, consigning it to the 'Imagination' as a passive capacity to be conditioned by experience. It was then easy to see the traditional faculty of Reason—bereft, too, of Ethics and Theology—as confined to an area of relative triviality. Its reputation was not helped by the increasing popularity of the old theory that 'Truths of Reason' are linguistic: that, as Hobbes puts it, 'we learn by reasoning nothing as to the nature of things, but only as to their appellations'. If language itself is learnt by conditioning, *a priori* knowledge too becomes a consequence of habituation.

On the other hand, objection may be taken to Hume's 'psychologism'. His treatment of 'causal reasoning' may thus be taken to be a contribution, not to psychology, but to a 'logic of confirmation', to the elucidation of *a priori* principles determining what are good inductive reasons: the criterion lying, for example, in the number, or the number and the 'range' of observed instances of a law. Some take the heroic step of regarding these principles too as linguistic, hinging on the meaning of such words as 'probable'. But another line of thought leads from the premise that principles of reason, whether of deduction or induction, are normative, to the conclusion that they are no concern of psychology. This seems to impugn the very notion of a rational faculty. The argument might run as follows: that a bit of thinking occurs is a natural fact, but that it constitutes good reasoning is a non-natural fact, and so the fact that it constitutes an exercise of the faculty of Reason is a non-natural fact; but a non-natural fact cannot figure in the explanation of a natural fact. Such a conclusion, baldly presented, seems so counter-intuitive that it may increase the temptation to explain rationality 'naturalistically' as mastery of linguistic rules, whether of ordinary language, or of any language, or of some preferred ideal language.

The question whether the rationality operative in *a priori* reasoning is sharply distinguishable from that which operates in causal reasoning, and the question whether the former is explicable as linguistic competence, are themselves both, if any question is, abstract, philosophical and *a priori*. But their answers surely have important implications for psychology. For example, if *a priori* insight is merely an aspect of linguistic competence, it must be a mistake to propose an explanation of the acquisition of language that contains *a priori* insight even as a minor part. On the other hand, if such an explanation of linguistic competence is a compelling possibility, the fact will help rebut the philosophical reduction of rationality to that competence.

What arguments can be brought to bear on the question whether the ability to reason deductively, or to spot logical consequences, inconsistencies and *non sequiturs*, is to be explicated as a form of linguistic competence? My own intuitive discomfort with the theory seems to have two, almost opposed sources. The first line of objection, I believe, is ultimately inadequate, and leads into the traditional deadlock. It runs as follows.

There seems often to be a clear distinction between understanding an argument as a bit of English, and understanding or getting the point of the reasoning. A failure to reason correctly seems so far from being a sign that the sentences in question are not fully understood, that, unless they are fully understood, the case cannot be one of invalid reasoning. Hence a man who does not follow the reasoning of 'All men are mortal; Socrates is a man; therefore Socrates is mortal' because he does not understand these English sentences has not failed to grasp the validity of a syllogism, any more than someone who does not follow the argument because he does not hear it properly. There is the related and traditional point that 'a Frenchman and a German are able to reason in exactly the same way about the same things'.[1] Moreover, the *construction* of a proof obviously involves more than a facility with language, so that it is natural to distinguish a facility with *ideas* from linguistic competence, and to identify the former rather than the latter with rationality as traditionally conceived in relation to abstract reasoning.

Counter-arguments are readily forthcoming. For example, it may be said that, while the ability to think up the steps of a proof may be deemed a part of man's 'rationality' and cannot simply be included under the aegis of 'understanding a language', yet the only factors determining the validity or 'rationality' of any step, once made, are meaning-rules. Hence to make or accept the step non-accidentally is to demonstrate possession of these rules. The case might be compared with an argument by analogy or counter-example. It may be admitted that an extra-linguistic gift is required to think up appropriate and cogent examples, but argued that what makes an example an instance of, say, 'negligence' or 'knowledge', and so appropriate and cogent, is the meaning-rules governing these words.

Again, it might be admitted that truths of reason need not be self-evident or obvious, if the linguistic facts that they illustrate are complex, and argued that it is for this reason that understanding premise and conclusion is not a sufficient condition for seeing the logical connection. The kind of insight and intuition possessed by one who does see the connection is still insight into the structure of language, and support for it must come from the making explicit a series of steps each of which cannot be denied by anyone who understands the language. Producing these steps may be a difficult business, but following them must not be for anyone who

[1] Descartes, *Objections and Replies III*.

knows their meaning. Moreover, a Frenchman and a German may have the same insight, because the insight is into linguistic rules, which different languages may have in common.

Behind such counter-arguments there lies the most persuasive of all considerations that can be adduced in favour of the linguistic theory. Since Hobbes it has never been found difficult to pour scorn on the suggestion that infants and animals or beings without language reason syllogistically, or indeed make deductive inferences at all. One might as well claim to be doing mathematics asymbolically. Cats cannot be supposed to count in the same sense as we do, even if they do know when one of their kittens is missing. And under what conditions could an otherwise 'intelligent' ape be supposed to see, or to fail to see, that all brothers are male, or that identity is a transitive relation?

There is, however, a seemingly different source of objection to the linguistic theory, the feeling that in an explication of rational insight reference to rules of language is simply circular. For language does not even seem to be the kind of thing that could be learnt by rote or habituation like some pointless noise-game or ritual. The distinction between following a proof and understanding the English in which it is expressed may not, after all, be nearly so sharp as my first line of objection suggested, not because there is no more to following the proof than understanding the English—a way of putting it that implies that 'reason' is here a superfluous faculty or else has been explained away as linguistic competence—but because comprehension of a more or less difficult issue may be requisite to understanding the language in which it is stated—a point that leaves reason enthroned. What needs to be grasped is that this point does not presuppose that the issue could equally well have been comprehended without language at all.

A subtle train of thought may well require intricate language, even if no unusual words or senses are involved. Certainly the mastery of technical terminology characteristically requires an intelligent grasp of subject-matter or, indeed, of techniques. Yet there is neither a sharp nor an obviously significant distinction between the technical and the everyday, the abstruse and the ordinary. To instruct a child in some points of language may *seem* to be merely to tell him what accords with the etiquette of the language-game: 'Don't say "He what did it" but "He that did it " '. But even the explanation of such a thing as the difference between the perfect and the pluperfect tenses, however informally it is done, involves not *merely* an exposition or illustration of syntactic rules, but also an invitation to grasp the point or significance of the difference between using the one tense and using the other. This seems not very different from the fact that nobody could understand what lawyers currently mean by 'negligence' or philosophers once meant by 'substance' who is intellectually incapable of following the arguments that have historically determined that meaning. Consequently the notion of understanding a language may be closer than is often supposed to the concept of understanding that has the connections, so important for classical Rationalist philosophy, with the notions of explanation, insight, 'seeing why' and so with justification and knowledge in a different sense from that of mere competence or knowledge how to play a game with sounds.

The question raised in the last two paragraphs lies at the heart of John Wisdom's philosophy as it has developed since the influence on him of the later Wittgenstein. In the early stages of this progress, Wisdom was prepared to suggest that an *a priori* proposition can be explained as a way of making 'the same factual claims' as a contingent statement about language, in so far as its justification lies in 'what people say'.[1] But at the same time, in his treatment of philosophical questions and of this very question, he recognised that as a rule both the arguments for and against a philosophical position have some cogency: so that there is no difference in kind between the weapons even of the paradox-monger and his opponent. But this consideration throws doubt on the appeal to 'what people say', pointing towards a very different view of the relationship between rationality and language: ultimately to the view that what men say and hold to be correct may be more or less reasonable, that even established ways of talking can be rationally criticised, and that language can be rationally extended, whether permanently, as perhaps Freud has extended it, or *ad hoc*, to make a point.

Many of the examples that originally directed Wisdom's interest derived from Wittgenstein, but whereas Wittgenstein treated most if not all philosophical or conceptual argument as an aberration, Wisdom has come to regard it, even when extravagant,

[1] *Philosophy and Psycho-Analysis*, p. 62.

I

as the same in kind as the sort of reflection essential to intellectual progress. His examples have become correspondingly less trivial. The emphasis has moved from 'Is a tomato a fruit or a vegetable?' and 'Can you play chess without the queen?' towards legal reasoning, Cantor, Einstein and Freud. Most significant advances in human thinking are accompanied by disputes over the use of words which are like some trivial disputes, but are not trivial. A current example is the dispute over whether 'knowledge' is the right word for what Chomsky calls 'innate knowledge'. The danger is now seen by Wisdom to come not, or not only, from those who give such disputes a too portentous aspect, but from those who would sweep them aside before they have done their work.

The view that conceptual questions are to be settled by reference to meaning-rules or definitions supplies a traditional motive for holding them in contempt. For it becomes easy to suppose that only those who are not clear about their meaning could become involved with such questions. But it is possible to retain a belief in the decisive relevance of linguistic rules, and yet regard conceptual issues as interesting and difficult. For if the rules to which appeal must be made are complex, it may be difficult to achieve explicit knowledge of them without careful analysis. Some such thought is characteristic of much recent philosophy, and is presupposed, for example, in the transformational grammarians' criticism of 'ordinary language philosophy' for not being systematic enough about meaning. Philosophy, we are told by J. J. Katz, has been 'puzzling about words for over two thousand years', and we shall remain condemned to 'endless quibbling' in the absence of a theory of language that will enable us to 'extrapolate from the clear cases in such a fashion as to extend its generalisations to the unclear cases, thereby utilising our strong intuitions about clear cases to compensate for our weak intuitions about unclear ones'.[1]

It would be in the spirit of John Wisdom's philosophy, as I understand it, to reply that, since abstract argument began, about mathematics, law, natural science or anything else, men have not only appealed to analogies with clear or, let us say, agreed cases in support of their judgment of disputed cases, but have also

---

[1] *The Philosophy of Language*, pp. 286–7, cf. pp. 92–3. (Harper and Row, New York 1966).

offered hierarchies of generalisations embodying their interpretation of 'clear' cases. The generalisations are not intrinsically stronger than the analogies, but are equally open to dispute. No solemn pronouncement that they are meaning-rules—a trick that has also been tried for centuries—will cut the process short. That is just as well, since what is interesting and important in the question about Chomsky's 'innate knowledge' is not a merely linguistic question as to whether the word 'knowledge' and its synonyms are applicable without solecism or ambiguity, but in part at least a question as to the exact nature of what is being postulated, which is not quite like anything previously postulated and strikingly unlike at least much of what is 'indisputably' knowledge. This issue, from which the question whether Chomsky's claim is justified cannot be disentangled, rests on the significance of the difference, and cannot be seriously considered without the gamut of cases, clear and unclear, of what is and what is not knowledge. The conclusion to be desired is that the conclusion will reflect our increased comprehension. It is not necessary that our concept of *knowledge* should remain totally unaffected by the issue. For the fact is that the jaundiced view of the history of philosophy as a history of puzzling and quibbling over words is quite misconceived, drawing support from blind alleys in the past and bad history in the present, but rebutted by the conceptual advances achieved, as measured by our increased grasp of the world in which we live and of the problems that face us. (Which is not to say that philosophical fashions are never retrograde.)

Generalisation is not a bad thing, but the right arm of reason, although useless or inconceivable without reflection on the cases. Nor is reflection on 'what we say' a bad method. Wisdom has said that it can help us to 'catch logical connections'. Insight into conceptual connections consists in grasping how and why 'what we say' is reasonable—or, perhaps, not so reasonable after all.

Wisdom's characterization of *a priori* reasoning carries with it a conception of a rational faculty that is significantly more comfortable than the traditional one in a number of ways. Reason no longer appears as an infallible, rule-following, uncreative faculty, spinning its conclusions from its own entrails, those intuitively known principles supposed definitive of its nature. We can reject the Cartesian psychology that explained erroneous reasoning as always due to the interference of prejudice in rational processes, and we can reject that 'principle of principles, that principles must not be questioned' fittingly derided by Locke. When 'deduction' is seen as just one possible aspect of the rational process, the concomitant of reflection on examples and generalisation—the validity of the inference itself being subject to such reflection—it is no longer difficult to see how the same general faculty operates in all branches of knowledge, for example in ethics and natural science. The difference between 'causal reasoning' and *a priori* reasoning can be seen to lie primarily in the fact that in empirical science the cases by which generalisations are suggested and tested are data actually observed, and cannot be merely supposed. The *natural* significance of an analogy cannot be decided *a priori*. Finally, to suggest that the traditional eye of Reason is basically an eye for significant analogies and differences is to suggest a link with a more down to earth notion of intelligence that may intelligibly be supposed to extend beyond possessors of language.

If it is true that language is essentially open to extension or modification or moulding as a part of rational reflection on something other than language itself, it seems not unlikely that in the acquisition of language rationality or general intelligence will play a related role. For the learner who for the first time comes to grasp an established area of language does not seem necessarily different in kind from the competent speaker who gets the point of another's novel utilization of language. It seems dangerous, therefore, to base a psychology of language on a theory that treats a language as an inelastic system of rules, and the acquisition of language as involving no more than the 'internalisation' of these rules.

On the other hand, language has very many features that could not be grasped in anything like the way in which a conceptual connection or the point of a paradox or of a bit of classification could be grasped. Such features do not in the same sense have point, even if in some sense they serve a purpose. A phonological rule, for example, or rules for pronominalisation, may at best seem natural, but hardly rational. The question raised by *a priori* reasoning is therefore somewhat different from one that has received some discussion by Chomsky and others, as to whether a child's acquisition of language as a whole could be accounted for by a general faculty of intelligence.

The opposition standardly identified by the modern argument

for innate ideas is behaviourist learning theory, but a different view of what is involved in intelligent hypothesis might propose the model that the mind unconsciously operates in relation to rules of language as it does in science, by speculative hypothesis suggested but not mechanically produced by the data and open to experimental confirmation, modification and so forth. Children do sometimes seem to get things wrong in an orderly way. The proposal is made by Chomsky himself, but he argues that unless we suppose a set of innate 'organising principles' or 'restrictive conditions' on the form that such hypotheses could take, it remains incredible that the data should provide the basis for a speculative hypothesis with more than the slightest chance of being right. It is therefore not surprising that he should be found frequently to stress the evidence that the acquisition of language is a 'species-specific capacity that is essentially independent of intelligence'.[1]

There may be problems about this formal model for a largely unconscious process, but I am interested in its relationship to another claim of Chomsky's about intelligence or reason. This is the claim that the study of the principles that determine the form of grammar, called by Chomsky 'universal grammar', is concerned with 'the nature of human intellectual capacities'. The linguist, at this level, is 'trying to establish certain general properties of human intelligence'.[2] There seem to be two separable points behind such an assertion. I shall simplify the first rather crudely: if we regard 'intelligence' simply as the sum of non-physical learning capacities, if we regard every non-physical competence as 'intellectual', and if there are innate structures that make it possible to learn one sort of abstract system but not another, then the principles of that sort of system reflect properties of human 'intelligence' and help define the human 'intellect', *in this sense*. By thus postulating that Chomsky uses 'intelligence' ambiguously, we can at least account for the fact that he both regards linguistic competence as essentially independent of intelligence, and also regards the study of 'universal grammar', the key to linguistic competence, as the study of the structure of human intelligence.

On the other hand, it seems that Chomsky is making a more impressive claim when he says that the linguist studies the

[1] *Language and Mind*, p. 68. (New York 1968).
[2] *Ibid.*, p. 24.

structure of human intelligence: at the extreme, he might mean that the linguist studies the innate mechanisms that determine the way we reason, or what we find reasonable. We may recall Katz's claim that the systematic and empirical study of the structure of language should enable us to resolve *a priori* disputes. It is also relevant, of course, that Chomsky associates his theory with the classical theory of innate ideas, the chief point of which was to explain our knowledge of truths of reason. The study of innate principles was indeed thought to be the study of the structure of human rationality.

One difference is that Chomsky offers an explanation of the same form for all aspects of linguistic competence. The phonological, syntactic and semantic components of linguistic descriptions are all thought to be represented at the level of universal grammar. But in his favourable commentary on Rationalism he does not seem merely to be drawing a general analogy between his theory of grammar and the classical theory of innate *a priori* knowledge, but rather to see himself as offering a more comprehensive theory that includes the old theory, doubtless open to modification as progress is made. It is true that he says little about 'truths of reason', but this seems to be because their explanation is supposed to lie chiefly within the 'semantic' component of grammar, a region in which, as Chomsky admits, 'we soon become lost in a tangle of confused issues and murky problems'.[1] In view of the general prevalence of the linguistic theory of *a priori* truth it is hardly surprising if he makes such an assumption. Although he rejects the Empiricist's 'reductive' view of linguistic competence, it remains doubtful whether his general theory could possibly do justice to *a priori* rationality.

One objection is that he must treat the 'intuitions' of reason as on the same level as linguistic (or merely linguistic) intuitions: he must treat what is perspicuous as requiring the same sort of explanation as what is not perspicuous. A non-perspicuous intuition would be the rejection of the deviant sentence 'What boy did he believe the claim that John made about?' which Chomsky locates in the class of those that are 'quite impossible, although it would be clear what they meant, were they grammatically permissible'.[2] Here we have an 'intuition' in a fairly ordinary sense:

[1] *Ibid.*, p. 50.
[2] *Ibid.*, p. 42.

as it were, a dependable feeling of wrongness, without our being able to say why. How we know that something is wrong is obscure, and a suitably complex analytic explanation of the wrongness may support the thesis of innate principles. But with 'John is taller than Mary, although Mary is taller than John', the feeling of wrongness is quite different, so that if we talk of 'intuition' the word is used more as Locke used it, for recognition of the obvious. There is not the same mystery about our knowledge. That is, there is not the same foothold in the content of our knowledge, in respect of that feature of the sentence that makes it unacceptable, for the argument that we are being guided by a possibly complex system of rules. There may of course be *other* mysteries, from the point of view of psychology.

One way of putting the point is to allow a certain distinction between the judgment that a sentence is grammatical and the judgment that it 'makes sense'. The deviant sentence 'John is more good at puzzles than Bill is good at puzzles', while execrable English, 'makes sense' in a way in which 'John is better at puzzles than Bill is better at puzzles' does not. The argument for innate structure—semantic structure, at least—seems to presuppose that behind the judgment that a sentence does or does not 'make sense' lie implicitly accepted linguistic rules, and nothing else. Yet behind the judgement that the first sentence 'makes sense' there lies recognition of the simple possibility that levels of excellence should be compared—no more a grammatical fact than is the possibility of any quantitative comparison. If it seems mysterious or empty to talk of such recognition in this case, consider 'John is better at reading by more than Bill is better at writing', 'John is better at reading by more than Bill is better at reading' and 'John is more better at reading than Bill'. Someone hearing these sentences might easily have the intuition that all are deviant, but only the last of the three is in fact deviant, and all can be regarded as 'making sense'. To grasp that the first is not deviant it is necessary to grasp the possibility of comparing the degree to which John excels at one accomplishment with the degree to which Bill excels at another. With the second, we must grasp the possibility of comparing the degree to which John's ability at reading exceeds another of his abilities with the same degree in the case of Bill's ability at reading. Since it is easy to suppose that someone should, through lack or temporary failure of intelligence, be incapable of grasping or slow to grasp these possibilities, it is plausible to conclude that, in interpreting what is said to him, the child has in his armoury not only linguistic intuitions, however acquired, but *also* his intelligence or capacity for seeing what 'makes sense'.

When evaluating the classical arguments over innate knowledge, it is essential to be clear that the dispute is exclusively about 'intuitions' of this second sort. It thus concerns the very part of Chomsky's theory, call it the semantic component, in which he confesses there exist no clear specific arguments for innateness. Considerations of phonology and 'mere' syntax seem incidental. Seen in this light, Locke's philosophical position has an important bearing on the issue that I am trying to raise about rationality and linguistic competence.

There are two major distortions of Locke's position in the usual criticisms from Chomsky's point of view. The first consists in the old claim that Locke does not even consider the possibility of dispositional innate knowledge. The truth is that Locke has an explicit conception of dispositional or 'habitual' knowledge, which allows us to see very clearly why only memory-knowledge could for him count as such. His presupposition is that Descartes was right about the nature of knowledge: knowledge consists in 'seeing', and *ipso facto* understanding, relations between ideas. That is to say, Locke held an 'Intuitionist' theory of knowledge, and reasonably supposed that an 'intuition' or 'perception' of intelligible relations must be conscious. The connection of *knowledge* with *understanding*, on this conception of it, can be illustrated by Locke's own example of Newton's *Principia*: a man *knows* Newton's conclusions to be true only if he has followed the proofs, although it is not necessary for 'habitual knowledge' that he should now 'have in actual view that admirable train of ideas'.[1] But in the concept of 'innate knowledge' the connection with understanding and rational 'perception' is broken completely. How then could such a concept explain our 'perceptions'? This makes it intelligible that, in the knockabout rhetoric of Book I of the *Essay*, Locke should deride the theory as if it attributed learned insights to infants.

The other distortion puts him in the camp of Empiricism. The

[1] *Essay*, Bk. IV, Ch. I.

'Empiricist', in denying innateness, is supposed to lean towards a theory of learning that ascribes all concepts and knowledge of language-rules to 'inductive generalisation and association',[1] the former being represented on Humean lines as a kind of habituation or conditioning through the force of experienced instances: a theory certainly having easy links with behaviourist psychology. But the existence of a very different, very limited kinship between Locke and his arch-critic Hume hardly justifies the extraordinary suggestion that learning-theory is a precise statement of something implicit in Locke, who is a full-blooded Rationalist, and a very important and great one, in the only significant and useful sense of the term. He assumes that the universe is an intelligible system of substances, which interact in accordance with their actual structure or essences. The system is 'intelligible' because the interactions are logically entailed by the essences of the substances involved. The essence is *actual* structure, because *powers* must be explained by, and so cannot constitute, essence. The chief work done by the principle that all our ideas came from experience is to support his thesis that we do not have the key to this system. What is given in experience is knowledge of effects and powers, and the concepts of a limited number of sensible qualities. Speculations about underlying structure, such as the atomic theory, are limited by this restriction on our stock of concepts. In arguing that human knowledge is limited, Locke was not breaking away from Rationalism. Spinoza and Leibniz were of the same opinion, if for different reasons.

The point of all this is not to quibble over the terms 'Rationalist' and 'Empiricist', but to allow us to see that Locke's objections to innate knowledge have nothing whatsoever to do with the view that some notion of habituation will satisfactorily account for the learning of language. Locke's view is that all our actual and limited knowledge can be explained in terms of a basic stock of experiential 'ideas' together with a *general* faculty of Reason or capacity for 'seeing' conceptual relationships. Consequently he represents an alternative opposition to the theory of innate knowledge; or at least a likely source of qualification and clarification that cannot be dismissed with the bald assertion that talk of 'intelligence' or 'reason' is too general or vague or lacking in explanatory power. There is no need to subscribe to Locke's

[1] v. Katz, op. cit., pp. 240–82.

theory of ideas as objects of intuition in order to feel that there is
at least as much justice in his own chief complaint that talk of
innate, implicit principles offers no explanation of how we *know*
and can *see* that such principles, and their specific applications, are
true.

For this last criticism can be transposed into a discussion that
assumes a much closer dependence of the ability to think rationally
on the ability to talk intelligibly than Locke would have allowed.
The notion that our ready acceptance of the principle, e.g., 'If A
is greater than B, and B than C, then A is greater than C', is due
to an implicit recognition or knowledge of a set of grammatical
rules that we are unable to state, does not do justice to its 'evidence',
to the fact that we do not feel its correctness only obscurely or, in
the ordinary sense, intuitively. For we can consciously understand
the relation, seeing that and why it holds for 'greater than' even
without generalising our thought to all comparatives or all transitive relations. If knowledge and understanding of the specific rule
derived from implicit and innate knowledge of some more general
rule, the former would be merely intuitive and could not be
recognised as justified at least until the general rule itself became
explicitly known.

Here it is pertinent to recall that an important and neglected
part of Locke's attack on Innatism is his criticism of the doctrine
that implicitly accepted general 'maxims' usefully underlie the
simplest and most evident inference made at a more specific level.
The truth that our low-level inferences may be in accordance with,
or instances of high-level principles Locke regards as of interest
to the systematising logician rather than to the psychologist and
epistemologist. (The interests of these last surely converge here,
for a man's knowledge cannot owe its status as justified belief to a
reason that is not psychologically operative, and there is no
necessity to go beyond what justifies his belief in order to explain
it.) Locke's Intuitionism leads him too far towards the conclusion
that knowledge of more specific truths and knowledge of general
principles are mutually independent, whereas, to my mind, an
analytic examination of any conceptual argument provides convincing evidence that, from the point of view of epistemology,
principles and examples prop one another up. Yet if it can be
shewn to be a false assumption that the possession or grasp of
general principles must be postulated to explain particular non-

accidental inferences and insights that are, from the point of view of logic, in accordance with them, one of the chief classical arguments for innate ideas is utterly demolished. An account of *a priori* justification such as John Wisdom's shews how the objection could be made independent of Intuitionism. For Wisdom eschews the assumption, central to Intuitionism, that *a priori* knowledge rests on insights that can be neither questioned nor justified, the *terminus a quo* of all reasoning. But if the objection can be sustained against the classical theory, it can be sustained against the modern theory precisely to the extent to which the latter offers to explain conceptual knowledge.

A promising line of speculation concerns the possible extent and limits of the role that reflective rationality plays in language acquisition. I call it 'reflective rationality' rather than 'intelligence' not because it is a different faculty, but (as I have tried to explain) because of its 'direction'. If our model for language acquisition presents the learner as making intelligent guesses at the rules of language, systematising the data as one might the moves of chess-players in order to arrive at the rules by which they play, we are assuming that his intelligence is aimed directly towards linguistic structure. But in the region of 'semantics', at least, the intelligence is characteristically directed outside language, e.g. towards a set of instances which the learner must succeed in seeing as members of a single class. The classical theory of innate ideas, of course, included the doctrine that we are predisposed to view the world through the medium of basic concepts or categories, e.g. the concept of a *thing* or *substance*, a causal agent having an essence explanatory of its powers. Whereas in Locke's complex treatment of such concepts, we find the general suggestion that they contain nothing that cannot be explained as a result of rational reflection on experience; they simply represent the only way of making sense of reality as experienced.

It is not easy to see how this issue, which had largely to do with philosophy of science, might be related to grammar. But one apparent connection concerns the relationship between the 'syntactic' and 'semantic' components. It does not seem possible to keep in separate compartments knowledge of the sense of a word such as *cat*, or *runs*, or *red*, and knowledge of the part that such a linguistic element can play in 'deep structure'. We might attempt to summarise the latter knowledge as knowledge that *cat* falls into the category of *thing* or *physical object* (or perhaps even *living thing*), that *running* is an *action* or *activity*, and so on. Wittgenstein adduced this sort of consideration in his attack on the notion of logical simples, and on a certain view of the role that 'ostensive definition' plays in concept acquisition. For if knowledge of 'grammar' is included in possession of the concept of *cat*, or *running*, or *red*, it may seem incomprehensible that any such concept could be straightforwardly transmitted by ostensive definition or acquired by 'acquaintance'. Knowledge of word meaning thus appears derivative from knowledge of sentence meaning. There may be a truth behind this: one can hardly imagine a man with a large vocabulary but no syntax, any more than the reverse. Yet the argument can be stood more or less on its head. For 'ostensive definition', formally or informally done, obviously does play a large and essential part in language acquisition and, as far as I can see, a primitive part. Single words uttered in appropriate circumstances do as a rule come first. The notorious 'idea that the meaning of a word is an object' is not based on nothing—nor are associationist theories of meaning. Now the achievement of grasping the point of similarity between a number of cats seems to me to presuppose no knowledge of grammar, and is reasonably classifiable as an exercise of intelligence. The same goes for the similarity between running animals. But in that case, is not the grasp of the significance of '(The) cat (is) running' *also* something that is intelligible as the exercise of general intelligence independently of knowledge of grammar? There exists the possibility of these different modes of comparison, which itself seems to generate, rather than merely reflect, the possibility of a fundamental syntactic relationship. Certainly something very different seems involved from, e.g., rules for pronominalisation. Nor should we ignore the fact that, in so far as it is perfectly natural to suppose that the child comes into the world armed with a specific capacity to appreciate it for what it is, e.g. as a world in which physical objects interact and there are other beings like himself, it would be very unnatural to treat such an instinctive power as linguistic, i.e. as exercised only when language is acquired and peculiar to human beings. (Not that some philosophers have not suggested that we are indebted to sentence-structure for the concept of a physical object.)[1]

[1] e.g. Ayer, in *Language, Truth and Logic*, p. 42. (London 1946).

How much weight this line of argument will bear, or how far it reaches, is not clear to me. It does seem relevant to some of the claims made. Katz argues, for example, that the ordinary English imperative, e.g. 'Help the man', must be grammatically conceived of as being derived from an underlying structure or phrase-marker with 'you' as subject. This 'unobservable' feature contributes to the meaning, so that argument continues, and thus must be known somehow by one who knows that meaning. Since the feature is unobservable, it cannot be allowed that a Humean conditioning process leads the speaker to predict, e.g., that only 'will you?' or 'yourself' will ever be correct after an imperative, never 'himself', 'will he?' and so on.

Now the principle that 'you' is the subject of an imperative has a decidedly *a priori* air. It would be difficult to distinguish a child's realisation that the imperative 'Jump!' has *you* as unheard grammatical subject, from his realisation, given knowledge of the sense of the verb *jump*, that when authority says 'Jump!' the person addressed is expected to jump. But the latter realisation is likely to come when he sees the others jump, the impatience of the speaker directed towards non-jumpers and so on—provided that he has the intelligence to propose such a mildly creative inter-pretation of the whole situation. We can then understand why 'Dress yourself' should appear to him unexceptionable, while, if he has a grasp of reflexives from other contexts, 'Dress herself' should appear not to 'make sense', or else not to be an imperative. Thus there is no need to postulate, as Katz does, that the child has unconsciously derived the given final phrase marker by implicitly recognised principles of derivation from an underlying phrase marker constructed on implicitly known principles of universal grammar. Such a portentous interpretation seems, indeed, to rely on an unrealistic abstraction from the situations in which signific-ance is grasped; the 'input' is artificially impoverished.

There *may* be areas in which it is not easy to see whether features of 'what we say' are governed by conceptual or by merely grammatical considerations.[1] But the existence of such difficulties does not undermine the distinction between the two sorts of consideration, or between 'logic' and 'grammar'.

Finally, to return to a simple and probably the most influential

---

[1] And these *may* correspond to that possible domain to which Chomsky refers, where 'semantic and syntactic rules interpenetrate'.

stumbling-block in the way of the view that I am proposing. This is the argument that, given that a being without language cannot meaningfully be supposed to be contemplating such a truth as that if A is better than B then B is not better than A in the same respect, it seems impossible that he should either see or fail to see its truth. It therefore seems impossible that such an insight or failure should be operative in the acquisition or failure to acquire the language to express it. This looks conclusive but is not. We may take note of the fact that it is not entirely unnatural to explain a failure in language-learning or concept acquisition in such terms even as 'He cannot understand that all brothers are male'; or a success by 'At last he realises that not all women are mothers'. There may be something quaint and overformal in this character-isation of the learner's mistake, but it contains something that is missed by such accounts as 'He uses "brother" to mean *sibling*', or 'He no longer takes "mother" to mean *woman*'. For the inability to extract a principle, or significant likeness, from suitable examples is a failure of understanding, and overcoming this failure is an exercise of rationality. There is an analogy with the learning of mathematical symbolism, an area of language from which 'mere grammar' is virtually absent, and which may invite the same paradox: if a mathematical truth cannot be grasped without symbolism, or by one who does not understand the sym-bolism, how could the failure to grasp a part of mathematics ever be operative in a failure to learn the symbolism? But in so far as the conclusion of this argument seems to exclude the possibility that the same intelligence or insight that operates in grasping a mathematical truth should figure in the explanation of the rapid acquisition of mathematical concepts, it surely must be sophistical. Katz, in explaining the model, *input→language acquisition device →output*, offers the fact that 'a very intelligent person can obtain the solutions to certain mathematical problems (the output) given just the barest formulation of the problems (the input) whereas a very unintelligent person might have to be virtually told the solutions before he gets them'. The reflection that mathematical symbolism too has to be learnt should perhaps have moderated his zeal for innate principles. Leibniz thought that the whole of mathematics is innate in us, but that, I imagine, is not a doctrine likely to be embraced by modern psychology.

VI

INCORRIGIBILITY, BEHAVIOURISM AND PREDICTIONISM

GEORGE W. ROBERTS

1.   I̲N̲ T̲H̲I̲S̲ essay I explore an argument against behaviourism
     suggested by the writings of Professor John Wisdom but
never developed by him. This argument assumes the incorrigibility of statements about one's sensory states of the moment and
concludes that statements about one's behaviour in its relations to
one's circumstances, not being incorrigible, cannot be equivalent
to those statements. I submit first that this argument does follow
but destroys its own premiss, the incorrigibility-doctrine about
sense-statements; then I discuss some, but not all of the reasons
given by the late J. L. Austin and by Wisdom for rejecting the
incorrigibility doctrine, and add some reasons of my own devising.
I extract the anti-behaviourist argument partly from an anti-
phenomenalist argument Wisdom gave, so some aspects of that
argument are further examined. Also I transform the incorrigibility argument against behaviourism into a related, sound argument from the impredictiveness of sense-statements, and I
explore at length some issues about non-predictive error and
predictionism related to that argument.

2.   In his 'Philosophical Perplexity' (1936) Wisdom offered
an argument against the view that statements about material
things are analysable into statements about sensations. The
argument is to be found in the following passage:[1]

> Thus the sceptic's pretended doubts amount to pointing out
> that, unlike statements descriptive of sensations, statements
> about material things make sense with 'perhaps he is mistaken'.
> And the sceptic proposes to mark this by an extraordinary use
> of 'know' and 'probably'. He proposes that we should not say
> that we know that that is cheese on the table unless it is
> entailed by statements with regard to which a doubt is not

[1] *Proceedings of the Aristotelian Society*, 1936–37. Reprinted in *Philosophy
and Psycho-Analysis* (Blackwell, 1952), in which the passage occurs on page 71.

merely out of the question but unintelligible, i.e. such that where S is P is one of them 'S is P unless I am mistaken' raises a titter like 'I am in pain unless I am mistaken'. 'That is cheese on the table' is not such a statement and so of course it does not follow from such statements—otherwise a doubt with regard to it would be unintelligible, i.e. it would be absolutely certain in the strict, philosophic sense.

If this argument is sound, it follows that no material-thing statement is entailed by, and so that no material-thing statement is equivalent to, any statement about sensations. It also follows that no material-thing statement entails any statement about sensations; for the negation of a material-thing statement is a material-thing statement and the negation of a statement about sensations is a statement about sensations,[1] so that if a material-thing statement entails a statement about sensations then the negation of that sensation-statement entails the negation of the material-thing statement and hence a sensation-statement entails a material-thing statement.

3.　It seems to me to be remarkable that no one, not even Wisdom, has noticed as well as he might have that given its premisses this sort of argument does at least appear to disprove analytical behaviourism, whether or not it disproves phenomenal-ism[2]. It appears, that is, to disprove the doctrine that every statement about minds is equivalent to some statement about material things. In fact if its premisses are sound this sort of argument appears to show more than that behaviourism in this sense is false; it appears to show as well that no statement about behaviour in relation to circumstances can entail any statement about sensations.

If the premisses of the argument are true the argument appears to establish these conclusions; but are the premisses true? It is assumed now, and argued later, that material-thing statements are corrigible in the sense in question. The question now is

[1] This can be put: category-status is negation-invariant, at least for the categories of statements about material things and statements about sensations. The category of material-thing statements does not differ in any respect that matters here from the wider category of statements about the external world.
[2] The warning word 'appears' is needed here, as will appear. I argue that the premisses entail the conclusion only if the incorrigibility-premiss is false. So if the intended deduction is valid, an essential premiss must fail, and if both premisses are sound, the argument does not follow; the argument cannot therefore prove its conclusion.

whether statements about sensations, as Wisdom used that phrase in the quoted passage, are incorrigible. I shall argue, first, that this incorrigibility-premiss is inconsistent with the deductive validity of the argument that deploys it, and second that this premiss is in any case false. The question will then arise whether any similar argument can be given, whose deductive validity does not impugn one of its premisses; and I shall argue that an argument from the impredictive character of sensation-statements meets this condition. Statements about one's own sensations of the moment are not incorrigible, but are non-predictive in a sense in which material-thing statements, or at least those plausible as behaviourist *analysantia*, are predictive. Moreover, such features as non-predictiveness must be shared by equivalent statements.

4.   First, then, I must explain how the principle in accordance with which Wisdom's anti-phenomenalist argument and the parallel anti-behaviourist argument follow eliminates the incorrigibility-premisses of these arguments. The principle of these arguments is in effect this: if 'He thinks that p but perhaps he is mistaken' makes no sense and p entails q, then 'He thinks that q but perhaps he is mistaken' must also make no sense.[1] In a word, ' "Perhaps he is mistaken in thinking that p" makes no sense' is entailment-hereditary. It follows trivially that ' "Perhaps he is mistaken in thinking that p" makes no sense' is equivalence-hereditary or, as I like to say, equivalence-invariant. The latter principle appears to be weaker than the former, but we shall shortly see that this is not really so. Now these principles have entirely negative consequences for the incorrigibility-notions they contain, as philosophers have almost completely failed to notice. I will begin to show this by pointing out that it makes perfectly good sense to say of someone 'He thinks that Goldbach's conjecture is true but perhaps he is mistaken', or indeed to say 'He thinks that the circle cannot be squared but perhaps he is mistaken' (though for the knowledgeable it is wrong to say this). Now take this latter case; if the equivalence-invariance principle for the notion in question holds true it follows that 'He thinks that t but perhaps he is mistaken' makes sense for any *a priori* true statement t, for any two such statements are logically equivalent: it cannot be true that one of them is true while the other is false.[2] So even 'He

---

[1] The words 'in effect' cover the change to the third person.
[2] It might be held that equivalence-invariance holds for the incorrigibility-

K

thinks that one and one make two but perhaps he is mistaken' *makes sense*, though perhaps it is a little difficult at the start to think of a conceivable situation in which this form of words would properly be used meaning what it now does. Since it makes sense to say 'He thinks that p but perhaps he is mistaken' for at least some *a priori* false statements, it must make sense for all of them. But we can go further still: it makes sense to say 'Perhaps he is mistaken in thinking the circle cannot be squared'. By a well-known property of equivalence a logically true statement can be eliminated from a conjunction without diminishing its logical content; so 'The circle cannot be squared and f', where f is any statement as to the facts, is equivalent to just f. But 'Perhaps he is mistaken in thinking the circle cannot be squared and f' makes sense, for 'Perhaps he is mistaken in thinking that' makes sense as applied to at least 'The circle cannot be squared' and so to its conjunction with any other statement. Now by equivalence-invariance for ' "Perhaps he is mistaken in thinking that p" makes sense', it follows that 'Perhaps he is mistaken in thinking that f' must make sense as well. It should also be noticed that this shows that equivalence-invariance implies entailment-hereditariness for the notion in question. Since ' "Perhaps he is mistaken in thinking that p" makes no sense' is necessarily not instantiated the two conditions must be satisfied in just the same cases, namely none.[1]

The notion we have just been considering should be contrasted with another very similar one, *viz.*, 'He cannot be mistaken in thinking that p.' Plainly there are some statements of which this holds true, *viz.*, *a priori* true statements and such statements as 'I think' and 'I exist', the Cartesian favourites. As for some points of similarity, I have argued elsewhere that this notion too has no application outside that narrow circle, so that 'I am in pain' for example is in this sense corrigible.[2] It follows that the notion is not only equivalence-invariant but entailment-hereditary, and so

---

notions and the substitutes I propose for them only with 'equivalence' used in a stronger sense. For the substitutes I propose this is patently absurd; for the incorrigibility-notions I reply for now only that these notions form part of the verificational logic of statements and that this logic follows equivalence in the sense given.

[1] It may be objected that it is (necessarily) a contingent matter that a form of words makes no sense. The discussion required to deal with this sort of objection would lead us too far afield here.

[2] In 'Some Questions in Epistemology', *Proceedings of the Aristotelian Society*, 1969–70.

that these conditions are equivalent for it as well. It is easy to find exceptions for entailment-hereditariness for 'He cannot be mistaken in thinking that p' if, for example, 'I am in pain' falls under that notion, for no one would maintain that 'Someone is in pain', which is entailed by 'I am in pain', is in this sense incorrigible. But if only the likes of 'I think' fall under the notion such exceptions cannot be found; 'I think that someone thinks' cannot be mistaken any more than 'I think that I think'.

5. I should return, however, to a detailed examination of the contents of Wisdom's anti-phenomenalist argument. In the first place, we may very reasonably suppose that by 'statements descriptive of sensations' (as by 'sense-statements' elsewhere) Wisdom here meant to refer to statements about *one's own* sensations *of the moment*. Otherwise what the sceptic is said to point out is quite obviously false. Clearly it will not do to suggest that '*He* is in pain unless *I* am mistaken' 'raises a titter like "I am in pain unless I am mistaken "'. Nor will it do to say that 'I *was* in pain unless I am mistaken' 'raises a titter like "I am in pain unless I am mistaken"'. Even if, as Wisdom said in the paragraph preceding that quoted above, ' . . . "He says he is in pain, but perhaps he is mistaken" has no use in English', we may still refuse to allow that what is "absolutely certain", in the sense cherished by the sceptic, is *for each person* anything more than statements like 'I am in pain' (and perhaps logico-mathematical truths, which Wisdom mentioned elsewhere in 'Philosophical Perplexity'). *We* may perhaps be "absolutely certain" that *he* is not mistaken about *his* pain, in the very special sense that 'He is mistaken' makes no sense in this connection. But we, that is we *others*, can *not* be "absolutely certain" *that he is in pain*; for 'He is in pain unless I am mistaken' and indeed 'He is in pain unless we (others) are mistaken' make sense, just as does 'That is a cheese unless I am mistaken'. Even I cannot be "absolutely certain" that I *was* in pain at a certain past time; though supposedly I could not have failed to be "absolutely certain" that I was in pain at that time.

These considerations enable us to show what sort of phenomenalism might be refuted by Wisdom's argument. At best the argument appears to refute what might be called private phenomenalism of the present moment, which is the sort of reductionistic, phenomenalistic theory that corresponds, not to solipsism *simpliciter* but to solipsism *of the present moment*. That is, it is the analytical doctrine that corresponds to the solipsistic existential denial in the form 'Nothing exists except me (as I now am) and my sensations of the moment'. I do not want to deny the philosophical interest of solipsism of the present moment, but it is obvious that phenomenalism is not at its most plausible or popular in its corresponding form. Phenomenalists do sometimes equivocate over public and private phenomenalism, but in neither case are they drawn at all often to a phenomenalism of the moment. Clearly, then, on the face of it Wisdom's argument is at least misleadingly presented. As presented it applies, correctly, only to the most peculiar, extreme, and infrequently held form of phenomenalism. Yet it is presented so as to suggest the idea that phenomenalism in every form can be refuted by reference to the peculiar character of statements descriptive of sensations, *i.e.*, really, as we have seen, statements descriptive of one's own sensations of the moment. It is indeed the use of the words 'statements descriptive of sensations' in this peculiarly limited way, to refer not to any and every statement about anyone's sensations at any time, but only to one's own sensations at the moment, that may have suggested the unfortunate idea that the argument applies against all forms of phenomenalism. But the argument fails to affect public phenomenalism, or even private phenomenalism not merely of the present moment. 'Statements descriptive of sensations' in the wider, more proper, and natural sense relevant to those theories are not all incorrigible by any means; the argument fails then in these cases through the manifest failure of its crucial premiss. Statements about one's own past or future sensations and statements about the sensations of others are not incorrigible; even if statements about one's own sensations of the moment are incorrigible that is no reason to suppose that statements about material things are not reducible to, or at least entailed by, statements about sensations in general, whatever the creature or time. After all statements about one's past, present, and future sensations need not be incorrigible even if they are constructed out of statements about one's sensations all of which are at some time incorrigible. Consider, for instance, 'Yesterday I had a pink rat hallucination, I have another now, and tomorrow there is yet another in the offing'. On an incorrigibility-doctrine each component is incorrigible for me at the corresponding time, but the whole statement is never incorrigible for anyone.

6. I proceed, then, to a review of some of the considerations that led Wisdom and others to subscribe to incorrigibility-doctrines about sense-statements. In the first place, it was thought that statements about one's own present sensations are not revocable on the basis of future sensations or the sensations of others; and it was thought in addition that there was no way that a statement could be mistaken, at least no way in which a genuine statement could be genuinely mistaken, except by way of mistaken expectations involved in the acceptance of it. But there was a further reason as well for the incorrigibility doctrine about sense-statements, and the explanation of this reason helps make more explicit what is involved in the notion of incorrigibility, of the impossibility of mistake or error.

When he wrote the 'Other Minds' articles Wisdom would have said that 'I think I am in pain but perhaps I am mistaken' makes no sense unless a use is carefully provided.[1] It is worth considering what was covered by the phrase 'providing a use' as employed here. First, it was meant that the words 'I am in pain', say, could be used in such a way that I would not qualify as being in pain, properly speaking, unless I had more than a momentary twinge, so that I could after all be mistaken in a predictive way when I say on the basis of my current sensation that I am in pain. But this was not, perhaps, the only thing that was meant by providing a use for 'mistaken about my pain now'. Another way in which a use was to be provided for such words was to employ them to refer to errors that are, or were supposed to be, merely verbal, and not real errors. In Wisdom's well-known words, I could be mistaken about my current pain, but the mistake would be like that which I would make when I call Jack Alfred knowing very well his name is Jack or not caring what his name is. Again, I say 'I feel well' meaning 'I feel ill' when I do feel ill, and so by a slip of the tongue use the wrong word; I am then mistaken but only verbally.

Austin made some well-known objections to these Wisdomian views about sense-statements.[2] I should like now to consider an

---

[1] The series is in *Mind* (1940–43) and reprinted in Wisdom's *Other Minds* (Blackwell, 1952).
[2] Wisdom's words were in 'Other Minds VIII'; Austin's criticisms in his 'Other Minds' symposium article, *Proceedings of the Aristotelian Society*, Supplementary Vol. XX (1946), reprinted in Austin's *Philosophical Papers*, 2nd edition (Oxford University Press, 1970).

objection to the incorrigibility doctrine suggested by Austin's remarks. Even when it is a question of the character of my own sensation of the moment I can, in Austin's view, be genuinely mistaken: I can mislead not only others but also myself. For instance, I can ask myself 'Is it aqua or turquoise?' of one of my current after-images or hallucinatory rats and be uncertain in my judgment and finally mistaken; I can misclassify the image in respect of its colour and so be wrong about it. The difficulty with this objection to the incorrigibility of sense-statements is not that it is mistaken but that it is liable to be dismissed as referring to purely verbal error. This can happen because the sort of case in which we most readily conceive of and concede the possibility of error about whether a current sensory image is aqua or turquoise is that of an image whose colour is *borderline*; and the question 'Is this rat-image aqua or turquoise?' asked of a borderline case can very readily be re-presented in the form 'Is this rat-image aqua, or *shall I say* turquoise?'. This transformation readily prompts the description of the question as verbal, and this in turn may prompt its description as not a real question and so the conclusion that answers to such questions are at worst verbally wrong.

Now as Austin, and later Wisdom might have insisted, such a borderline-aqua rat-image may be one for which, if I must obtain a verdict, I can toss a coin, but it may not be. If not, then my choice of an appellation may assimilate the image's colour to what resembles it least and so misclassify it, and in that way distort my apprehension of its colour and represent a mistake, a genuine enough mistake about its colour even though a mistake that is not at all a matter of prediction or expectation. At any rate the mistake will not be a predictive mistake in the way that 'It is a pain' said at the first twinge may be, in the usage explained earlier, mistaken in respect of my expectations. So the sort of error suggested here by Austin's objections to incorrigibility may be genuine enough, even if such errors can correctly be described as verbal because of the transformability of the corresponding questions into the 'Shall I say?' form. For such errors may nevertheless not be merely verbal but also real. They may be genuine cases of mistaken apprehension in a way in which a mere slip of the tongue, say 'I feel well' for 'I feel ill', is not. Such errors may be plain cases of misapprehending what is before me;

and even when the predicate is something very obvious such as 'red' and the matter something very immediate such as an hallucinatory rat-image there is still room for error in some cases at least, error not of a predictive but of a purely recognitional sort. This is error regarding what Professor H. H. Price called primary recognition and distinguished from secondary recognition; the latter, Price said, might involve predictive error as it was recognition from signs.

7. So really even 'He thinks he is in pain but perhaps he is wrong' is not so hopeless as Wisdom and others have suggested. Still, there are further arguments to be given against incorrigibility-doctrines; I choose now to give three of them, the first given by Wisdom, the second and third my own though not unrelated to the first.

The first argument might be called the argument from complex cases. In his 'Price's *Thinking and Experience*' Wisdom said that Price seemed to him to be mistaken in the supposition that primary recognition cannot be in error.[1] Now this assertion really had as part of its point the denial of the incorrigibility of sense-statements, which are the extreme case of statements that concern simply what is before one, namely statements that concern only those sensations before one at the moment. The argument Wisdom offered against Price was an argument by example. Is it not possible, he asked, to be mistaken as to whether the pattern before us is that of a willow-pattern plate?

In his unpublished Virginia Lectures *Proof and Explanation* Wisdom presented the examples of the Royal Arms and the Stars and Stripes;[2] it is possible to be mistaken, *e.g.*, in respect of the relative position of the Lion and the Unicorn in the first case, and in respect of the number of stripes, or the colour of a border stripe and so the stripe-sequence (red-white-red, *etc.*, or white-red-white, *etc.*, from the top down, say). The point here is that in these cases, in the case of these complex patterns, it is possible to be taken in, to fail to recognize some anomaly, even in the most favourable circumstances for applying or withholding a predicate such as 'Stars and Stripes'. It makes no difference at all here if the

[1] In Wisdom's *Paradox and Discovery* (Blackwell, 1965). Verbally, Price is not mistaken; if I recognize I get it right, and strictly too 'misrecognize' may be solecistic. No matter for now.
[2] Lectures delivered at the University of Virginia in 1957; a mimeographed version has been circulated.

pattern in question is that of a plate or an after-image; the same sort of misrecognition, of misapprehension can take place with one's sensation of the moment as with one's plate of the day.

Take the case of the Royal Arms. When an after-image is before me after I have taken a certain drug and I am asked 'Is it the Royal Arms?', I may reply 'Yes'. Then I am asked at once 'Ah, but weren't the Lion and Unicorn reversed?', and reply 'Oh yes, you're quite right'. Here we have a straightforward case of my misdescribing, because I have not properly taken in, the character of the sensation before me, even though I have been giving full attention to the task of describing these after-images, as I have been told to do so as part of an experiment. Only now do I learn that the scientist has given me a drug with a selective reversal effect on after-images, which causes the Lion and Unicorn to appear in reversed position on the third occurrence of the after-image, as I failed to note. This is a preposterous story of course (though who knows what clever scientists will be unable to do), but not at all because it is inconceivable that things should be so. Here then, in these complex cases, it is clear that misrecognition and failure to recognize one's momentary sensations are conceivable, and it is clear too that these are in no sense verbal errors, but genuine errors as to matters of fact. There is certainly real error, with the temptation not to recognize it as such removed by the fact that unlike error in the 'Shall I say?' cases we cannot call it verbal in any sense; though as we have seen there may be recognitional error even in borderline cases.

But now I propose to give a further argument, which will I think show that the same sort of radical, non-verbal, unmistakably real error of recognition is possible even in the simplest cases; even when the question is one of recognizing one's sensation, one's after-image of the moment, say, as red in colour, for example. I am saying, then, that recognitional error of this radical sort is in principle possible here just as in the complex cases like the after-image of the Royal Arms; the simplest and the complex cases are not in principle different in this respect.

Perhaps this argument can be presented more plausibly by a somewhat roundabout route. I want to begin then by putting before us a remark made by Professor P. F. Strawson. Strawson wrote:[1]

---

[1] *Introduction to Logical Theory* (Methuen, 1952), p. 97.

The stroke-formula has an especial charm in that it illustrates with peculiar clarity the remoteness of the conception of definition within a formal system from the ordinary conception of verbal elucidation of meaning. For one is inclined to say that it can be *explained* only in terms of the notions (negation and conjunction) which it is used, within the system, to define.

What Strawson's words here suggest seems to me to be false. I think there is no good reason to suppose that the stroke-operator, which we read as 'not both . . . and . . .', could not *conceivably* be introduced into a natural language prior to the notions of negation and conjunction. I hold that in a logically possible natural language those notions could be introduced by definition in terms of the stroke operation, and indeed named derivatively from that operation in such a language: negation, for instance, might be called 'reflexi-strokation'. For that matter we can imagine a conceivable Strawson brought up in such a language saying:

This definition-formula for strokation in terms of negation and conjunction has an especial charm in that it illustrates with peculiar clarity the remoteness of the conception of definition within a formal system from the ordinary conception of verbal elucidation of meaning. For one is inclined to say that they can be *explained* only in terms of the notion of strokation which they are used, within the system, to define.

I think then, contrary to Strawson, that there is really every reason to suppose that every possibility of definition 'within a formal system' (this phrase being a red herring I cannot pause here to show up) corresponds at least to a *conceivable* course of verbal elucidation of meaning for its *definiendum*. In a word, every equivalence of meaning is a two-way semantic route, available at least in principle not only in formal systems but also in natural languages. Whatever meaning-conferring procedure is or can be employed in a language for introducing an expression in a certain meaning, could in principle be used *mutatis mutandis* to introduce any equivalent expression. We can indeed actually deduce the way the primitive procedure might conceivably be applied to the defined expression, from the way in which the procedure is employed primitively with the defining expressions. In the case here, if we suppose that 'not' and 'and' are introduced by an ostensive procedure of a simple sort, say the utterance of 'not-p' when not-p and the like, it is not at all difficult to imagine the game beginning instead with 'stroke' as a symbol defined ostensively in the corresponding way. We should not really be put off here if we think that this is not or could not be the whole or even a part of the primitive procedure by which 'not' and 'and' come into our language.

These remarks can be related to the question about incorrigibility. First, it is perfectly possible to define extremely complex predicates in terms of simple words for colours, shades, *etc.*, that express a gerrymandered re-classification of the colour-manifold. Moreover, it is possible to produce such a new system of colour-descriptions with the property that, *via* long chains of complex definitions, the present simple colour-concepts can be introduced into that system. If I am right about the conceivable inversion of any semantic introduction-route expressible in equivalences, there is no reason in principle why we should not acquire by examples the use of the colour-words whose definitions in our colour-words are highly complex, and then by definition or in some other manner acquire our present simple colour concepts on the basis of them, as equivalents to elaborate constructs from the gerrymandered colour-divisions. We can easily enough conceive of mistakes with the highly elaborate concepts; so by equivalence-invariance mistakes with the present simple concepts should be possible, too. Actually, this conclusion follows by equivalence-invariance from the possibility of finding equivalents in terms of the complex concepts, equivalents about which no doubt we can be mistaken, for our simple basic colour terms such as 'red'. But if someone says 'One can't really have the complex concepts without first having the simple, and one can't have the simple unless one doesn't make mistakes with them' the treatment I have given here is one way of undermining his objection.

I do not say that Austin or even Wisdom would have accepted my drastic anti-incorrigibility arguments and conclusions, though Wisdom was committed to them by his anti-phenomenalist argument in 'Philosophical Perplexity'. Still it is worth remark that the corrigibility of statements about complex momentary sensory states can be used in an argument for radical anti-incorrigibilism, and used without invoking a principle such as equivalence-invariance for the notions in question. Given the corrigibility of sense-statements about complex patterns I can ask 'Where do you draw the line?'; this is indeed what Wisdom called it, 'a common metaphysical weapon of great power'. Wisdom is one of those who have taught us to regard its use in philosophy with no little suspicion. It would be regrettable, however, wholly to eschew its use; deplorable as it is to commit the borderline fallacy, in cases in which there *is* no line, not even an indefinite one, or rather in which there is no *relevant* line to be drawn, the question and the argument it represents are entirely proper. I believe the simple-complex distinction to be like that for the logical possibility of error, both in the case of sense-statements and in that of the *a priori*.

8.   One aspect of the notion of incorrigibility that has so far been neglected is reflected in a further inadequacy of Austin's sort of account of mistakes about one's current momentary sensations. Austin does not sufficiently guard against the suggestion that these mistakes are merely the result of an incompletely developed understanding of terms, as for instance 'turquoise'. Again I do not think the rejoinder need apply against the counter-examples to incorrigibility derived from Austin's remarks; but the rejoinder is plainly avoided by examples such as the Royal Arms images derived from Wisdom's Virginia Lectures, for which clearly we can very well know what the thing is like and yet make mistakes over recognizing it.

Hesitant reactions to Austin's counter-examples are apt to be overdetermined; partly the mistakes are thought to be verbal because they show inadequate understanding of the terms misapplied, partly because they are thought to concern borderline cases and so to resolve into mere matters of words. These reactions are by-passed by the Royal Arms images, but there is another rejoinder closely related to the claim that mistakes about current sensations show misunderstanding of terms that can be raised even against such cases. It may be said that though we understand the 'Royal Arms' and are attending to the image we are not *actualizing* our understanding of the terms when we fail to notice that the lion and the unicorn are the wrong way round for the Royal Arms. I do not think this rejoinder will do; I am inclined to say 'This is just refusing to speak of "actualized understanding" unless there is no mistake'. To deal with this rejoinder more adequately, a roundabout route may be used once more. The route is indicated by the equivalence-invariance argument against incorrigibility from the possibility of mistakes about the *a priori*.

Strawson,[1] commenting on my claim that the logical possibility of mistakes exists even in the simplest *a priori* cases, *e.g.*, 'One and one make two', said that at least no mistakes could be made here if one had a complete and fully actualized understanding of the terms involved. But I deny even this, for the following reasons. First, even the simplest *a priori* truths are logically equivalent to the most complex, so by the appropriate equivalence-invariance principle 'One and one make two' does not admit of mistake for one with a complete and fully actualized understanding of its terms if and only if complex and difficult mathematical truths, for example Green's theorem, do not admit of mistake for one with a complete and fully actualized understanding of their terms. But this is surely false; surely I can perfectly well understand the terms of Green's theorem, that understanding may be perfectly lively, perfectly in evidence, as I consider the theorem, yet I may for some reason wrongly think the theorem false. It is important to notice that we have some inclination to say that if I think Green's theorem false I do not yet have a *perfect* understanding of it, though it is perfectly true that I understand.

This brings me to something said by Dr. Anthony Kenny about Descartes' notion of indubitability.[2] For Descartes, as Kenny reminded us, infallibility is only guaranteed when one's ideas are *perfectly* clear and distinct, when, that is, one perfectly well understands what is involved in an issue. Now perhaps Descartes was right to think that he could ascribe indubitability or incorrigibility to, for example, 'I exist' or 'I think', and to mathematical and logical truths, at least to simple mathematical and logical truths. It is important to grasp just how this is right. If I have an *absolutely perfect* understanding of what is involved in *any a priori* statement, however complex, then indeed I cannot be wrong about it (perhaps because being right is logically part of perfection, but this sort of point I somewhat neglect here). Indeed we may go further; if I have an absolutely perfect grasp of what

---

[1] Strawson was in the chair when 'Some Questions in Epistemology' was read to the Aristotelian Society on November 10, 1969, on the 350th anniversary of Descartes' three dreams.

[2] In discussing 'Some Questions in Epistemology' in Oxford in January, 1970.

is involved in a statement about my current sensory states, *e.g.*, 'I have now before me a twelve-column porch image', then too I cannot possibly be mistaken about it (Descartes himself did not fail to recognize the similarity).

If, that is, I am entirely in command of *all* the meaning-connections of a statement, both those to other statements and those to immediate sensory conditions of applicability, then I cannot be mistaken about either *a priori* statements or statements about my own sensory states of the moment. Making *any* mistake about what a statement involves, its meaning-connections, is adverse to its being the case that one understands it, even though one has enough things right about it to qualify beyond peradventure as, in the ordinary way, understanding it, or even perfectly understanding it. Now one may, in the ordinary way, be mistaken about a statement by making some wrong connection involving it when one has yet made enough connections right to count as understanding it. We may, in the ordinary way, say truly 'Now I understand the question "Is Green's theorem true?" perfectly well', and go on to give the wrong answer, still understanding perfectly well. But in the new, metaphysical, Cartesian usage, which we all (even, as we have seen, Strawson and Kenny) have *some* inclination to indulge in, the understanding we have when we have made any misconnection and got the thing wrong is less than perfect, less than absolute.

The slide found here resembles the slide described by Wisdom in 'Other Minds VIII', in that both proceed by counting as fatal what is in any degree adverse. Both slides lead to what is, in the ordinary use of language, an incorrect conclusion, but both too reveal a connection, a continuity apt to be missed in the ordinary way of speaking. In the present context this is the continuity between the cases in which we truly say we understand but give the wrong answer through some reflective inadequacy, and the cases in which we do not understand. As I have pointed out, the same thing applies to one's statements about one's current sensory states as to the *a priori*, "honest error" is impossible, error is impossible that does not in some way, to some degree count against one's grasp of the notions involved. With all other statements error that does not in any way reflect on one's understanding of what is at stake is entirely possible.

9.   As I have indicated, the premiss of the incorrigibility

argument is now unacceptable to Wisdom. So it may seem that, though Wisdom doubtless missed a dialectical opportunity when he failed to exploit the incorrigibility argument against the behaviourists, perhaps through excessive sympathy with their position, the matter is no longer of much importance in connection with his philosophy or indeed with behaviourism. Why should we saddle behaviourism with the objection from the incorrigibility of sense-statements when (i) the behaviourist is not committed to the doctrine of sense-statement incorrigibility; far from it, for as we have seen his doctrine is actually inconsistent with it; and (ii) the incorrigibility-doctrine is after all recognized to be not even true?

But this would be a mistake. Of course this suggestion is quite right in that the incorrigibility doctrine is now out of court where behaviourism is concerned. However, both the doctrine and the argument admit of reformulation into something acceptable; I mean that a related sort of argument against behaviourism can be constructed on the basis of considerations some of which are brought forward by incorrigibilists. Such considerations are prominent in Wisdom's exposition of the incorrigibility doctrine in 'Other Minds VII', and elsewhere in the 'Other Minds' series.

The considerations I have in mind are these: sense-statements are, though liable to error, not liable to *predictive* error at the time they are about for the person whose sensations they are about: not liable, then and for that person, to error *via* mistaken expectations associated with them. In contrast, any statement about the material world is at least conceivably liable to predictive error at any time.[1] With any material-thing statement anyone could at any time conceivably be in such a position that he is mistaken about it through having mistaken expectations about his sensory states. This observation does not imply that every material-thing statement must be predictive in the sense that every such statement is liable at some time to error by way of mistaken expectations. Nor does it imply that every such statement must be predictive in that it cannot conceivably fail to be liable *ad infinitum* to expectational error. It merely implies that no material-thing statement can fail to be conceivably liable to expectational error at any moment to which any sense-statement refers. Thinking there

---

[1] The exceptions, if there are any, do not include any statements plausibly cast as behaviourist *analysantia*.

is a frown on my face, I look into a mirror expecting not to see my usual smile; but surprisingly there it is grinning out at me. If this surprise continues I will properly become convinced I was wrong about whether I was frowning; an astonishing error but conceivable nevertheless. With statements about my present sensory states I will never properly be convinced I was wrong about them by further sensations *in the way in which* the mirror-sensation and its *sequelae* entitled me to believe myself mistaken about the look on my face.[1]

Given that I have now had such-and-such sensations it is conceivable that I should go on to have such further sensations as disallow any material-thing statement. Given that I now have pain-sensations it is conceivable that looking in the mirror I seem and again seem to myself to wear a happy face. Such further sensations could evidence to me the most perfect comfort-behaviour on the part of my body altogether consistently with my present pain-sensation. Later I may come to doubt that pain as the memory of it fails, especially if the records of the contrary bodily behaviour are kept well; but this does not affect the point that the pain-sensation for me is logically consistent with further and even present sensations for me as of bodily behaviour at the time indicating the most perfect comfort, and sensations indicating subsequent bodily behaviour entirely suggestive of former comfort. This is not the argument against behaviourism by lie direct, that any sensation is compatible with any bodily behaviour (or potentialities of it) on my part. It is the argument that any sensation I now have is compatible with adequate past, present, and future sensory evidence for me of past, present, and future, actual and possible bodily behaviour on my part that indicates that I do not now have that sensation. In particular, given my present sensations further sensations may show me that my body behaves in a way discrepant with those present sensations; but given my present sensations no further sensations can show me that I do not have them. If this contrast holds between statements about my current sensations and statements about my body, then surely it also holds for any statements about my body in relation to its circumstances and indeed for any statement about the material world. None of this

---

[1] Much turns on the italicized phrase. One way of making the contrast it indicates is developed in the remainder of this section; another is developed in the final section.

rules out the idea that my sensory states through a given moment may conceivably preclude my subsequent sensations giving an adverse verdict on a material-thing statement; all this argument requires is that my sensory states through a given moment may conceivably *not* preclude an adverse verdict from subsequent sensations on any material-thing statement. Evidently, too, the verificational properties involved in this contrast are equivalence-invariant. Doubts about the equivalence-invariance of incorrigibility may not be altogether inappropriate, but no similar concession need be made for the equivalence-invariance of impredictiveness, as I call the incorrigibility-surrogate now under discussion.

It should be emphasized how easily we might have allowed ourselves to be thrown off the track of the impredictiveness argument by the idea that statements of material fact are not necessarily predictive, in the sense that not all these statements necessarily generate expectations for every future moment, expectations liable by their disappointment to disprove the statement regardless of the degree to which previous sensory states have been favourable to it. In a word it would have been very easy for us to miss the argument due to interference from the predictionism controversy.

Here, finally, is a related anti-behaviourist argument whose independence of the predictionism controversy is still clearer. Given one's sensations of the moment, whatever those sensations may be, the truth or falsity of any statements about one's sensations of the moment is determinate. Now it may be allowed for the sake of argument that given one's sensations of the moment, the truth or falsity of some statements about the material world is determinate, provided that those sensations are sufficiently favourable or unfavourable to the statement in question. But those sensations at that moment might be otherwise than as they are; and if they were otherwise, the truth-value of that statement about material things would conceivably not have been determinate on the basis of them. Now if the material-thing statement were equivalent to a statement about one's sensations of the moment its truth or falsity would be determinate given one's sensations of the moment, regardless of the character of those sensations.

10. The substitutes for incorrigibility proposed here do not then require predictionism about material-thing statements for

use with them in anti-behaviourist arguments. It would be as well, however, to reflect further here on predictionism and the notion of non-predictive error.

Predictionism is the doctrine that every statement not about one's own sensations has infinite consequences for the future, in the sense that every such statement whatever its *prima facie* temporal reference has consequences for every future time *ad infinitum*.[1] Wisdom supported this doctrine in the 'Other Minds' series; the best known attack on it is again Austin's 'Other Minds'. Austin's main point is really that, in the case of some material-thing statements, there may come a time after which whatever happens we may not allow that it disproves or even calls in question the material-thing statement in question. The bird may begin to translate from Swahili, the toy duck may explode or sprout the wings of an eagle; but a toy duck it was all the same despite its now unorthodox behaviour. A sufficiently orthodox pattern of appearance and performance through a sufficiently extended, but still limited period of time will, in the case of some material-thing statements, put them beyond peradventure. No doubt their subsequent behaviour may be extremely surprising, but it will cast no doubt on our previous identification of the objects. I need not, and when the past history has been good enough cannot, cast doubt on the identity of the thing as, say, a duck. A curious sort of duck no doubt, one that sprouts eagle's wings and carries off the maid in its talons; but still, it *was* a duck, whatever it is now, despite the unexpected ambitions it has developed.

However, the fact, pointed out to me by Wisdom, that future evidence may not only run counter to a material-thing statement but actually tend to disallow past evidence of it, does not tend to

---

[1] *A priori* true statements are meant to be excepted, but not any statements as to the facts not *merely* about one's own sensations.

In this essay I employ with some indifference formulations in terms of consequences *simpliciter* and formulations in terms of experienced or experience-able consequences. In fact this really makes no difference to the arguments used, as these go through *mutatis mutandis*; but the matter deserves further discussion. Something like this is also true of my use of 'sensation' and 'sensory state'.

Also, Wisdom is now very well aware that the consequences *ad infinitum* may not need to be such that their failure disproves or even casts doubt on the material-thing statement; the falsity of the consequences given a sufficiently favourable evidence-history to preclude a verdict reversal or even a verdict-doubt may be held nevertheless to be adverse to the statement. The stronger notion is, however, required for Austin's criticism to be relevant, and it was implied in 'Other Minds VII' predictionism.

show that this Austinian objection to predictionism is incorrect. To use a terminology I would recommend, this is unsound as an answer to Austin's objection because it depends on a shift of verificational perspective. When the evidence in question is the evidence of the present moment, when the perspective is that of the given moment, then no doubt things may occur that do cast doubt on the past evidence of any material-thing statement. It does not make the slightest difference if the past evidence was perfect; it can itself, in the present evidence perspective, come into question (or for that matter in the present and future evidence perspective). If so, then the present evidence perspective can conceivably have such contents that any material-thing statement is cast in doubt in the light of it. It is a serious deficiency in Austin's account that he does not mention such possibilities; Wisdom was quite right, to this extent, in bringing the point against him. Still, the point is not the slightest use if the question is not 'Can I conceivably come to doubt a material-thing statement once I have had perfect evidence for it and be justified in so doing?', but rather 'If perfect evidence for it is before me can I conceivably come justifiably to doubt a material-thing statement?', where the justification of the doubt has to be some item of evidence that tends at least to reverse the verdict. Of course the most perfect evidence can cease to be before me, if that means that my present evidence of the relevant evidence past and present can re-shape the picture I have of the evidence, however perfect it has been in the past.

The perspective in which the latter of the two questions is to be understood may be called the continuing account perspective: appearances to me, or appearances to all creatures, are entered in the record, and the question is whether any series of entries however favourable and long so long as it does not extend into the infinite future justifies beyond peradventure any material-thing statement. Austin is perhaps right that there may come, with some material-thing statements, a time at which with sufficiently favourable evidence through that time I cannot justifiably raise the question whether the material-thing statement in question is true on the basis of further evidence *on the same scale* as the sensory evidence that might have justified me, in the face of a less adequate previous basis of the material-thing statement, in raising some question about it. Perhaps *local* evidence can no longer discredit the statements in question. Perhaps discrediting evidence would have to be something far more drastic and comprehensive than Austin imagines, for a sudden flow of Swahili does not mean it was no duck, though Austin rather suggests we might not know what to say.[1] But I should maintain that *global* evidence always can. A sufficiently thoroughgoing change of the right sort in the course of my sensory experience can always reverse the verdict on a material-thing statement even in the face of *any* previous course of such experience whatever. This point does not depend on a shift, overt or covert, to the present evidence perspective.

The sort of case I have in mind here should be briefly indicated; I mean, for instance, brain in the bottle cases. Suppose I suddenly find myself on an operating table surrounded by laughing surgeons, who tell me the course of my experience hitherto was simply programmed by a computer, that it was really an illusion, that only now am I walking into the real world. I may at first think this is an illusion or a nightmare but in time I may very properly agree.[2] Nor will I necessarily allow that the computer did too good a job, and that there really were such things as I once thought I perceived, that the creation of such sensory states for me was tantamount to the creation of a world, albeit one curiously though causally related to the world in which I awakened. I should at once add that we are all perfectly entitled to suppose that any such turn of events is out of the question, that we will in fact never awake and be shown the bottle wired to a computer, *etc.* It may be I would at first be justified in supposing that someone was pulling my leg; but in the end I might well not be justified in continued scepticism about it, if this curious world into which I had awakened went on in a suitable way, coherent and all that; it need not even be too like or too different from this one.

Apparently then, there is a consequence-relation between any statement about material things and some global statements about sensory evidence for any future time. But this consequence-relation is neither entailment nor the verification relation. It is

[1] Actually we would say a talking duck; I think Austin confused our being rendered speechless with our not knowing what to say when we found our wits. Also there may be a difference between what we would say in the astonishing yet conceivable situation and what we would say about the situation when merely reflecting on it as a possibility.

[2] Those who are inclined to suppose otherwise should ask themselves whether no conceivable continuation of my experience in such a case would and should lead me to agree with the surgeons.

not the verification relation, by which anyone anywhere in time may conceivably have a sensory state sequence that verifies for him any material-thing statement at all; at least the verification of no state of affairs is necessarily precluded by mere remoteness in time or space. The consequence-relation is not that sensory states at any time or place *may* exist to verify or justify the assertion of any material-thing statement about the past, present or future. The consequence-relation is also not entailment. If the consequence-relation were entailment, then the falsity of the sensory state statements that are consequent on a material-thing statement would itself guarantee beyond peradventure the material-thing statement's falsity. But that would be incompatible with the very thing I am asserting here, namely that *no* statement about sensory states, local or global, can guarantee against future reversal in a continuing evidence account of any statement about material things. The global evidence can *always* reverse the verdict; hence the verdict reversed by any given global evidence can be restored by further global evidence and so on *ad infinitum*.

11. Now to sum up the main points made so far about behaviourism. The incorrigibility argument against behaviourism is parallel to an argument given by Wisdom against phenomenalism, though Wisdom himself never applied the argument against behaviourism. Quite unexpectedly this style of argument commits one to denying its incorrigibility-premisses; if the arguments follow there can be no contrast between incorrigible sensestatements and corrigible statements about material things or behaviour for the arguments to exploit. Other reasons have also been mustered against the incorrigibility of sense-statements. Certainly the challenge to provide an acceptable incorrigibility-characterization that applies to *all* sense-statements (and to logical-mathematical statements as well) has not hitherto been met or even fairly faced.

To the rescue of this type of anti-behaviourist argument comes, however, a recognizable substitute for the incorrigibility-premiss; *all* sense-statements (not just the simple ones) share with logical and mathematical truths the feature that they are not liable to predictive error for one person at one moment at least, and differ in this respect from all statements about material things. So the incorrigibility argument is transformed into the *impredictiveness* argument. This analogue of incorrigibility is doubtless equivalence-invariant, and we have at last a style of anti-behaviourist argument that is valid, non-circular, and sound in its premisses. Curiously, though Wisdom never used the incorrigibility argument against behaviourism, he did sense the applicability of something like the impredictiveness argument. Discussing predictionism he says:[1] 'The subtle and conflicting connections between what we have been saying and behaviourism we must look into later'. But while what he goes on to say in the 'Other Minds' series does not fail to shed light on this matter I do not think Wisdom gave any other evidence of an appreciation of the sheer incompatibility between behaviourism and the impredictiveness of sense-statements. He has put us in a position to give the impredictiveness argument, but he has not given it himself. Sense-statements and behaviour-statements differ in potential predictiveness-for-me, and so cannot be the same in meaning. Unfortunately Wisdom failed to grasp how the conflict with behaviourism here need not depend on predictionism, but could be brought out in terms of mere possibility of predictions. Neither Wisdom nor Austin saw that the contrast between sense-statements and behaviour-statements could be put as that between statements necessarily not liable to predictive error and statements necessarily liable to predictive error. That is, to make the contrast we need not characterize statements about behaviour as necessarily liable to be shown up by future sense-contents. Nevertheless a case can be made, *contra* Austin, for predictionism; though Wisdom himself has not stated it.

12. The impredictiveness premiss of this anti-behaviourist argument needs further examination, however. That premiss is that there are statements about mental states, *viz.*, statements about one's own mental states of the moment, that are not even conceivably liable to predictive or expectational error. But I have also argued that even those statements are, except for some

---

[1] 'Other Minds VII,' in *Other Minds* at page 167. Wisdom might in fact have given an anti-behaviourist argument turning on the supposed contrast between the infinite corrigibility of material-thing statements and the incorrigibility of sense-statements. But the truth of the incorrigibility premiss would have rendered the argument invalid and both premisses are questionable. I defend a version of predictionism here, but I do not elaborate the anti-behaviourist argument that could be stated in terms of it; instead I concentrate on the safer impredictiveness argument, which is very similar except that it more readily stimulates an examination of notions of non-predictive error.

Cartesian favourites, liable to error.[1] Is it true that such errors *cannot* be predictive errors? In this discussion I use 'exempt from predictive error' and similar expressions to mean 'exempt from predictive error for one person at one moment at least'. The phrase without the implicit qualification applies only to *a priori* statements; and then perhaps, as with the formula that covers sense-statements as well, only with the further qualification indicated in what follows.

Let us consider again the experiment with image-altering drugs. Suppose, for instance, that I think I have before me an image of a porch with twelve columns, partly perhaps because that is how many it seems to me there are, but partly also (perhaps I hesitate to answer for myself about their exact number with so many) because that, I take it, is how many the scientist said there are. But in the case I am now describing there are not twelve columns, there are thirteen, and I did not just fail to estimate the number correctly for myself (perhaps I was not even trying), I also got it wrong because the scientist said there were thirteen, not twelve as I supposed he had said. It is not difficult to describe a similar error with an *a priori* question, as for example this one: I think I have done my bridge-calculations wrongly when I hear news of a bridge collapse on that river the day of the grand opening. But the papers that evening reveal it was the old bridge on the same river that collapsed, or a careful check on the site reveals that the surveyors were mistaken about the river's width; the calculations were perfectly correct. There is an old story from which this example is adapted, which really bears the same moral: two engineers watch the ribbon-cutting ceremony, the bridge collapses, one says to the other 'Damn! I *knew* that plus should have been a minus'.

So 'not liable to predictive error' does not apply to one's statements about one's momentary sensory states, or even to *a priori* statements. But the fact that not even the *a priori* is exempt from predictive error in this sense encourages us not yet to be satisfied that nothing can be made of the notion of 'non-predictiveness' here.

Now I introduce the notion of statements not liable to *purely* predictive error (for one person at one moment at least), which

---

[1] Again in 'Some Questions in Epistemology'.

will definitely serve to distinguish statements about momentary sensations with *a priori* statements from all others.

A statement is not liable to purely predictive error for a person at a certain time whenever any error he makes about it at the time must involve an element of reflective error, of mismanagement or misapplication of concepts. If this is so, then whenever there is an error about the statement it could conceivably be remedied, or could conceivably have been avoided, by appropriate reflection without further investigation. A logical or mathematical error may be made on account of a predictive error, an error involving mistaken expectations, as the bridge case shows; and it may not only be made in this way, it may very reasonably be made in this way. But the error in the bridge case can be remedied by going over the calculations; it can be made sure that there is no mistake by a purely reflective procedure.[1] Now take as well the somewhat more elaborate case with the scientist giving drugs to affect, *e.g.*, my hallucinatory images. Here I may be mistaken because I mishear the scientist telling me my porch-image has thirteen columns; but I might conceivably remedy the mistake by coming to have a better grasp of the image before me, by an improvement in my recognitional capacity or in the exercise of it (where the recognition is what Price calls 'primary recognition'). Now it is true that in the *a priori* case the error is *connective*, while in the momentary sensation case it is *applicative*. But in both cases correcting the mistake need not be a matter of coming to have the right expectations.

Should anyone protest that I have not yet described *a priori* errors, or errors about one's current sensory states, that *involve* or even *lead to* predictive errors, it is perfectly easy to turn the examples round. I suppose the scientist said 'thirteen' instead of 'twelve' because I think that to be the correct number of hallucinatory columns, which he would surely know and not deceive me about; or because I have the calculation wrong, I suppose that the bridge will not collapse. But we need not straighten out these notions any further just now. If anyone objects that the sorts of error I have just described about *a priori* statements, or one's present-moment sensation statements, are not really predictive errors about these sorts of statement, or so far as they involve

---

[1] There are various sorts of mistakes over calculations; but there are some sorts that can be described in these terms.

these sorts of statement, I will not here inquire further whether he is wrong. Instead I will simply say that he must accept the first, unqualified formulation of the epistemological feature common and peculiar to the *a priori* and present-moment sensation statements, *viz.*, 'admit only non-predictive error' *simpliciter* (but with the qualification 'for one person at one moment at least').

Furthermore, it is very plausible to suppose that the notion of a statement not liable to purely predictive mistakes is equivalence-invariant. Yet the notion does not go through all the hoops of any of the arguments using equivalence-invariance to destroy the notions of the incorrigibility family. For instance, just as the conjunction of a statement not allowing predictive error (if there are any such statements) with another statement need not be a statement that is liable only to predictive error, so the conjunction of a statement admitting only errors not *purely* predictive may admit purely predictive errors. In this not admitting (purely) predictive error is unlike admitting error, for the conjunction of a statement liable to error with any other is itself liable to error. So either of the favoured notions here can be used in an anti-behaviourist argument without generating the contradiction involved in such a use of any incorrigibility-notion.

'THIS IS VISUAL SENSATION'

J. M. HINTON

I WISH I could offer for this occasion a unified essay of sufficient substance solely in appreciation and criticism of Wisdom. Instead, in the hope that something of the sort might usefully be added to what he has written about perceptual claims and related statements, I have tried to look searchingly at the thought expressed by my title.

There is, however, a question I want to raise briefly first. It is a much-discussed one. Is there a type of statement, on which 'the statements we make about physical things' are non-deductively based? That Wisdom thinks there is, seems clear from many contexts—for instance, from the essay on 'Mace, Moore and Wittgenstein' in *Paradox and Discovery*.

I take it to be certain that there are such things as perception-illusion disjunctions—propositions which you can compose by twice inserting a suitable proposition, such as 'A light is flashing before my eyes', instead of p in 'Pip v Iip', where 'Pip' is 'I perceive that p', and 'Iip' is 'I am being illuded that p'.[1] Such an either-or proposition, using the truth-functional 'vel', is among the things that can be true of one. Indeed, it is among the things one can say and think—as are both its limbs or disjuncts, incidentally, since 'illusion' here has its proper sense, as in 'optical illusion', of being at most so to speak tempted by a false belief, and not the transferred sense of false belief itself. Moreover, if by a 'sensation-statement' or whatever—let us say, an S-statement—we were to mean a certain kind of perception-illusion disjunction, then there are two things which would turn out to be facts, and which might give rise to the idea that the statements we make about physical things are non-deductively based on S-statements. It would turn out to be a fact, and indeed a logical platitude—

(i) that whenever a perceptual claim which entails some physical-thing statement is made and is true, there is at least one

[1] Or perhaps the second disjunct is 'Ii(Pip)'.

S-statement which is true and but for whose truth the perceptual claim would not be true, yet which might be true even if the perceptual claim were false; and

(ii) that whenever a perceptual claim which entails some physical-thing statement is made and is true, and is not the most specific perceptual claim the perceiver could have made with truth, there is at least one true S-statement which neither entails nor is entailed by the perceptual claim which is made, but which is entailed by, without entailing, the most specific perceptual claim the perceiver could truly have made.

Those are logical platitudes when for 'S-statement' we read 'perception-illusion disjunction', the relevant S-statements then being, of course: the perception-illusion disjunction whose disjunct of perception is the perception-proposition asserted as the perceptual claim, in the first case, and the perception-illusion disjunction whose disjunct of perception is the most specific perception-proposition the perceiver could truly have asserted, in the second case.

However it hardly seems that Wisdom would be satisfied with those platitudes, as the truth in or behind the thesis that the statements we make about physical things are non-deductively based on S-statements. For it seems that those platitudes fail to identify anything that you could call 'the sort of thing which in the end is the ground for any statement of the type in question', the type in question being physical-thing statements. And in stating those platitudes, we certainly do not 'trace further than does the orthodox logician, the justification-refutation procedure proper to statements of the given type'. We do not trace anything further than the orthodox logician does, and it hardly seems that we trace that procedure at all. (The expressions quoted are from the title essay in *Paradox and Discovery*, p. 120.) So, while those orthodox-logical platitudes might help to produce the idea that there are such things as S-statements, the 'ultimate grounds' of our physical-thing statements in Wisdom's sense, they could hardly justify that idea.

Does anything justify that idea? It is true that, under pressure from the queer kind of histrionic credulity we keep miscalling scepticism—the sort of 'scepticism' that Wisdom calls superstition with the signs reversed—we tend to stage a pretence-retreat from some unambiguous perceptual claim, 'I perceive that Q', to an ambiguous something; which perhaps we call an S-statement, and which perhaps is expressible as 'Seemingly I perceive that Q'—same Q. Still, this unusual movement of the mind hardly seems *bound* to uncover anything of a sort that we ordinarily base ourselves on, in our statements about the physical; or anything of a sort that in the end is the ground for those statements. And sceptics in no merely academic or archaic sense of the word, Ryle, Quinton and Austin for instance, want to know what exactly this so-called S-statement is.

It might, I take it, be the same thing in other words as the perception-illusion disjunction whose disjunct of perception is the original perception-proposition, 'I perceive that Q'. It might alternatively be the same thing in other words as some other perception-illusion disjunction; one whose disjunct of perception is some more specific perception-proposition, in virtue of whose truth the proposition, 'I perceive that Q', was true if it was true at all. Of course the thing might again be various other things, but one may not see, among the things it might be, anything of a kind on which 'the statements we make about physical things' can be said in a general way to be based non-deductively.

As well as being the ultimate grounds of our statements about the physical, S-statements for Wisdom are propositions about which we can ask, without too much absurdity, whether the statements we make about physical things are *analysable* into that sort of proposition; though Wisdom does not accept the affirmative answer. Now it would surely be too absurd to ask whether physical-thing statements were analysable into the relevant class of perception-illusion disjunctions, since in every such disjunction a physical-thing statement occurs as a constituent—though not as a conjunct. (For that matter, the same is true of 'Seemingly p' and 'Seemingly I perceive that p', where p is a physical-thing proposition, even if these 'seem'-statements are not explained as perception-illusion disjunctions; important as the distinction between a primitive operator of seeming and one thus explained is, in some ways.) We could still ask whether the speech-act of asserting a series of S-statements approached as a limit the speech-act of making a perceptual claim, but it would be misleading to put this question in terms of analysability.

Nor is it clear that the question as to analysability can really be less absurd if the case is this: that every so-called S-statement which can be thought of as supporting a perceptual claim can, in a way, be distinguished from all statements that contain physical-world statements as constituents, but only by adverting to the verbal form chosen by the speaker for the so-called S-statement. At any rate, when what a given so-called S-statement cannot be distinguished from, except by adverting to its wording, is a perception-illusion disjunction, then I feel that we may well want to decide that that particular S-statement just is that particular perception-illusion disjunction, less perspicuously expressed. For this decision will at least put it beyond all doubt that the so-called S-statement has some of the properties commonly claimed for such statements, at the price of entailing that it lacks others of those properties. Yet the properties it lacks are of course vital. If S-statements, when at all relevant to physical-thing statements, are complexes of these, then Phenomenalism has a shorter refutation than it is commonly given—or than it is given by Wisdom.

So much for the bone I thought I would pick with Wisdom before beginning the main part of my essay. It is not quite a matter of first disagreeing about chalk, and then going on to make what one hopes will be some acceptable remarks about cheese. The two topics are connected in a way I shall mention at once. It will turn out in the very end that they are connected in such a way that disagreement on the first produces partial, even if not very substantial, disagreement on the second.[1]

*   *   *

The general reader may form the impression that from a Wittgensteinian point of view and kindred points of view, there is supposed to be something badly wrong with the thought, '*This* is visual sensation'—or with something like this thought, or with certain ways of using this thought or something like it. He may be puzzled by this, because the thought is one which comes to us naturally enough in certain situations. Someone may have been saying how difficult it is to define visual sensation, or to say what you mean by it, or to say what it is. It is not unnatural for the hearer then to widen his eyes and say, beneath his breath perhaps, '*I* know what visual sensation is, *this* is visual sensation'. Again, the impulse may arise as a reaction to someone's questioning whether there really is, as Wisdom claims, a kind of statement that

---

[1] The foregoing, like the rest of this essay, was written before writing a book entitled *Experiences*, which has already appeared.

can be called a sensation-statement, on which statements about the physical are non-deductively based. Some people, though hardly Wisdom, may feel like retorting, '*This* is visual sensation, of a particular kind, and any statement which says that something of this kind is occurring is a sensation-statement, for a start'.

The speaker here intends the paraphrase, 'sensation, as distinct from perception'. Given the context, sensation-statements are to be distinguished for his purposes from perceptual claims, since statements about the physical are often deducible from these. In the first context, however, the person who has the thought that 'this is visual sensation' may not want to make any such distinction. His thought may be that 'this is visual sensation, sense-perception'. After all, the one who provoked the retort, by talking about the difficulties of definition, may have made no distinction between sensation and perception. For that matter he may, with or without making such a distinction, have addressed himself specifically to the notion of perception; where the 'perceived' is, *ex vi termini*, something whose existence or occurrence does not entail that anyone is in any way aware of its existence or occurrence.

I will first use most of my space to scrutinise the thought that 'this is visual sensation, sense-perception', and then I will say something—very little, as it turns out—about the thought that 'this is visual sensation, *as distinct from* perception'.

'*This is visual sensation, sense-perception*'

I shall consider a number of objections that might be made to this statement or thought, and then give my own assessment of it.

Objection 1

Perhaps the least ambitious objection is, that the person who makes the statement or has the thought has simply missed the point in the situational context we have supposed. The fact, where it is a fact, that 'this is visual perception', does not make it less true that visual perception is hard to define, any more than the fact that 'this is a man' makes it less true that Man is hard to define. The objector may add more aggressively that if there are x ways in which 'visual perception' can be verbally defined and understood, then there are not less than $x+1$ ways in which '*This* is visual perception' can be understood; the extra way being to take it that the speaker is trying to assign a meaning to the expression 'visual perception' for his own benefit and 'before all worlds' so to speak, rather than being content to use it in any meaning it may already have. I shall leave on one side the whole idea of an attempt at 'private ostensive definition' in this narrow sense. It is, of course, a much more inviting idea where 'sensation, as distinct from perception' is concerned than in the present case, but I shall not discuss it at all in this essay. Restricting ourselves, then, by the assumption that the speaker or thinker, for whom '*this* is visual perception', thinks he is *instancing*—giving (himself) an example of what 'visual perception' stands for, in a meaning it has, as a pre-established social fact independent of his present volition; what should we say about the objection?

On the tentative assumption of other things being equal, we should surely repeat some of the things Wisdom has said about defining and instancing. The instancing here, if that is what it is, does not altogether miss the point if the person who talked about the difficulty of defining visual perception seemed to imply that there might be no such thing. To any such suggestion, the instancing opposes the perfectly germane retort, that a definition of the general term would fail of reportive correctness by excluding the given case; a retort which need not be infallible in order to be true. As for the idea that there may be many ways in which 'visual perception' can be understood; since we have firmly tied the verb to a full, undebauched, external or objective sense we can say two things: that in advance of investigation one cannot know whether there is more than one objective sense of the verb; and that even if there is, this has no tendency to show that the instancing statement is not true in one sense or more.

In short, the act of would-be-instancing which we are scrutinising does not, necessarily and altogether, miss the point in the situational context we have supposed, in which there has been talk of the difficulty of defining visual perception.

Objection 2

An objection which may appear important is that the instancing statement or thought begs the question against the metaphysical sceptic.

Now to 'beg the question', to assume the very point which is at issue, to ask or expect your interlocutor to concede at the outset the very thing he happens to require to be convinced of; this is to break the rules one must follow if one is to produce rational conviction in the mind of that man—and hence, the rules one must follow if one is to be judged to have come off best in the disputation with him. It is therefore no absolute or logical mistake, but a fault relative to the would-be helpful and/or combative confrontation with a particular type of interlocutor, one for whom the point in question is—the point in question. We are not, however, always confronted by the so-called 'metaphysical sceptic', nor is there any special reason to assume that the person, whose thought is that 'this is visual perception', must be involved in such a confrontation. Not only is he hardly addressing himself to any other person, but also the other person who occasioned his response may not be playing that particular philosophical role.

It is true that someone who is playing that role, an *alter ego* perhaps, may always intervene, and it is true that the thought we are examining would beg the question against such a one. However this is no criticism of the thought; every thought begs the question against some conceivable interlocutor. We ought to add that the person who has the thought may be perfectly aware that he is thereby making a *claim*, even if only to himself. He may be quite well armed against the general suggestion that one should make no claims, and the equivalent suggestion that one should make them only when, *per impossibile*, they follow logically from what are not claims but 'infallible reports of introspection'.

It is, then, a fact, but we need not think it an important fact, that the thought we are scrutinising 'begs the question against the sceptic'.

Objection 3

From a different, though nowadays equally familiar, quarter —for these objections are, of course, not necessarily all available to the same objector—comes the accusation that the person who has the so-called 'thought' is just saying to himself a sentence which has no use, and consequently no meaning. Another way of putting the charge is, that the utterance cannot be given a context; that there is no situation in which it would have a point, or in which it would sprout up as a living use of language.

Since the utterance does, as we have said, sprout up naturally enough in the context we have mentioned, the real work of this objection is done by a rider which the objector will add; that no amount of sprouting counts if what sprouts is philosophical. Assuming for the sake of argument that the utterance we are concerned with always does deserve that classification, and assuming in the same way that we may accept the general principle of the objection; we would surely have to know something about philosophy which some of us do not think we know, in order to accept the rider. If we knew for instance that philosophy, when not confused or deluded, must always be either the criticism of philosophy or else the characterisation of non-philosophical linguistic usage; then the point might be made, since the utterance in question hardly seems to fall into either of those categories.

Also it is neither quite clear that we ought to accept the general principle of the objection, nor quite clear that the accused utterance is always and only philosophical. Can something not be true unless there is, in some context, some point in stating it? And anyway might I not quite pointfully say 'This is visual perception' when I had just been shown how to see the composition in a picture or the geological structure of a landscape?

On present and certain knowledge at least, it seems that the objection, that the utterance 'does not have a use', ought to be rejected.

Objection 4

I would also reject the objection that—'You cannot answer the question, "How many instances of visual perception occurred in the last two minutes?"'. If I call this undeniably correct statement an objection, and mention it here, this is only because I think some people may feel as if it might somehow be an objection. There is certainly no truth in the idea, which its being thought to be an objection seems to imply. I mean the idea that if the statement-form 'This is an instance of ϕ' is to express a truth, then the general term, 'ϕ', must be one in whose case it makes sense to ask how many instances of ϕ there were or are in such and such a spatial or temporal context. All colour-terms, all stuff-terms, most abstract nouns and various other general terms refute such an idea.

Objection 5

Someone who objects to the remark we are concerned with on the ground that it is 'based on introspection' obviously means, that it belongs to a class of remarks unacceptable to him and commonly or sometimes said to be so based. He may also mean that nothing relevant is properly called 'introspection', but that whoever makes the remark has to claim mistakenly that it is based on something properly so called.

If the objector means the first of those things without meaning the second, then he ought to tell us why the relevant class of remarks is unacceptable to him. (It will be a class sometimes, rather than commonly, said to be based on 'introspection', since the noun commonly means brooding on one's character-traits, and it will no doubt be a class that includes such statements as 'I am having a mental image of the place where I used to live', 'I am having yellow, blue and mauve after-imagery', and 'I have got a slight headache'.) If what the objector has against the relevant class of statements is that when someone makes them to someone else the latter cannot verify them, then one of two things is true. Either he is confusing our present, philosophical, context with one of experimental psychology, in which it may be desirable to deal only with statements which the experimenter, who is observing a subject, can verify; or else he is taking for granted a particular kind of logico-philosophical verificationism about the conditions under which a thing can be a true statement. That particular kind of verificationism is itself quite unacceptable to many people, including most of those present-day philosophers whom some people might call neo-positivist.

If the objector means that nothing relevant is properly called introspection, but that anyone who says '*This* is visual perception' has got to claim that his statement is based on something properly so called; then this gives us two questions to consider. Is there in fact a looking inward which tells me that 'this is visual perception'? And if not, must I claim that there is, in order to make the statement? On the first question: it is of the essence of the most usual philosophical notion of such a looking inward, that this act always produces a finding which does not stand to be corrected in all the ways in which a perceptual claim stands to be corrected. So, if 'This is visual perception' is thought to be based on introspection in that sense, then it must be thought to be so based indirectly, by being based on something else, something properly a finding of introspection; something like 'This is visual sensation, as distinct from perception'. It is not yet time for us to consider this statement as such, but we can nevertheless ask whether 'This is visual perception' is based in any way, directly or indirectly, on any kind of looking inward.

If it is, then this is not just because it is a visual perceptual

M

claim. Ryle is surely right: claims to perceive visually are not in general based on introspection, though they had better be accompanied by extrospection. The idea that they are all based on introspection seems, as Ryle says, to be itself based on our merely refining upon, instead of courageously abandoning, the false and unhelpful analogy between our seeing things and the things we see. True, it would be a harmless analogy to speak—and think— of 'seeing' one's seeing, if a satisfactory account could be given of what the second-order so-called 'seeing' actually was; just as there is no harm in thinking of someone as looking inward when he is brooding on his own traits of character. But it is notoriously difficult to give a satisfactory account of second-order 'seeing'. Does 'seeing' one's seeing mean thinking about it, pondering or meditating on the fact of one's seeing? If not, it is perhaps a glossogenic figment, in part the result of the unwarranted assumption that the common noun an 'experience' exemplifies all or most of the same rules when seeing is called an experience, as it does when we apply the term to, say, being operated on. On the other hand, if 'seeing' one's seeing does indeed mean pondering on the fact of one's seeing, then this is not the characteristic basis, or even accompaniment, of a perceptual claim. Still, such pondering does happen to be characteristically involved in this particular instance, where someone's thought is that '*this* is visual perception'. So we could say, in a sense, that this particular perceptual claim was based on introspection, or at least was a rather introspective one, without giving our assent to the controverted idea, that every instance of perception is not only an instance of awareness but also the object of an instance of second-order awareness. To the extent, then, that there is any need to claim that the statement, 'This is visual perception', is based on introspection; to that extent, the claim seems to be a defensible one.

To think of one's seeing as if it were something one saw is admittedly a pervasive error, which human fallibility can hardly avoid at all times. The person who has the thought '*this* is visual perception' may, like anyone else, fall into that error. Indeed his demeanour, if he cries out loud that '*this* is visual perception', may give some ground for the suspicion that he is falling into it. Yet the reason why he is focussing his eyes with such avidity on some part of his environment, or surveying much of it with such abandon may not in fact be that he supposes himself to be focussing non-physical eyes upon, or letting them rove freely across, his seeing.

It may simply be that, in and by using his actual eyes in this way, he occasions the seeing, the visual perception, whose occurrence he emphatically asserts. After all, the pronoun 'this' does not universally mean 'this which I behold'.

In sum, it seems unsatisfactory to reject the statement that 'this is visual perception' on the ground that it is or is meant to be based on introspection.

Objection 6

The statement we are discussing is that 'this is visual perception', and not that 'this is visual perception, without being perception of anything specifiable'. Nevertheless, a natural uneasiness may find expression in the remark that perception is always perception of something specifiable.

It is partly that I have kept calling the statement a 'thought'. This raises the question: granted that in a literal sense of the verb, 'to say', you can *say* 'This is visual perception' without *saying* what 'this' is visual perception of; can you *think* that 'this is visual perception' without *thinking* that 'this' is visual perception of some specified thing?

Surely you cannot, but surely I have not implied that you can. 'This is visual perception' may be what I have called it, a thought, and yet be a thought which it is impossible to have without also having some other thought, of that more specific kind. But what sort of impossibility is this? Are we referring to a psychological law? No, rather it is true *ex vi termini* that you cannot—cannot be said to—think 'This is visual perception' in a coherent way, without thinking either 'This is visual perception of St. Paul's', or 'This is visual perception of a newly-washed cathedral', or 'This is visual perception that St. Paul's cathedral has newly been washed', or something like that.

To see how it is true *ex vi termini*, it may be useful to note the following facts. You can say, 'Something, as distinct from nothing, *phies*' (that is, '*Phi*-ers are non-null', '($\exists$x) (ϕx)') without saying either 'Something, for instance *alpha*, *phies*' or 'Something, though I have no particular instance in mind, *phies*'. However you cannot think the first of those things without also thinking one of the others. You cannot, you cannot be said to, we will not let you be said to, think only that *phi*-ers are non-null. For it is a fact that either you have at least one particular instance, *alpha*, in mind as *phi*-ing or you don't. And if you do, we will say your whole thought is 'Something, for instance *alpha, phies*', while if you don't, we will say your whole thought is 'Something, though I have no particular instance in mind, *phies*'. (This does not mean that you can only say, not think, that 'for some x, x is an egg-laying mammal'. It does mean that this cannot be your whole thought, so that in a certain sense you can think it only as a consequence, even if you set it down as an assumption.)

In the case of perception there is further the peculiarity that in virtue of the meaning of the verb 'to perceive', you cannot—because we will not let you—be said to have a coherent thought, 'For some sort or kind *phi*, though I have no particular sort or kind in mind, I perceive a *phi*-er' or 'For some proposition p, though I have no particular proposition in mind, I perceive that p'. (Of course *words* may fail you; then you have something in mind.) It follows that the so-called thought, that 'this is visual perception', can—if it is coherent—only be the thought, 'This is visual perception of something, and for instance of a *phi*-er', or '. . . and for instance that p'. Or '. . . and for instance of alpha', where this is a non-descriptive singular term; except that in a limited sense you can think 'For some x, though I could not say what for instance, I perceive *x*', if you mean that you perceive no individual but one whose name you do not know.

Still, this does not show that there is anything wrong with the non-specific statement, 'This is visual perception (of something)', or with the more specific thought, which must lie behind such a statement if it is to have any chance of being true.

Objection 7

An interesting objection or batch of objections centres on the accusation that the person who says or thinks, '*This* is (an instance of) visual perception', is not actually referring to anything; or at any rate, not to anything which he can truly declare to be an instance of visual perception. There is more than one ground on which this may be alleged.

It may be alleged on the ground that the man cannot show us what he is referring to, unless he is referring to something other than an instance of visual perception. However, it is surely illegitimate simply to assume that one must not, may not, take oneself to be referring to anything unless one can show others what one is referring to.

Again, the allegation that there is no reference to an instance of visual perception may be based on the fact, or idea, that there is no possibility of the perceiver's reidentifying the particular instance of visual perception he is referring to. However, it seems merely wrong to assume that there is no reference unless there is the possibility of reidentification: I can surely refer to a particular flash of light.

A third way in which the allegation may be supported is by arguing like this. If a statement is true, or false for that matter, and contains a term, t, which is used with the intention of singling something out to say something about; and if this purpose is achieved; then the object of reference, to which t refers in the context, will answer to some description—apart from the description 'sole object of reference of that term in the context'—to which no two or more things could answer. For if this were not so, then it would be impossible, even for omniscience, to answer a question which might be asked by someone who did not understand the language of the statement, but who had been told that t, in the context, had a sole object of reference; namely, the question what the sole object of reference of t in the context was. And if omniscience could not answer that question, then there would be no sole object of reference of t in the context. Now it does not seem—the objection continues—that there is any description, to which no two or more things could answer, and by means of which that question could be answered where t is the term 'This' in the context 'This is (an instance of) visual perception'. It seems that there is, in that sense, no possibility of identifying what is supposedly being referred to, and cited as an instance of visual perception, here.

The general principle, which this objection takes for granted, is less questionable than the principle that a speaker must always himself, in that sense or way, be able to identify what he is referring to. Yet the principle assumed is still a bold one. It stands no less opposed than that more questionable principle does, to our strong tendency to think of 'This!' as a paradigm of identification. We tend to feel that 'This!' is sometimes the best conceivable answer to the question as to what has been or is being referred to, and that the question, 'What am I using "this" to refer to?' is sometimes absurdly self-answering. It may well be right to oppose that tendency of ours. Candidly, it must be right to oppose it. However, I do not think it is necessary to discuss the matter of general principle here; the point is in any case not made by the principle assumed.

For in the first place, the object of reference of the word 'this' in 'This is visual perception'—if there is one, and if the statement is true—will answer to the description, 'A's visually perceiving (whatever it was) at time t'. And that is a description to which no two or more things could answer.

Someone may retort that it is, in a more or less self-explanatory sense, a 'referential tautology' for the man to say that his visually perceiving whatever it was, was an instance of visual perception. This retort surely contains an objection; yet it is not completely obvious what the objection is exactly, since on the general principle which is being assumed here, each and every instancing statement that is true must correspond to at least one 'referential tautology'.

The objection may be this: that the instancing statement had better be paraphrasable otherwise than as a referential tautology, and yet by means of a descriptive singular term instead of the pronoun. Why had it better be? Various reasons might be advanced. That if a statement refers to anything at all, then it refers to something—the same thing—whether it is true or false. That an instancing statement can always be false without failing of reference; instancing implies the possibility of mis-instancing of that kind or in that sense. That this particular statement, anyway, if it is a statement at all, can be false without failing of reference. Leaving open the question whether all or some of those ideas are correct, and the question whether it would indeed follow from them that the statement in question had better be paraphrasable in the manner indicated, let us just say that—other things being equal—the statement is in fact so paraphrasable. Define 'visual experience' simply as the logical sum, the *vel*-class, of visual perception with visual illusion, and the statement can be paraphrased as 'A's visually experiencing whatever it was, was an instance of visual perception'. This is not a 'referential tautology'; it would be false without failing of reference if A's relevant visual experience were illusion.

I do not think *that* way of supporting the charge, that there is no reference to any instance of visual perception here, is successful. However, there is a fourth way in which the charge may be supported. It involves challenging, not before time perhaps, a phrase I have used freely.

What *is* 'an instance of visual perception'? A few lines above, I equated it by implication with 'an instance of someone's visually perceiving something, of something's being visually perceived by someone'. This is surely quite a natural way of taking the phrase. It is one in which the word 'case' could be used as naturally as the word 'instance', and it is one which goes with our ordinary, everyday talk about how 'in this case', or 'in this instance', something is or is not so. We have a so-called case or instance of visual perception, in this sense, when from what was so, in the case, it follows that something visually perceived something. For instance Jack's perceiving Margaret was, if visual, an instance of visual perception in this sense. That is one way of taking the phrase, 'an instance of visual perception'. There is another way of taking it. It can be taken to mean, something which in all strictness of speech 'is a visual perceiving' of something by something. These two conceptions of 'an instance of visual perception' need not converge; one may not think that a so-called case or instance of something's visually perceiving something is, in all strictness of speech, to be called 'a visual perceiving of something by something'.

You will not think so, if you think that unlike Jack and Margaret, Jack's visually or otherwise perceiving Margaret is a sort of un-thing, the illusory appearance of reference to which is dispelled when one expresses oneself as clearly as one can. On this view, Jack's perceiving Margaret was neither a visual perceiving nor anything else, if we are to speak strictly.

But it is not only on that assumption, that the two conceptions of 'an instance of visual perception' fail to converge. Without assuming that the appearance of referring to such objects of reference as Jack's perceiving Margaret is always illusory; and without assuming that nothing can in all strictness of speech be called 'a visual perceiving'; and given that Jack perceived Margaret visually; one may still not think it true in all strictness of speech that 'Jack's perceiving (of) Margaret was a visual perceiving of something by something'. For one may understand this statement as, at best, an unclear way of giving the information that, from what was so in the case mentioned, it follows that something was visually perceived by something. In other words, one may see the statement as at best an unclear way of saying that Jack's perceiving Margaret was a so-called instance of visual perception, in the first of the two senses. One may see the statement in that light; and I, for my part, do. That is how it looks to me; not because I think I know something general about expressions like 'Jack's perceiving (of) Margaret'. and not because I think I know something general about expressions like '. . . is a perceiving'. It is not that on some ground of that sort or some other sort, I see the statement in that light; it is not that, faithful to some idea, I see the statement in that light. I just see it in that light, that is my understanding of it. This is another way in which the two conceptions of 'an instance of visual perception' can fail to converge.

Since there are those two conceptions of 'an instance of (visual) perception' which may fail to converge, a question can be put to the person who wants to say that '*this* is (an instance of) visual perception'. We can ask him whether he just means, a case or instance of visual perception in the first of those senses. Putting the same question in another way, we can ask him whether, and if so how exactly, he wants to distinguish between '*This* is (an instance of) visual perception', on the one hand, and on the other hand, 'Something is *now* the case from which it follows that something visually perceives something' or '(From) the way things are *now*, (it follows that) something is visually perceived (by something)'.

I believe that most of the people who feel like saying '*This* is visual perception' would also feel, at least after reflection on the matters that have been touched on above, that they would be grappling with unfamiliar problems if they insisted on making a distinction, there. That is certainly how I feel myself. It seems to me to be altogether safer, easier and more natural, not to attempt to make any such distinction. Indeed I think that my own wishes, if someone has been going on and on about how hard it is to know what visual perception is, would be just as easily satisfied by saying 'Something is being visually perceived at this very moment, and without too much difficulty I could tell you what and who by', as by saying '*This* is visual perception'.

This objection, or challenge, about what is meant by 'an instance of visual perception', has therefore at least achieved a fair degree of incidental usefulness. It has shown that the statement, '*This* is (an instance of) visual perception, visually perceiving', is not exactly as it seems, in that it is neither easy nor, really, necessary to distinguish it from things from which it might have seemed to be distinct. But does the objection or challenge

show what it was tabled as trying to show: that there is no reference, in the statement, to an instance of visual perception? This
seems a less than crucial question. The objection or challenge
shows, at any rate, that it is not easy to claim that there is reference
to an instance of visual perception in the statement, unless in a
sense in which we might say that there was reference to an instance
of visual perception in 'Something saw something', and even in
'Jack saw Margaret', whether or not these statements entail that
anything is in all strictness of speech 'a seeing' or 'a visual perceiving'.

Objection 8

The final objection I want to consider is not exactly an
objection to the statement, sketched in broad strokes, that *'this
is visual perception'*; the formally ambiguous assertion that *'this
is visual perception—it is happening at *this very moment*, I myself
am *now* visually perceiving various things, and I could tell you
what for instance'. It is an objection to this assertion when it is
accompanied, as it commonly is in our times, by the thought or
statement that visual perception is of course a physical process in
which light initiates changes in the retinas, optic nerves and
brain. 'Objection' may not be the right word exactly; the response
I have in mind is simply—'How do you mean?'. This will
probably seem like an objection to the speaker, who may rightly
believe that many people would regard his statement as requiring
no clarification.

I want to respond as well as I can to this 'How do you mean?'
response, since I am one of the many who find it natural to make
what I have called the formally ambiguous assertion, with that
addition—which is not much less formally ambiguous. (By a
formally ambiguous assertion I mean any assertion whose logical
form is not obvious, including one whose logical form is unfixed
in the following sense: that any decision by the speaker, about the
logical form of his assertion, will be a decision as to what logical
form or forms the assertion shall have, rather than a decision as to
what logical form or forms it had already. Even in that special
case, a formally ambiguous assertion need not be anything we
would normally and naturally call ambiguous.)

The minimal content of the first part of the statement being
that the speaker visually perceives something, what are the minimal
contents or commitments of the addition? They are surely those

which the context gives to the 'is', or better the 'X-ing is Y-ing', of a familiar kind of statement, the kind we call 'a scientific account of what happens when X-ing occurs' or '. . . when, as we (ordinarily) say, X-ing occurs'. The speaker who makes the addition is adding that 'what happens when, as we say, visual perception, or seeing in that sense, occurs, is that light initiates changes in the retinas, optic nerves and brain'. Yes, but what are the minimal commitments of that? I think there are two posits which its proponent must intend to make, and one negative condition which he must fulfil.

1. He must mean to assert what few in our culture will be found in essentials to deny, that unless light initiates changes in the retinas, optic nerves and brain, no visual perception occurs. Hence by his whole statement, including the addition, he must mean among other things that such light-initiated changes are taking place in his own head at the time of speaking or thinking. (This may partly account, by grammatical attraction, for the continuous present which the verb 'to perceive' tends to be given in the combined statement.)

2. Unless his use of the 'what happens when' formula is eccentrically weak he must, I think, also mean this: that with enough knowledge we could state, for an indefinite number of sorts of visual perception which occur, laws which mention an environmental-cum-physiological condition sufficient for that sort of visual perception; the physiological part in conjunction with the absence of the environmental part constituting a condition sufficient for the illusion of that sort of visual perception. None of this would be implied if the 'what happens when' formula could be taken *au pied de la lettre*, but then it seems independently obvious that this cannot be done.

Although this second posit does not, perhaps, have the near-irresistibility of the first, it does seem sensible to make it until we find some reason to believe that nature is harder to understand than this.

3. Those two conditions do not exclude the speaker's adhering to the philosophy known as Psycho-Physical Dualism. On the other hand his use of the 'what happens when' formula, unless it is a very eccentric or at least a very misleading use of the formula, does. We must therefore lay it down further that the speaker does not adhere to that philosophy; though we need not

make it a condition that he adheres to no philosophy. Adherence to Dualism is admittedly not a simple on-off business; not everyone is as much of an adherent as Descartes, or as much of a nonadherent as Ryle. It will surely be hasty, for instance, to call someone a Psycho-Physical Dualist simply and solely because he thinks this: that if you take a particular subject's visually perceiving something at a particular time, and if you take any part or the whole of the more or less simultaneous environmental-cum-physiological process, then that makes *two* of some classification which we still use when we express ourselves as clearly as we can. (I do not happen to see such a classification myself; but it might be hasty to acquit me of Dualism for that reason alone).

Given that the language, in which the environmental-cum-physiological process would be described, is the language of exact science, while that in which we speak of 'visually perceiving', or of 'seeing' in that sense, is not; and given that there is no need to assign different spatio-temporal co-ordinates to the 'perceiving' and the later part of the environmental-cum-physiological process; there do not seem to me to be any further conditions, beyond those three, which the speaker or thinker must satisfy, in order to be making a normal 'X-ing is Y-ing' statement of the scientific 'what happens when' sort here.

On the other hand there are, of course, many further conditions he may fulfil, and many further commitments he may intend. I will just mention three of these.

(a) He may intend to assert that his visually perceiving (whatever it is that he visually perceives at the time) *is numerically identical with* some part of the relevant environmental-cum-physiological process. It is natural that this thesis should be keenly discussed, since anything about identity is interesting, even when it is not about mind and matter as well, as this is. However I shall not discuss the thesis here.

(b) He may intend to assert that, in visually perceiving whatever it is that he does visually perceive, he *is experiencing* the whole, or some part, of the relevant environmental-cum-physiological process. The conditions lexically required for the truth of this assertion would seem to be (i) that his visual perception is pretty directly due to that process and (ii) that his visual perception has some sort of appropriateness to that process; an appropriateness which makes it proper to regard the visual perceiving as a sort of indistinct awareness of that process, as well as a distinct awareness of whatever it is that he visually perceives. (The further lexical condition, that the 'experiencing' should constitute some sort of test or trial of the subject, is seldom insisted upon nowadays.)

(c) He may intend to assert that he *feels the light* reflected from some object or originating at some source. This bold usage, by analogy with 'feeling the heat' of or from something, can be appealing; particularly if it is begun in the case of something dazzling, like a fire. (It would be rather too startling to begin with 'feeling the light from a white cat', let alone 'feeling the light from the immediate environment of a black cat'.) Language is made to be stretched, one of the things Wisdom emphasises; and I want to make the point that this particular stretch, which surely helps to explain a philosopher like Quine's saying that we are always talking about our 'surface irritations', is not based on general knowledge alone. There is an experiential stretching here. I do not mean to imply—nor, I think, does Wisdom in what he says about paradox mean to imply—that the language must 'snap back' after the 'stretch'. The point is not to advance some kind of conceptual conservatism. The point is that the development—whether current or past, whether historical or biographical or only a fictional reconstruction—has got to be understood, if we are to decide whether what emerges is a new concept or only a muddled notion.

This (instance of) sensation, 'feeling the light', like feeling the heat, will be a case of 'sensation, sense-perception', not 'sensation, as distinct from sense-perception'. At least it will be, if the distinction is made in the only way I have mentioned; which is also the only way I am here and now concerned with. For although there are various ways of trying to define 'sensation, as distinct from sense-perception', the relevant one is one in which this would, by definition, not be a relation between the subject and his environment—the physical world in which light modifies photographic plates and the bodies of plants and animals. Still, though 'feeling the light' is perception in the relevant sense, the actual word 'sensation' and its cognates, through their connections with 'sense-organ' and with 'feeling', play a vital role here.

* * *

Having considered all those objections to, or queryings of, the statement or thought that '*this* is (an instance of) visual sensation,

perception', the conclusion I draw is that with those reservations
—which, however, one might hesitate to describe collectively as
minor reservations—there is nothing seriously wrong with the
thought.

It can nevertheless be misused in our thoughts about the
visual perception of others, in the way that Wisdom has illuminated by what he has said about pictures which are idle, or which
do not lead anywhere. When my thought is that the other, like
myself, now visually perceives whatever it may be, and when at the
same time I think '. . . and *this* is visual perception (of whatever
it may be)', then I tend mentally to use a picture, static or moving,
of (whatever it may be) as a sort of ideogram for 'He now perceives
(whatever it may be)'—placing the picture in a thought-balloon
above the other's head, so to speak. So far, the only objection is
to the relative ambiguity or imprecision which such an ideogram
has in comparison with a string of spoken words, unless and until
it is designated by convention to be the written form of such a
string of words. However a more objectionable development
tends to supervene. I tend to feel as if the ideogram were a
comparative standard, blueprint or pictorial specification which
one ought to be able to use in confirming or disconfirming one's
statement about the other's visual perception—and *not* by finding
that the other's central nervous system contains a structural
analogue of the ideogram. This unwarranted way of thinking—
why ought one to be able to put the ideogram to such use?—may
issue either in a bogus 'scepticism' or in a genuine and deplorable
non-scepticism. The 'scepticism' develops when the feeling that
one ought to be able to use the ideogram in some such way is
accompanied by the more or less distinct awareness that God
himself could do no such thing, the combination presenting as—
'We cannot really know whether, and if so what, another visually
perceives'. The non-scepticism develops when there is the vague
feeling that somehow, someone must have succeeded in putting
the ideogram to such a use, with a confirmatory result. This non-
sceptical feeling is often combined with the use of a more than
usually ambiguous ideogram; as for instance in the reading, if not
the writing, of the Sunday-supplement article in which we learn
that 'we see the field-mouse like this (soft-focus photo) but the
herring-gull sees him like this (sharp-focus photo, every hair
visible)'. An adverse verdict on those ways of thinking, in which

a non-criterion is thought of as a criterion, does not depend on the assumption that no statement can have a truth-value unless it has a criterion or verification-procedure.

'*This is visual sensation, as distinct from perception.*'

As relevantly intended, this statement means neither that the case is one of illusion, nor that it is not one of perception. It might simply mean that this is, or that here we have, whatever else we may have, a case of visual sensation; where the subjective verb, 'to sense visually', can be distinguished from the objective verb, 'to perceive visually'.

However, as a general rule it means more than that. It must mean more if the speaker has it in mind, like Wisdom, to ask the question whether statements about the physical are analysable into reports of sensation. It must in that case, and in any case it usually does, mean at least that the subjective verb, 'to sense visually', can further be distinguished from the disjunctive verb, 'to perceive or be illuded visually', as well as from any physiological or physiological-cum-behavioural verb. This already begins to be controversial—though the statement, 'I see, visually sense, or have got, *muscae volitantes*' perhaps involves such a distinct verb, since the 'flying flies' seem like a far-fetched simile rather than a reference to anything one might be tempted to believe.

But there is usually still more in the statement. For instance there is often the thesis which Wisdom advances in effect, that some of the specifying uses of the relevant verb, some of the uses in which one says what or how one is visually sensing, are non-deductive grounds of a kind always available for perceptual claims. Or there may be the still more problematic thesis, which one does not find in Wisdom, that this role of non-deductive ground for perceptual claims, or some other role, or no role, is played by certain alleged happenings which cannot be described more specifically than as 'visual sensations' or 'instances of visual sensing', in the relevant alleged sense of the verb. To get anything more problematic than that, we would surely have to go as far as the thesis which some philosophers, strangely, appear to regard as non-problematic though unsatisfying: that some non-thought or other, 'This is——!' or '!', can relate to an event of which one is the conscious subject, but which cannot be described at all.

VIII

THE TEXTURE OF MENTALITY[1]

KEITH GUNDERSON

'WHAT appears to you, who yourself are spirit, when at the standpoint as spirit, appears from the outer standpoint as the bodily substratum of this spirit.' (G. T. Fechner in his *Elemente der Psychophysik*.)

'For it's not merely that a condition fulfilled in the case of inference from the outward state of a house or a motor car or a watch to its inward state is not fulfilled in the case of inference from a man's outward state to his inward state, it is that we do not know what it would be like for this condition to be fulfilled, what it would be like to observe the state of the soul which inhabits another body.' (John Wisdom in *Other Minds*.)

I

Introduction: Concerning Walls. There is a poem by the contemporary Polish poet Zbigniew Herbert which is as follows:

WOODEN DIE

A wooden die can be described only from without. We are therefore condemned to eternal ignorance of its essence.

[1] Earlier versions of this paper were presented at the University of Chicago and the University of Wisconsin philosophy colloquia, and at the 1971 meetings of the American Metaphysical Society (held in Toronto) and the American Philosophical Association, Pacific Division (held in Los Angeles). I have personally benefited from the critical suggestions of various commentators and audience gadflies, but especially from general remarks made by Professors Fred Dretske and Paul Ziff, and, as usual, from very detailed hestitations communicated to me by Professor Charles Chastain. Unfortunately the paper as it now stands has not similarly benefited. I have been remarkably slow in assimilating these criticisms and have not yet seen my way clear to modifying the paper in the light of them without indulging in darkness elsewhere. I hope to do better later, and I view this paper as part of a 'work in progress' to be called, when complete, *The Mind as an Object of Knowledge.* The first part of this has been published in similarly unsatisfactory form as 'Asymmetries and Mind-Body Perplexities' in *Minnesota Studies in the Philosophy of Science Vol. IV*, pp. 273–309 ed. by M. Radner and S. Winokur (Minneapolis, 1971). The third and final part will be called 'Other Mirror-Images' in which I explore a range of cases where one *approximates* direct knowledge of the mind of another (meaning by this something quite different from telepathic knowledge or co-consciousness).

Even if it is quickly cut in two, immediately its inside becomes a wall and there occurs the lightning-swift transformation of a mystery into a skin.

For this reason it is impossible to lay foundations for the psychology of a stone ball, of an iron bar, of a wooden cube.[1]

And if this reason *is* a reason we may surely add as caboose to that list of 'of's' 'of a human being' and thereby inflate to its limits the sphere of our psychological ignorance. For Herbert's reason is, roughly, the reason used by the sceptic who wishes to persuade us that we cannot know the mind of another: Try to describe a man's mind sufficiently from 'without'. Enumerate his movements, gestures, looks, and speech. All that is still description 'only from without'. At each stage of our verbal chippings we are left with a wall and 'the lightning-swift transformation of a mystery into a skin'.

How, more precisely, are we persuaded that we will forever bump up against a wall and fall short of knowledge of the mind of another? Professor Wisdom has written:

> . . . this is easily done. For a person, A, is said to learn the correctness of a statement to the effect that he, A, will have a certain sensation largely by having that sensation, while another person's, B's having that sensation is of course not called his learning the correctness of the statement about A. And if asked who knows best how a man feels, he himself or someone else, we readily answer 'The man himself'. It then remains only to call the way a man knows his own feeling, his own mind, the only real, direct, way of knowing his mind, and it follows at once that no one can have direct and real knowledge of the mind of another. Reached by this route 'We cannot know the mind of another' is a necessary truth in that natural development of ordinary language which its proof persuades us to adopt.[2]

And it is, I think, Wisdom who has provided us with both an impressively comprehensive account of the way in which certain

---

[1] From his *Selected Poems*, translated by Czeslaw Milosz and Peter Dalee Scott (Baltimore, 1968). In order for the poem to be put to use at this point ths reader must suppress for a few lines any antagonism he may harbour toward, panpsychism, and think happily upon the mental life of a stone ball, iron bar or wooden cube.

[2] *Other Minds* (Oxford, 1956), pp. 206–7.

philosophical starting points necessitate a wall, as well as a recording of how philosophers who accept those starting points may yet seek, always unsuccessfully, to penetrate that wall or clamber over it.

Of course one *need* not accept those starting points. One need not 'call the way a man knows his own feeling, his own mind, the only real, direct way of knowing his mind'. And then we would not be faced with a wall, but something else. These alternative architectures are also painstakingly blueprinted by Professor Wisdom.

But wall-lessness commands its own price which turns out to be an appalling lack of privacy. Pushed to extremes it may even force us to treat with a straight face and not as a joke the *obvious* joke mentioned by Professor Ziff in his article 'About Behaviour-ism'[1] where one behaviourist meets another on the street and says 'you feel fine. How do I feel?'. For if we accept movements, gestures, looks and speech *not* as after all is moved and gestured looked and spoken still leaving us with a 'lightning-swift trans-formation of a mystery into skin', but as bestowing upon us knowledge of the mind of another, there remain the difficulties of explaining how we know our own mind. For obviously we don't know *we're* in pain by harking to our howls or glancing at our grimaces in a mirror. And so we may be led by our conceptual choreography to dance in other directions: by saying that in our own case there is no use for the utterance 'I know I'm in pain' since there is no use for its contrast utterance 'I don't know if I'm in pain'; or by claiming that the word 'pain' (as well as other mentalistic words) means one thing when used in first-person psychological reports and something else when used in statements describing others; or by attempting to 'hold out' for there being only one meaning to 'pain' and trying to make that compatible with two radically different sets of criteria for applying the word: one set for me to me, another for me to another.

Each move brings with it a train of difficulties, couplings after couplings of implausibilities, and each linkage we find inspected and tested in Wisdom's brilliant *Other Minds*.

These dialogues and essays are concerned primarily with problems of knowledge: knowledge of knowledge, knowledge of

[1] In *Analysis*, XVIII (1957–58), 132–6. Ziff, however, sees the joke as embodying two bad arguments against behaviourism.

N

the external world, knowledge of the future, or the past, etc., and the ways in which these are or seem like or unlike knowledge of our own minds and knowledge of the minds of others. All this is brought to focus on the wall between ourselves and others.

This wall, however, is not only of epistemological moment. It also casts a long shadow over that philosophical weed patch known as the mind/body problem. In particular, it seems to stand in the way of making plausible a certain characterization of the mind/body relationship otherwise attractive in the 'isms' it isn't, namely, the characterization of mental states, events, or processes as being identical with certain subsets of physical states, events, or processes (which thus avoids the difficulties of Cartesianism, epiphenomenalism, etc.). But how could this (physicalistic) characterization of mentality be compatible with the existence, forever and a day, of a wall between ourselves and the mind of another? For should it not seem the case that *if* mental states, events, and processes are certain physical states, events, and processes, then there *might* be a time (The Age of Utopian Neurophysiology) when we should simply see, and thereby know the mind of another?[1] (Consider: electron mindoscopes.)

Yet a stubborn resistance remains. And even the foremost proponent[2] of physicalism will not, I think, wish to say that we might at some stage simply see and thereby know without need of further inference, the mind of another. And one way to summarize his resistance to relinquishing this need of further inference is to say that even in the era of Utopian Neurophysiology there would persist the feeling that whatever the nature of a man's mind, it differs, radically, in texture from whatever it is we might some day

---

[1] But notice, even if we could make sense out of 'simply seeing' the mind of another the sceptic might well not be satisfied with an alleged penetration of the wall. For it would still be open to him to contrast 'simply seeing' the mind of another with the sort of direct non-inferential knowledge we would have of our own mind, and then insist that only the latter is real knowledge. This move, which has been so deftly described by Professor Wisdom, certainly bears on what follows. But I want to emphasize why few if any would initially grant that we could make sense out of 'simply seeing' the mind of another. As it turns out this unwillingness is not independent of the sceptic's propensity to wed knowledge of minds *simpliciter* to direct non-inferential knowledge of one's own mind.

[2] Professor Feigl seems to me to be the foremost proponent of physicalism, and I know he wouldn't say this and insists on the need for something like an argument from analogy to justify belief in the existence of other minds. But I also know, from conversation, that he is not altogether comfortable in so insisting. See his *The 'Mental' and the 'Physical', The Essay and a Postscript*, (Minneapolis, 1967).

come to observe going on in, for example, someone's central nervous system.

In what follows it will be an alleged difference in texture between the mental and anything physical on which I shall concentrate. But in passing I shall want casually to map some of the issues involved on to those issues which arise in the philosopher's hungering after 'perfect knowledge' and thus show the extent to which the reasons why there is this matter of a wall constitutes as well many of the bricks and mortar of the mind/body problem, and *vice versa*. That is, I will suggest that the wall between ourselves and others is one with that sense of differences in texture between the mental and anything physical. And what this sense of difference derives from I shall try to make plain. Hence, I'd like to explain *why* it's the case, as Wisdom convincingly argues, 'that here in the fact that there is something that it is not self-contradictory for one man to know directly, while it is self-contradictory for others, we have a characteristic difficulty of the logic of the soul.' Once this is done I think it will become apparent that paradoxically and after all the wall between ourselves and others is not only compatible with the truth of a physicalistic characterization of the mind, but in some sense a consequence of it.[1]

If nothing else I'll hope to hint in passing how Wisdom's wisdom continues to impinge on current approaches to the mind/body problem, such as those of Professors Feigl, Meehl, and Sellars, *et al.* But I'll begin by going way, way back.

II

Possible Sellarsian Ancestors. Amidst the rather toned down metaphysical temper of our time it's *almost* refreshing to recall the sweep of Anaximenes' unbashful contention that 'Just as our soul, being air, holds us together, so do breath and air encompass the universe'. Air, according to Anaximenes, is both material and animated. It's said to be related to the whole of the observable world in the same manner that an individual soul is related to a particular body. With similar scope Democritus claimed that the soul (or mind) was composed of 'fine-grained' atoms whereas Epicurus supposed the soul to be mortal and composed of atoms

---

[1] See the last part of section III.

most similar to the atom of air. When these atoms are scattered, death is said to result.

But why, we can ask, should breath or air be repeatedly chosen as the element with which the soul or mind is identified in Greek thought? And, similarly, why should Democritus wish to describe the soul or mind as being composed of smooth or 'fine-grained' atoms?

There is, of course, the obvious association of breath with a living as opposed to a dead body. And this may, in some instances, be sufficient for explaining the tendency to associate the soul or mind with breath (or air) if one views the soul or mind as the animating force of a body. (Note: in Homeric Greece it was the *thymos* or 'breath-soul' which was credited with feeling and thought, and not one's *eidolon* or shade. The former disappeared upon death.) On the other hand, such an explanation may not seem entirely satisfactory. For many features other than breath are allocated only to living bodies, though these have never been said to be the substances of which souls consist. So a further suggestion is this: a *rationale* for souls or minds having been identified with breath or air might be that one wished somehow to maintain that souls or minds were constituents of the world while at the same time holding that they were not as *conspicuously* in the world as, say, rocks or rivers, tunics or trumpets. Democritus, however stalwart his search, would never *see* the mind of another. Nor, indeed, would it appear accurate to say he could see his own! (Compare: there is nothing (wintry days aside) which we *see* which is breath. So too, 'Where is the wind?' 'In the trees'. 'But where, exactly?' 'Nowhere exactly'.) In short, if the soul or mind is thought to have a texture which makes its presence in the world somehow less forward than rocks or rivers, tunics or trumpets, this difference in texture should be expected to transfer to the sort of atoms—albeit atoms—of which the soul or mind is said to consist. Thus special atoms for souls or minds: 'fine-grained' or smooth ones.

Were this (casually risky) exegesis correct, an interesting, though probably inadvertent, partial continuity might be exhibited between the motivation for Democritus' (*et al.*) characterization of the soul or mind as 'fine-grained' and the so-called 'grain-argument' which Professor Wilfrid Sellars is said to have used against the thesis that mental states are identical with certain subsets of neural states. The simplest gloss I know of on this criticism of the identity thesis is provided by the foremost proponent of that thesis itself. Thus Professor Herbert Feigl in his recent article 'Reduction of Psychology to Neurophysiology' writes:

> How could the smooth expanse of a colour in the visual field, the rather unitary experiences of anger or elation, etc., be identical (i.e., to be sure, empirically identical) with the referent of a complex set of physical functors which we would normally interpret as describing a highly complex pattern of neural excitations?

and

> As W. Sellars used to put it in discussions, the 'grain' is different in the two cases. This has led him (and no doubt others before him) to espouse a theory of the 'emergence' of raw feels. According to this view, there are neurophysiological events which are irreducible to the concepts of the physics which is sufficient for the explanation of inorganic (and very likely large parts of organic and living) nature.[1]

Or as Professor Paul Meehl expounds Sellars' objection in his (Meehl's) searching analysis of Feigl's position, 'The Compleat Autocerebroscopist: A Thought-Experiment on Professor Feigl's Mind-Body Identity Thesis':

> Roughly put, 'grain' refers to an admittedly vague cluster of properties involving continuity, qualitative homogeneity, unity or lack of discrete parts, spatio-temporal smoothness or flow, and the like, which many raw feels possess in ways that their corresponding . . . brain states do not. Thus a small phenomenal red patch is typically experienced as a continuous expanse of red hue. The identity theory makes the phrase 'phenomenal red patch', in the revised theoretical language, refer both to this entity and to that 'gappy', heterogenous, discontinuous conglomerate of spatially discrete events. . . .[2]

[1] In *Philosophy of Science* 2, edited by Philosophy of Science Society, Japan (Tokyo, 1969), pp. 163–84.
[2] In 'The Compleat Autocerebroscopist: A Thought-Experiment on Professor Feigl's Mind-Body Identity Thesis', p. 167, in *Mind Matter, and Method*, edited by Paul K. Feyerabend and Grover Maxwell (Minneapolis, 1966).

As an aside I would suggest that the implausibility which Sellars has been said to attribute to any identification of mental states with subsets of physical states may in part mirror the manner in which Democritus, for example, would have resisted the identification of the mental with conglomerations of 'coarse'-grained atoms. But the pivotal point is that between early Greek thought and the present the notion seems to have persisted that there is something peculiar about the texture of mentality which should lead us to resist identifying thoughts, feelings, and the like with the (admittedly varied) differently textured things, processes, or events in the physical universe. It is this notion which I now wish to explore, explain, and assess. And it is this notion I view as of a piece with Professor Wisdom's claim that 'The peculiarity of the soul is not that it is visible to none, but that it is visible only to one.' If the soul were like in principle observable things, processes, or events in the physical universe, it would be like things, in principle, observable to all.

No doubt we do possess some at least vague intuitive idea of difference in textures. Some boring examples: we know that the texture of wool differs from the texture of silk, and that the texture of eiderdown differs from the texture of a bed of spikes. And we know that the differences between something which is bumpy and something which is smooth, or between something which is airy and something which is solid may also be counted as differences in texture. Indeed certain words probably function primarily as indicators of texture ('smooth', 'coarse', etc.). Yet it hardly seems called for to coin a linguistic category called 'texture-terms' and then attempt to tell exactly what that included. So I'll sidestep such strategy and proceed on the assumption that we do possess an intuitive idea of differences in texture, and that for present purposes an acknowledgement of this without exposition will suffice. The question to capture concern is whether an appeal to these assumedly recognizable differences can in certain cases be used to undercut various physicalistic conceptions of the mind.

I'll propose that no appeal to felt differences in texture between the mental and the physical *can* undercut a physicalistic conception of the mind. At the same time, however, I'll try to illustrate why a certain type of demonstration of identity between allegedly two items of differing textures could ever be given of the identity, if it be an identity, between mental states, events, or processes and various physical aspects of our bodies. And the reason why such a demonstration will never be forthcoming is, I think, exactly the same as the reason why 'when from a man's face or what he says we guess he's angry, we are not like one who from the outside of a house guesses that it is inhabited *and could make sure*'.

If I'm correct virtually all the identity-analogies hitherto harnessed in the service of physicalism are strategically impotent in a crucial respect. They are impotent insofar as *none* of the (admittedly diverse) ways in which, for example, lightning flashes can be shown to be identical with electrical discharges, water with H_2O, etc., could ever be available for demonstrating the identity between mental states, events, or processes and various physical states, events, or processes. To admit this impotence, however, is not in the least to show that the mental may not be identical with aspects of the physical in the way in which lightning flashes are identical with electrical discharges. Indeed it may be. Here I only submit as a supplementary supposition that we will be forever bereft of a certain way of showing it. (And for those same reasons we will be forever lacking a certain way of knowing the mind of another.) Although this lack can be used to cast suspicion over the entire physicalist programme in the philosophy of mind, it's exactly that sort of suspicion I'd like to snuff out.

So I shall first consider a case which has all the ingredients of (seemingly) two things which though possessed of differing textures can be shown to be identical. I shall then show why although a mind-body identity thesis could never be blessed with comparable demonstrations of identity, this lack does not count against the plausibility of such an identity.

It will become obvious that the example I have chosen to elaborate is more simple-minded than scientifically sexier examples involving, for example, cross-category identities, theoretical terms, etc. But I have deliberately avoided focusing on such cases because I believe they are unnecessarily complicated given the issues under discussion. Although action-packed, and rightly so, to a philosopher of science interested in reductionism in general, the non-simple-minded examples raise a number of problems which, strictly speaking, are quite independent of the mind/body problem. Furthermore, although I can't argue it here, I think that none of the non-simple-minded examples of identity provide us with any *added* advantage over my simple-minded case for proving the identity of mental states with certain physical states. All examples, for certain deep reasons, are equally unconvincing.

III

The Importance of whether a Poster Blow-up of Dick Tracy's Face Viewed from Eight Feet Away should be Deemed Identical with a Configuration of Hundreds of Little Dots. Consider a typical poster-sized blow-up of some All-American cartoon character, say, Dick Tracy. (For those appalled at the example a more aesthetic substitution such as a pointillist painting by Seurat may be made.) Viewed from eight feet off one might be said to see a 'smooth'-grained expanse which we call 'Dick Tracy's face'. If, however, we walk up to the poster and peer at it from eight inches away we will see that the face is made up of hundreds of little dots in a variety of colours. Without at first blush seeming ontologically nutty, we might say that Dick Tracy's face is identical with or the same as or made up of nothing but a certain configuration of hundreds of little dots. And we could add that this, surely, is a case where something with a 'smooth' grain (the face) is the same as something with a 'gappy' grain (the dots).

Admittedly, when we view the poster at what I'll dub the 'micro' (or dot)-level we'll not be able simultaneously to see it at what I'll describe as 'macro' (or face)-level. Hence we'll not be able to see the 'gappy'-grained expanse at the same time we see the 'smooth'-grained expanse. Yet we seem adequately blessed with an understanding of why these differences in perspective are infertile *qua* progenitors of ontologically distinct entities or entity-types. For we can explain the difference in grain in such a case as a function of different perspectives. No magician could build a career on such demonstrations. Who, for example, would expect a copy of *Playboy* or *The Daily Mail* to look the same when, say, viewed through a keyhole, or underwater, or from the top of the Empire State Building, etc. Different angles, distances, filters, and the like become for us means of discovering the different textural possibilities which an object has. So rather than suggest: 'Ah, two different textures, so there must be two different things' we say: 'When you look at *it* from over here, then *it* looks thus-and-thus, but from over there, so-and-so.' Were locutions such as the latter lopped from our discourse on lookings we would be albatrossed by the doctrine that any given object can be viewed from only one perspective. Rather, and more worsely accurate, we would be drawn to the denial of the possibility of viewing things from a certain perspective. For to grant any conceptual glamour to the idea of viewing something from *a* (or one) perspective necessitates a plethora of such to contrast with the one singled out. (Compare: We cannot single Martha out from the rest when she stands there, utterly alone, under the coconut tree on the desert island.)

One could, of course, worriedly ask, 'What is the object, this third thing, which, when viewed close up presents us with an array of little dots, and when viewed far off can be seen as a big comic strip face?' The source of such paranoia may derive from rude reminiscences of a *ding-an-sich*; or the haunting queries of, say, a double-aspect theory, such as 'What is *it* that these aspects are aspects of?'

I think, however, that such worries may be waived in the following way. There is no need to suppose there is a third thing or an object absolutely perspectivally neutral which underlies both the configuration of little dots *and* Dick Tracy's face. Although it's necessary to specify something other than dots or Dick Tracy's face in order to make sense of them each being a function of a particular perspective, this can be easily managed without reviving anything as unlikeable as a *noumenon*. For all we need mention in such a case is an unproblematic poster: thus we say, 'The poster when viewed from here is just an array of little dots, but from over there it's Dick Tracy's face'. And posters are in no way ontologically privileged compared with little dots or a big face. We posit a poster in this case simply because we then have a hook on which to hang our perspectives: these little dots are what the poster looks like from here, this face how it looks from there. But mention of a poster need not be mention of an object on which we have certain perspectives. In some contexts, of course, it might itself be the means of specifying a perspective: for example,'Ah, now I can see that piece of paper as a poster', etc. The point, in brief, is that such phrases as 'a poster' or 'a face' or 'an array of dots' can do (at least) double duty in our describing the ways our world is, or, if you prefer, the worlds our ways are. In some contexts such phrases can be used to pick out whatever we wish to talk about having a perspective on; in others we use the phrases to individuate the perspective itself. A normal constraint, a major limitation, upon when we use such phrases to do one thing rather than another seems often to be this; that if the phrase has already been used to indicate a perspective, it is not then used to specify the object which the perspective is a perspective of, and *vice versa*. Hence we avoid locutions such as 'Ah, now, from here, I can see this poster as a poster' etc. For if we have already indicated that we have seen a poster ('I can see this poster . . .') little if any informational utility accrues to adding 'as a poster'. The main moral, however, is simply that posters as distinct from arrays of dots as distinct from faces, etc., are not ontologically contrastive in any interesting or philosophically exciting sense. There is nothing here, for example, which even remotely resembles the contrast which Descartes makes between the mental and the physical. And the fact that in certain contexts mention of a poster may seem perspectivally neutral—that is, as indicating an object which one can view from different perspectives—in no way re-routes us to the mysteries of some exotic underlying substance or *ding an sich*.

Even if we felt compelled to admit that some third thing underlies a configuration of little dots and Dick Tracy's face, we could say precisely what it was: namely a poster. (Though we might also have said, and just as precisely, that it was something I bought in The Electric Potato Gift Shop, and so on and on and on.) Furthermore, if we wished, we could go on and say what a poster consists of: namely a piece of paper used in such-and-such a way. So too for what a piece of paper used in such-and-such a way is like. And so too for that so too.

IV

But what should be our summary description of the relationship between what is seen when we see Dick Tracy's face and what is seen when we see a conglomeration of little dots? There may still seem to be something wrong with blatantly identifying Dick Tracy's face with the little dots. But certainly there also seems to be something wrong with a blatant refusal to do so. Can we analyse these two wrongs so as to make a right?

What's wrong with any blatant identification apart from the blatancy (boo, hiss) is, I think, that the content of our visual experience or *what* we see (face or dots) is determined by a perspective, and in this case differing perspectives. Given that the perspectives are not identical, this non-identity can be shown, in a sense, to rub off on our description of what is seen: the face comes to be said to be what is seen when we are at some distance away, the dots come to be said to be what is seen when we are up close. And obviously in a literal sense *what* we see up close is not *what* we see see at a distance, so how could the face be identical with the dots? Let me characterize the sense in which what is seen up close and what is seen at a distance are not identical as *perspectival non-identity*.

On the other hand, there is something wrong with a blatant refusal to identify the face with the dots. That seems to be this: it is perfectly proper to say that this collection of little dots *is*, literally is, what we bought in the Electric Potato Gift Shop at a certain time in a certain single-purchase transaction, and that this copy of Dick Tracy's face *is*, literally is, also what we bought in the Electric Potato Gift Shop at the same time through that same single-purchase transaction. Hence, since the dots and the face both are, literally are, what we bought in the Electric Potato Gift Shop, the dots and the face are the same thing, identical. Here what has happened is that a reasonable identification between what is seen at a distance and what is seen close-up is established *via* the identification of each with something else which is referred to in a perspectively neutral way and hence in a way which deletes the perspectival features embedded in a characterization of either what is seen up close or what is seen from a distance. Thus, since things identical with the same thing are identical with each other we establish what I shall call a *non-perspectival identity*. The point of the parable should by now be transparent: viz., that items which are *perspectively non-identical* can be *non-perspectively identical*. And this, I believe is the correct way to characterize the relationship between Dick Tracy's face and the collection of little dots: *perspectively non-identical*, but *non-perspectively identical*.

If we speak indiscriminately about 'what is seen' we may overlook the essential ambiguity of the 'what' which may either refer transparently to the contents of a visual experience which is dependent on a perspective or obliquely to something which can be identified and characterized independently of any particular visual experience and its attendant perspective. Thus if we ask *what* was it you were looking at we might answer 'Dick Tracy's face'—i.e., something which depends on the content of that visual experience, or we might answer 'a poster' which in such a context is really independent of the contents of what we are seeing, i.e., Dick Tracy's face.

Or we can look at it this way. The *rationale* for identifying Dick Tracy's face with a configuration of little dots is one and the same with the *rationale* for talking about the existence of *an* object of investigation in the first place. We cannot make sense of an object being an object of investigation unless we admit that it could be looked at from various angles, distances, etc. But once we admit that admission we acknowledge, at least tacitly, an identification between what it is which is later looked at from a different perspective, etc. Hence a denial of an identification of Dick Tracy's face with an array of little dots amounts to a denial that we were involved in purchasing *an* item which could be investigated: i.e. looked at now from up close; looked at later from far away. *It is to treat the poster purchased as, in effect, resistant to investigation; as something which remains the same object only so long as we never alter our perspective with respect to it.* Obviously neither posters nor any other material entities are investigationally resistant in this sense. The capstone question to work up to, though, is whether the mind might be such an item and whether if it is this shows us something important about the mind/body problem, the 'grain argument', and other related matters.

An obviously crucial feature conditioning our willingness to identify (non-perspectivally) Dick Tracy's face with a collection of little dots is that as we walk up on the face the little dots emerge and as we walk back from the dots the face re-emerges, etc. I shall call this an *emergence relationship*. And I shall suggest that whenever an *emergence relationship* can be shown to obtain between two or more (or in some sense two or more) items those items can be shown to be *non-perspectivally identical*.

The importance of an emergence relation can be illustrated in the following manner. Suppose at the time we purchase the poster which we can identify with Dick Tracy's face we also purchase a stick of incense. Later on we identify (*non-perspectivally*) a collection of little dots with Dick Tracy's face *via* its identification with something (a poster) which we bought in the Electric Potato Gift Shop at a certain time. But why won't we identify the little dots with the stick of incense which we purchased at the same time in that same transaction with the clerk in the Electric Potato Gift Shop? The answer, I think, is fairly plain. An emergence relationship can be shown to obtain between the face and the dots which cannot be shown to obtain between the stick of incense and the dots. And whenever there is an emergence relationship[1] between (allegedly) two items one has sufficient reason for supposing that those two items actually occupy the same space and are hence (non-perspectivally) the same thing. How could such a relationship obtain unless those items did occupy the same space? (Try, for example, to illustrate an emergence relationship between any two things which do not occupy the same space, whether they be as dissimilar as a weasel and a watch or as similar as identical twins. It can't be done.)

Here, then, we have exhausted or at least been exhausted by an example where it seems that two items can be shown to be identical albeit non-perspectivally identical, even though rather radical differences betwixt them in grain obtain. It's now relevant to ask whether anything like the relationship which can be shown to obtain between Dick Tracy's face and hundreds of little dots can also be shown to obtain between mental states and neural states. My answer to this question is simply this: (1) our mental states may, indeed, be related to neural states in a manner which reflects or parallels the manner in which Dick Tracy's face is related to the configuration of little dots; but (2) we could never prove or as dramatically illustrate that they are because nothing remotely like the emergence relationship could be demonstrated as holding between mental and physical states. For nothing remotely like 'walking up' or 'walking back' can occur in connection with mental states and the neural states with which they are allegedly identified. (And for the same reason nothing remotely like coming to know another's pain less and less indirectly until we at last know it directly could ever transpire). This is so for the following reasons.

We are, as it were, the locus of any of our own thoughts, feelings, and sensations, and hence incapable of either walking up

---

[1] I am not claiming that an emergence relationship is a necessary condition for exhibiting an identity. Nevertheless I believe that the lack of such a relationship may tempt one to deny (wrongly) the possibility of an identity. This is especially so if one argues for an identity between two seemingly different items on the basis of analogies with other identities where it would be possible to exhibit an emergence relationship.

on them or walking away from them. What would it be like to walk away from a pain? How could we put ourselves at a distance from them and finally view them as a set of C-fibres being stimulated? Compare: 'Hey Martha, come look at your headache from over here and see what the aspirin is doing for it.' Or, what would it be like to walk up on the pain of someone else, so that we no longer see it as C-fibres being stimulated but rather confront that pain in the way the person having it does? Professor Wisdom has convincingly argued for the impossibility of coming to know another's pain directly. What I'm suggesting is that the aetiology of that impossibility also suffices for explaining the impossibility of knowing our own pains in any way other than directly—i.e. in any other way than by having them.

The needed perspectival shifts could never occur in connection with mental states and any physical states they might be identical with. As the locus of each of our thoughts, feelings, and sensations, we are trapped within a single perspective concerning them. Recall Leibniz's characterization of monads—centres of consciousness—as windowless. (Since that perspective amounts simply to being the loci, it is, of course, the limiting case of having a perspective.)

Even if, for example, we were equipped with a special 'inner eye' which could rummage around scanning our neural states or processes while we were in a state of pain it would be to no avail. We would still be stuck with an acute sense of there being two things with differing textures: (1) the pain we would be feeling, and (2) the neural events we were looking at. So even if we were in this bizarre manner to have two perspectives on our pain at once—as locus of them, and as observer—we would have no sense of them being identical. The case would still deviate from the Dick Tracy's face and little dots type example in that nothing like an emergence relationship could be exhibited between them. Nothing like walking up on, say, our neural states and seeing them blend into our feeling of pain, or *vice versa*, could ever occur. Similarly, there is no traversable continuum in this world which would permit us inch by inch to tread towards an ever increasingly direct knowledge of another's pain.

On the basis of the foregoing, then, I shall speak of us as being locus-bound to our thoughts, feelings, and sensations, and locus-detached from the thoughts, feelings, and sensations of anyone else. It is my contention that the difference in grain or texture between the mental and anything physical derives from our being locus-bound to our mental life and unable to view it as being like those physical processes, states, and events from which we are locus-detached.

It may well be that our thoughts, feelings, sensations, and so no are *non-perspectivally identical* with certain neural processes and events, but we cannot demonstrate ('show and tell') that they are. And it is our inability to do this which generates the 'difference in grain' which Sellars and others have noted.

With the exception of certain terminological disparities, what I've been saying probably echoes as well a variety of points which G. T. Fechner wished to emphasize in his *Elemente der Psychophysik*[1] when he wrote:

> When anyone stands inside a sphere its convex side is for him quite hidden by the concave surface; conversely. When he stands outside, the concave surface is hidden by the convex. Both sides belong together as inseparably as the psychical and the bodily sides of a human being, and these also may by way of simile (*vergleichsweise*) be regarded as inner and outer sides; but it is just as impossible to see both sides of a circle from a standpoint in the plane of the circle, as to see these two sides of humanity from a standpoint in the plane of human existence.

And:

> The solar system seen from the sun presents an aspect quite other than that which it presents when viewed from the earth. There it appears as the Copernican, here as the Ptolemaic world-system. And for all time it will remain impossible for one observer to see both belong inseparably together, and, just like the concave and the convex sides of a circle, they are at bottom only two different modes of appearance of the same thing seen from different standpoints.

I could, of course, have come at the problem that the grain argument poses for the identity thesis from the opposite direction. That is, I could have begun with the supposition that our thoughts,

[1] (Leipzig, 1907).

feelings, and sensations *are* identical with something physical such as neural events. I would then have asked the question of whether it would seem reasonable to suppose that *I* would have the same perspective on my thoughts, feelings, and sensations that someone else would have, and *vice-versa*. (Consider: the sense in which I can't but feel 'close' to my own pains.) And the answer to such a question, I think, is that the perspectives (mine and others) could not be the same. But if that answer is correct, we might well expect that the sorts of noticed differences in texture which often attend differences in perspective would crop up in the case of the neural events with which my mental states have been identified considered from my point of view and those same neural events considered from someone else's point of view. It's precisely these differences that I believe philosophers to be referring to when they talk about differences in grain. But if the identity thesis itself, together with the seemingly safe assumption that I could never have the same perspective on my sensations that you have, implies that a difference in grain will crop up, reference to differences in grain can hardly be used to undercut the identity thesis.

Yet it may be clarifying to comment on one interesting Houdini-like effort to circumvent the difficulties which are created by our being locus-bound to our mental states which in turn produces a sense of difference in texture between the mental and the physical. Here I have in mind Professor Feigl's celebrated conceptual 'invention' the autocerebroscope.

Why Professor Feigl's Autocerebroscope Could Never Help us to See that the Identity Thesis is True Even if it is. Because one could never 'walk back' from this 'macro'-level of one's own mind (if there is a macro-level of one's mind) to view it on a 'micro'-level (as brain states) and because one could never 'walk up' to the 'macro'-level (raw feels, etc.) of the mind of another, various interesting strategies have been employed to unpick the mind-body problem.

Professor Feigl, for example, has fancied for us the auto-cerebroscope. He says:

> We may fancy a 'compleat autocerebroscopist' who while introspectively attending, to e.g., his increasing feelings of anger (or love, hatred, embarrassment, exultation, or to the experience of a tune-as-heard, etc.) would simultaneously be

observing a vastly visual 'picture' of his own cerebral nerve currents on a projection screen.[1]

The fruit of this fantasy is its provision for at least some in principle possible observations of empirical regularities which would help confirm an identification of mental states with physical states and be in keeping with the allegedly empirical nature of that identification. The problem, however, is that any such observations would never tell decisively between, say, a psycho-physical parallelism and the identity thesis. This indecisiveness illustrates why even in the not-yet-dawning Age of Utopian Neurophysiology replete with autocerebroscopes we would lack any illustration of mind-body identity as powerful and persuasive as the illustrations of identity between Dick Tracy's face and a configuration of little dots. For the autocerebroscope does not provide us with anything like the investigational possibilities for what I have called 'walking up' and 'walking back'. They provide us at most with an analogue of the following kind: suppose I am glued to the floor eight feet away from the Dick Tracy poster. Then I am aware of Dick Tracy's face but not of the configuration of little dots. I cannot walk up on the little dots and see for myself that Dick Tracy's face is made up of them. Suppose, however, that a camera, two inches from the poster, were to project on a screen a configuration of little dots whenever I was seeing Dick Tracy's face. Then we would have an approximation to Feigl's autocerebroscopic situation. But note, we come by the approximation only through *weakening* our case for a persuasive identification between Dick Tracy's face and a configuration of little dots. This can hardly, then, be used to illustrate that we have possible illustrations of mind-body identity as powerfully persuasive as the *non*-weakened case of identity between Dick Tracy's face and configurations of little dots. Also, even the weakened case is at most an approximation. For it differs conceptually from the mind-body identity case in that we can easily imagine what it would take to convert the weakened case back into the strong case for identity; namely, simply imagining the feet becoming unstuck, and subsequently being capable of 'walking up' and 'walking back'.

Another way to put it is that we cannot 'autocerebroscopize' our way to an identity thesis resolution of the mind-body problem.

---

[1] In *The 'Mental' and the 'Physical'*, op. cit.

O

And this polysyllabic impossibility derives from the premise that my awareness of my own mental states, be they thoughts, feelings, or sensations, will always seem *to me* different in grain from whatever that utopian neuro-physiological device could present to me. So too, even if my neuro-physiological states could be made available to someone else, there would persist the suspicion on the part of that someone that *whatever* he was observing, he was not observing my thoughts feelings, or sensations. In other words, the wall would stand.

VI

Nevertheless, A Problem for the Thesis that Mental States may be Identical with Certain Physical States Based on the Temporal Irreversibility of our Precedent Awareness of Thoughts, Feelings, etc., as Opposed to Anything Described Neurophysiologically—All This Beginning with a Couplet of Pope's.

Alexander Pope asked a question and rimed an answer thus:

'Why hath not man a microscopic eye?
For this plain reason: Man is not a fly.'

Yet we can imagine the following being the case: that man evolves with a more fly-like eye such that various objects appear to him in the way they now appear to us only when, for example, we view them under a powerful microscope. We see H_2O, but we do not see anything like what we ordinarily see when we now see water. Or we see clusters of particles in suspension but we do not see anything which looks like what clouds look like when we now look at them. And so on. Now we can imagine, for one reason or another, someone inventing a *macro*scope so that we, with the aid of it, are able to see H_2O in the way that water ordinarily appears to us, etc. We can further imagine identity-relations between water and H_2O being touted for the same reason they are touted now. The point is we can imagine our arriving at such a conclusion from either direction: that is, by having first been aware of objects viewed microscopically, and then macroscopically, or *vice versa*. Similarly, we can imagine having first been aware of a configuration of hundreds of tiny dots, and then of Dick Tracy's face, or *vice versa*. The order in which the identity discovery is made, macro-to-micro or micro-to-macro, is essentially irrelevant. But is this similarly true in the case of the mental and whatever one might assume to be its analysis in terms of neurophysiological states, or whatever? It certainly does not seem so.

Let us simply assume that the mental does yield to some sort of analysis and that this is to be cast in terms of neurophysiological structure and activity. Note, if this is so, then I know my own mind on the macro-level, but yours only on the micro-level. So, then, the task for an identity thesis proponent is to explain *how* I can come, in my own case, to accept an identification between what I know on a macro-level with what someone else might know only on a micro-level. If this is so, then is it just a contingent fact about our discovery of the identity between mental states and neurophysiological states that we first were aware of mental states and only later came to be aware of the neurophysiological states of which they consist? That is, might it have been the other way around? If we think that the mind-body identity relation is like the dots and Dick Tracy's face, etc., we should be willing to say it might have been the other way around, but what could that be like? That is, what would it be like to be aware *first* of one's mind in terms of neurophysiological states without any awareness of thoughts, feelings, etc., and then afterwards *discover* that there were such things as thoughts, feelings, etc. (made up of such states)?

We can easily imagine being glued to the floor eight feet away from the Dick Tracy poster and hence being stuck with seeing the face, but then breaking away and running up on it and watching the little dots emerge. Or we can imagine having first been stuck with just an awareness of dots, being freed, and thus coming to see the face. But what would a comparable lack of incarceration in our own thoughts, feelings, etc., be like such that we might have first been stuck with only our neurophysiological states?

The impasse can be explained as follows. If we are talking about awareness of neurophysiological states we are already talking about awareness which is itself one of the sorts of things which we were trying to suppose we might only discover ourselves to have after having been aware (zounds) of our minds under neurophysiological descriptions. That is, talking simply about awareness (*of anything*) is already talking in pre-neurophysiological terms. Thus talking about our awareness of (whatever) neurophysiological states we might wish to identify our mental life with, presupposes the use of psycho-epistemic non-neuro-physiological terms.

We could not be stuck with knowing or being aware of our neurophysiological states without already also being stuck with knowing. But knowing, being aware, thinking about, etc., *are prime examples of those very things we were trying to imagine we might discover long after we had been apprised of our neurophysiological states.* This coupled with the fact that we are locus-bound to our own mental states and hence incapable of *seeing* them as being identical with our neurophysiological states (even if they are) is sufficient, I think, to explain the temporal irreversibility of our precedent awareness of thoughts, etc., as opposed to anything neurophysiological.

There is thus an obvious *epistemological* difference between the case of coming to identify Dick Tracy's face with a lot of little dots and the case of coming to identify mental states with neurophysiological states. But I fail to see any reason for believing this difference might be converted into an *ontological* difference. Mental states might, after all, be neurophysiological states. What we need to get used to is that even if they are, certain demonstrations that they are will forever elude us.

VII

Back to the Wall. So we return to Wisdom's remark that 'when from a man's face or what he says we guess he's angry, we are not like one who from the outside of a house guesses that it is inhabited *and could make sure*'. And this, I think, is absolutely correct. And for the same reason I would add that seeing our own minds as objects of knowledge—construed, for example, as neural states or processes—could not be like seeing from the outside of a house exactly how the timber, bricks and wiring all went together. We cannot with similar alacrity get outside ourselves. And because we can't there is this ineradicable sense of our minds differing in kind from whatever we might inspect from a distance including, for example, what Meehl has called a 'gappy', heterogeneous, discontinuous conglomerate of spatially discrete events'. And in seeing the correctness of this we should see as well why such mentalistic words as 'thought' or 'feeling', etc., cannot function as *just* theoretical terms which might some day be exchanged for observational terms: e.g. 'carrier-of-heredity' for 'gene', 'invisible germs in the blood' for 'those little critters you'll see if you look through this microscope', etc. For that would be to liken our knowledge of another man being angry to knowledge of a house being inhabited where we could some day go in and make sure, though maybe not now. And it would be to liken our knowledge of our own anger to something we might become detached from and hold up to ourselves for inspection in the way a repairman might inspect loose hinges on a broken shutter. Nor is the problem of inferring from a man's movements, gestures, looks and speech to what's behind that wall, like the problem of confirming the hypothesis that every Christmas there is a choir of ants which sing Handel's Messiah in the centre of the sun. For this is simply the problem of devising unmeltable instruments. And though we might never devise them we can at least in imagination produce the requisite super-asbestos which would settle the Singing Ants Hypothesis once and for all. But in the case of a man's mind nothing in or out of imagination could count as going in to see. It is not the indelicate problem of a retarded technology, but the delicate problem of the utter irrelevance of unretarded technology, something we've already sensed by noting the built-in philosophical obsolescence of Utopian Neurophysiology's autocerebroscope.

And all this, I believe, follows because nothing could ever count as one's being other than where he is, and being, say, the locus of another man's thoughts, or feelings. From our inability to be the locus of another's thoughts, feelings, and sensations, we can derive the problem of other minds, and from our inability to detach ourselves from the locus of our own, we can derive a sense of difference in texture between our own mental life and anything physical from which we are detached.

There is, perhaps, a disappointing drabness to all this: as if to say 'You mean that our being where we are and not where someone else is causes all these other minds, mind/body perplexities?' But that's like saying while looking at a fireworks display 'Just a lot of wick and powder behind it' or saying of the Mississippi when at its source in Itasca State Park (Minnesota) 'You mean that's all there is to it?' (pointing at a spring bubbling up).

The impressiveness of fireworks or the Mississippi like the intellectual excitements in the problem of other minds and the problem of mind and body lies not in their rather colloquial causes, but in the flowering and flow of those causes' effects.

IX

JOHN WISDOM AND THE PROBLEM OF OTHER MINDS

R. W. NEWELL

IT IS fashionable nowadays to break down old dichotomies by producing new relationships that fail to fit the traditional moulds of analytic and causal connections. Among the philosophical issues to which such moves appear as promising solutions is the problem of other minds, especially if the problem is seen as a puzzle about the relationship between statements describing a person's behaviour and those describing his mental states. In its more general aspect the problem seems intractable because of the impossibility of establishing a connection between these statements along inductive or deductive lines, if a sceptic's arguments are to be believed. If this is so, then the data of what a person says about his state of mind together with the circumstances of his saying it and the general background of his position lose their title as good reasons for a conclusion about the facts of his mental state. Reasons for a judgement are not good reasons, if reasons at all, unless they can be shown to support the judgement drawn from them. The sceptical thesis in this case is simply that the support is neither of a necessary nor of a contingent kind and that this exhausts the options it is possible to take. Within this framework the disclosure of an alternative and rationally acceptable connection differing from these but having the force of justification is a welcome event. If we can attribute the origin of this idea roughly to Wittgenstein, Professors Malcolm and Strawson have been principally responsible for its welfare.[1]

Yet it may be questioned at the start whether a strategy of this kind could succeed. Perhaps it would carry conviction in an issue in which a sceptic's attack draws whatever force it has solely from the point that neither inductive nor deductive methods of

---

[1] See Strawson, *Individuals*, Chapter 3; and Malcolm, 'Wittgenstein's *Philosophical Investigations*', *Philosophical Review*, 1954; 'Knowledge of Other Minds', *Journal of Philosophy*, 1958.

inference have application. But there is more to the issue about
other minds than this. Even if a conclusion reached about
someone else's mental state is a non-standard inference from
observations of his behaviour and circumstances, the person to
whom the statement refers can assess its truth in a way in which
other people cannot, a point obscurely expressed by the philosophical formula that a person has direct access to his own consciousness whereas the access achieved by anyone else is only
indirect. Nowithstanding that the difference between 'direct' and
'indirect' access is by no means clear, this feature has been taken
to support the view that a person's knowledge of his own mind is
certain in a way in which the professed knowledge of others about
his mind is not. And it is a short step to conclude that in the latter
case we cannot speak of knowledge. What emerges from this is
that the other minds problem has a special complexity of its own.

John Wisdom has emphasized the distinctiveness of the issue by
remarking that 'the peculiarity of the soul is not that it is visible
to none but that it is visible only to one'. How is this slogan to be
understood? Clearly we are not intended to take the reference to
the soul's being visible as meaning that it is perceptible by the
senses, for if this were so the soul could not be visible at all.
Misgivings soon arise: it is not, on the face of it, clear what Wisdom
means or that he is right, nor is it obvious how an understanding of
this point can lead to a solution of the problem of other minds.
Wisdom's impressive contribution can be brought into focus by
setting it beside the less elusive answers of Strawson and Malcolm.
One could, no doubt, attempt to adjudicate between them and
pick the winner, if there is one. Yet within the complexity of the
other minds problem there is ample room for compatible though
distinctly different manoeuvres. Selective sifting should disclose
that, far from their being rivals, each of the three answers comple-
ments the others.

To return, then, to Wisdom's remark. What we are being told
is that a person who is the subject of a statement ascribing mental
predicates is in a unique position with respect to its verification;
and we are left to conclude that this is not so, for example, in the
case of statements referring only to the subject's behaviour and its
background. Now if this is true a sceptic's position does not seem
much undermined; indeed his case seems strengthened, for it is
just this peculiarity that has been advanced as a ground for

philosophical doubt. The sceptical thesis this time is not merely that the reasons available to others are inadequate because they are unconnected to the conclusion in the traditional ways, but that they are inadequate because they inevitably fall short of the reasons that could be had only by the subject himself. And this suggests that attempts to defeat scepticism by using rational connections of an unorthodox kind are unsatisfactory in that they neglect the special position of the subject. To what extent is this criticism correct?

Professor Strawson has argued convincingly that mental predicates have the peculiarity that the recognition of their being both self-ascribable and other-ascribable is a necessary condition of understanding their use. One does not, according to him, in general ascribe states of mind to oneself on the basis of observation, but one does ascribe them to other people on the basis of observations of behaviour of a logically adequate kind. Thus its being correct for me to say that someone else feels depressed is in some way logically guaranteed if that person's behaviour and its background come up to a certain standard of adequacy, though I would identify my own feeling of depression in a different way. On this view the behaviour a person exhibits is not to be taken as a causal or inductive sign of his possessing a particular feeling or mental state. Nor do the facts of his behaviour and the surrounding circumstances, even if logically adequate, entail or formally imply a statement to the effect that the person displaying such behaviour actually possesses the mental state or feeling ascribed. Rather one would, or should, be prepared to ascribe, attribute or impute a particular mental state or feeling to someone else on the satisfaction of adequate behavioural criteria for reasons that could not be described as causal or contingent. We are being offered a general description of the conditions under which it would be correct to ascribe conscious states to others with the reservation that it is neither a causal nor an analytic truth that a mental predicate is correctly ascribed if the behavioural criteria are satisfied.

A different but not unrelated direction is taken by Professor Malcolm. Strawson, we find, is interested at least in detailing the conditions of correctly *ascribing* states of mind; yet it is not altogether clear whether he is also raising the thorny issue, into which Malcolm plunges, of the criteria for judging whether a person *actually possesses* the state of mind ascribed.[1] According to Malcolm the criteria of a person's having, e.g. a feeling of pain, are what the person says and does in certain circumstances, and their satisfaction establishes the existence of the pain 'beyond question', Now Malcolm is aware of the great and traditional gulf between (1) the question of whether we are justified in saying that a person has a certain feeling, or correct in ascribing that feeling to him and (2) the question of whether a person does (in fact) have the feeling we correctly ascribe or justifiably say he has. We might take him to mean merely that in appropriate circumstances we make no mistake in ascribing particular states of mind to others, and dismiss his flirtation with the stronger claim. Or we might take that claim seriously as an attempt to introduce a form of reductionism. But this would not, to be fair, get to the bottom of what Malcolm wants to say. Judgements about other people's pains are not, he says, logical consequences of any descriptions of their behaviour or circumstances. Nor does he allow that the two are causally related and so logically independent; for a causal connection, it is claimed, could obtain only if the criteria for the occurrence of pain have already been established. The relationship between a statement of the criteria of pain and the judgement that a person is in pain is not deductive yet is in some sense non-contingent. His proposal is that even if our judgements about the minds of other people are not formally entailed by the evidence for making them, and cannot be justified on inductive grounds, in some cases we can be sure not only that they are fully justified but also that they are true. Evidently, then, reductionism has been eliminated. By showing reductionism the door has Malcolm inadvertently ushered in scepticism? To say, as he does, 'If the criteria of (a person's) being in pain are satisfied then he *must* be in pain' conjures up the picture of a necessary connection or, failing that, at least a strong causal justification. And if these relationships are excluded it seems impossible to speak of being

---

[1] If I correctly ascribe a feeling of irritation to someone else am I (i) saying that he is irritated when I have really first-class justification for what I say, e.g. he says he is, looks as if he is and I have just cracked his best decanter; or am I (ii) saying he is with first-class justification when it happens, in fact, that he *is* irritated? Strawson certainly means (i) and possibly (ii) as well, which is the more important case. Much of the ambiguity comes from the expression 'correctly ascribe'. If you have cracked my decanter and I successfully feign irritation, is your quite justified ascription of irritation 'incorrect'? The answer is no, but this does not emerge clearly in Strawson's account.

certain. To this objection, as we will see, Malcolm has a cogent reply.

For the moment turn to the first of the two important questions that have been raised. If the behavioural criteria of a person's being in a particular mental state are satisfied, is the ascription of that state justifiable and correct? Strawson and Malcolm answer in the affirmative, and it is worth noticing why this answer is right and moreover why it could not have been wrong.

In the course of ordinary conversations about people the moment we are prepared to say that the criteria are sufficient we are also prepared to allow adequate justification. With our ears trained on common practice we detect a battery of platitudes: to say it is correct to ascribe a particular state of mind to someone else is to say that everything we can find out about the behaviour and circumstances of that person is favourable to the ascription; to say that it is reasonable to suppose but not altogether clear that the ascription applies, is just to say that on balance the facts of the person's behaviour and circumstances support the ascription; to say the ascription is incorrect or unjustified is just to say that the behaviour and circumstances of the subject are substantially adverse to accepting it. Disclosed here is the truism that if the criteria are satisfied then the ascription is justified.

Calling this a truism may be thought to be moving on thin ice. For surely, it will be objected, we never (and perhaps *cannot*) pin down exactly all the relevant constituents of behaviour and circumstances; some decisive fact may have escaped scrutiny (perhaps the subject was acting under post-hypnotic suggestion). Criteria, then, being too complex, remain indefinite, with the consequence that the guarded relation of 'logical adequacy' must do in place of unqualified logical sufficiency. This objection rightly insists that a judgement will not be *entailed* by an indefinite list. Yet this is deeply misleading. For we do, commonly, understand perfectly well when the piling up of facts about performance and context ('criteria') can stop and a justified judgement can be made. If I can be sure (straight away) that the man in front of me rather nastily sliced his hand when the pruning saw slipped, I can be equally sure (with a little investigation) that he has not been hypnotized, is not rehearsing for a stage play, and so on. Part of what is meant by saying that the criteria are sufficient is just that precautions of this kind have been taken. Of course the list of possible things I might have missed and that might impair my being justified will be indefinite, in the sense that when I have thought of all the ways in which my judgement could conceivably go wrong there will always be some I have not considered. Yet in deciding whether the criteria are sufficient we are not prevented from making a correct decision by the threat of logically possible flaws. If our conceptual scheme is a guide, these truisms *are* truisms.

But even if one's judgements are in some circumstances justifiably ascribed, does this meet a sceptic's challenge? The first hint of its inadequacy appears in the fact that the list of truisms above holds for everyone and not merely for all but one. If I cannot decide for myself, or as I please, about the correctness of ascribing a particular state of mind to someone else, I cannot so decide about the correctness of an ascription applied to me. For I am not in a unique position to say whether the criteria of my behaviour are satisfied on any particular occasion. Yet I am, it will be objected, in a unique position to say whether the ascription is true. And this is where the difficulty begins. For a sceptic takes his stand on an issue about the conditions of the truth of whatever we correctly (or incorrectly) ascribe. If Strawson's argument seriously impairs the claim, which has been made by some philosophers, that a person cannot justifiably ascribe mental states to others, it appears to leave undisturbed the stronger claim that the truth of the justified ascription can be ascertained only by the person to whom the ascription refers. And this is the posture a sceptic adopts. There is no formal inconsistency in denying that other people could be successful in finding out whether the statements they make about the contents of my consciousness are true and at the same time allowing that they are justified in making them. In fact, if I seriously set out to deceive someone about my feelings I should at least ensure that he is justified in holding his false belief. The second of the two principal questions has been passed by: if the behavioural criteria of a person's being in a particular mental state are satisfied, does this mean that the person is actually in that mental state? The answer seems to be no.

Malcolm, with one eye on Wittgenstein, rejects this answer. Of course, he argues, a sceptic's posture has the corollary that we can always envisage, without logical inconsistency, a case where a person feels no pain despite the satisfaction of the criteria of his being in pain. In *this* situation, Malcolm reckons, the only possible arguments impairing the judgement that a person feels pain are themselves based on a conceivable contrary state of affairs. He sees that the role of certainty, if it is to be understood at all, stops short of such a possibility. Doubts about people's feelings are intelligible insofar as they arise from questioning the adequacy of the criteria presented; but if the criteria of being in pain are satisfied further doubts simply cannot be understood in any ordinary sense. And this explains the force of Malcolm's remark that if the criteria of pain are satisfied a person *must* be in pain: we are obliged to conclude that he feels pain as an alternative to unintelligibility. If a sceptic cannot both have the concept of someone else being in pain and yet always doubt its application, as Malcolm claims, then scepticism must be incompatible with the conceptual background which makes it possible to talk of minds as we do, a consequence developed by Strawson, who sees a sceptic's conclusion as going wrong in an even more disastrous way. He believes, truly enough, that as a matter of logic we could not have the conceptual scheme we do have if it were rational to refuse to ascribe feelings of pain in the face of criteria logically adequate for their ascription. The existence of the linguistic structure in terms of which we identify and individuate persons, and in terms of which sceptical problems are stated, presupposes the irrationality of a sceptic's conclusion. Paradoxically a condition of the very formulation of scepticism is the acceptance of a conceptual scheme whose repudiation is a consequence of scepticism's being true. To hold the view that scepticism is correct *and* that it can be stated cogently is impossible; if Strawson is right, scepticism *necessarily* is either false or incomprehensible. Taken together these arguments amount to a decisive rejection of a sceptic's conclusion: sceptical doubts about other minds cannot be understood in any ordinary sense and cannot be formulated without fatally paradoxical consequences.

This victory over scepticism may well be accompanied by the reflection that perhaps it was won too easily. After all, it was clear from the start that a sceptic could not have been right. Long ago Moore remarked that 'philosophers have been able to hold sincerely as part of their philosophical creed propositions inconsistent with what they themselves *knew* to be true'. Now Moore, when faced with Russell's doubts about the external world and other people's minds took them quite literally in the way in which one would properly understand a remark like 'You've not had breakfast' said to a person who knows he has had breakfast. Obviously this remark is straightforwardly false if we understand by it what normally would be understood by such an utterance. And there is no reason in this case to understand it in any other way. Can the same be said, however, of a sceptic's doubts about other minds? Although a sceptic's words are paradoxical and false when taken literally it is open to us to ask whether they should be accepted at their face value. One main clue to how a remark should be understood is the background against which it is made, and the background to a sceptic's claim is distinctly odd (e.g. for one thing, Moore's point that it is not withdrawn in the light of facts of a kind that would lead me to say I was wrong about a person's not having had breakfast; for another, that it is sensitive only to *philosophical* argument). It is a reasonable assumption that there is something non-standard about the claim itself, that it is in a detectable way 'fishy'; and that it will not do to treat it in exactly the way we treat a preposterous but quite literal utterance.

John Wisdom has said that there is more to paradoxical doubts about other minds than the words a sceptic uses ordinarily convey. Yet apart from their being strictly false, what more could there be? Like Wittgenstein, Wisdom is interested in exposing the source of philosophical puzzlement. But the emphasis is different. For Wisdom it is less a matter of pointing to a philosophical mistake than providing a diagnosis of why the mistake was made, and in the course of this disclosing both the rights and wrongs of the argument behind the admittedly false conclusion. He does not, of course, believe that a sceptic's conclusion is in any way defensible, but views it as a distorted expression of a philosophical peculiarity which, when clearly reformulated, could not have been false. The outcome reveals a sceptic's arguments to be rather more valuable than his discredited results suggest. Consequently Wisdom insists that the chief target for scrutiny is the intricate network of reasoning propping up doubts about other minds. It would be neither necessary not profitable to rehearse the rich panorama of discussion contained in *Other Minds*, which, to be fair, at times submerges the outlines of Wisdom's own strategy. A better plan is to present the direction of his argument in a way that sets these outlines into relief. The first thing to determine is the sort of circumstances to which a sceptic's words refer.

We notice that the styles of reasoning falling under the label of scepticism vary a good deal. There are, to begin with, arguments originating from a preoccupation with the facts of mind and the probable (or possible) effects of scientific advances. For it is sometimes argued that unless, or until, the facts of mental phenomena are revealed by investigation to be other than they now appear to be, all talk of my being sure beyond doubt of how other people feel and think must be deferred. In this context of conservative scepticism there are two rival positions. The optimistic thesis is that there seems to be a genuine chance of this happening, e.g. the phenomena of telepathy might some day be confirmed, or advances in physiology and neurology may in future reveal the data of people's cerebral processes to be unimpeachable checks on their states of mind. And if this happened certainty would be within sight. On the other hand, the pessimistic variation, while agreeing that certainty would be at hand if things were different, sees no chance of a change. To say, as the optimist does, that the facts of mental life could be other than they are, is merely to say that it is not self-contradictory to envisage a more favourable state of affairs, e.g. in which telepathy is confirmed, or in which mental and brain states are discovered to be the same. Yet there is no more reasonable expectation of this happening than there is of the failure of the laws of nature. My being sure of the feelings of someone else, while not a logical impossibility, is ruled out as a consequence of the phenomena being what they are. In the view of the optimist a sceptic's conclusion is a statement which is likely to become false, and according to the pessimist it is a statement which, though at any time it might have been false, has been and always will be true.

To pin down these varieties in botanical fashion, both are representative species of the large and indefinite genus of *remediable* scepticism, whose members share the belief that the logical possibility of being absolutely sure is never closed. Yet we know from the history of philosophy that moderate views have a short life and are soon undermined. The two we have taken up are no exception. For the standard reply to their arguments is that even if the phenomena of mind were disclosed to be other than we think they are this would be insufficient to guarantee certainty.

The moderate sceptic must reckon with the objections of his hard-line colleague, the *irremediable* sceptic.

Telepathy, it will be argued, is no answer; any claim to have discovered 'telepathic phenomena' must rest on observed correlations between the avowals or actions of the people involved. Moreover a person could be confident about his own telepathic abilities only if he could distinguish between his imaginative and his genuinely telepathic experiences; yet to do this he must appeal for confirmation to the reports of the person whose mind he claims to know. And this is not relevantly different from our situation at the moment, in which the behaviour of others provides a basis for our claims about them. If, as might happen, telepathy were vindicated, we would continue to rely on the assumption that when a person says or in some other way shows that he has a particular feeling, he *does* actually have that feeling. But this is exactly the assumption at issue. As a move against scepticism telepathy begs the question.

Nor would the identification of sensations or thoughts with cerebral states take us any further towards certainty. What is supposed is that some day I will be in a position to say without any mistake whether someone else has a particular mental state, e.g. feels a pain, from observing the behaviour of (as it is said) the C-fibres in his brain; and that when this day arrives we can eliminate from language the referring use of expressions like 'I am in pain' ('He is in pain') and substitute for them expressions like 'My (his) C-fibres are firing'. The trouble here is that even if this situation were to come about it would not invalidate a sceptic's argument. In such circumstances I could tell whether the statement 'His C-fibres are firing', said of me, or 'My C-fibres are firing', said by me, is mistaken or correct in a way in which someone else could not; for in addition to the observations that he could make I can tell whether the statement applies by paying heed to, though not observing, the firing of my own C-fibres—or, as we would normally say, from the feeling I have at the time. But to allow that I can non-observationally report the firing of my own C-fibres is to allow that I can ascertain and report this particular fact by a procedure not available to others. And once this is permitted scepticism is given the premise it requires. It cannot be objected that I feel nothing when my C-fibres fire, for that would lead to the elimination of sensations; nor that my feeling is indirect evidence of their firing based on past correlations, for then my feeling and the firing of my C-fibres would not be identical; nor again that my feeling conclusively establishes the existence of my C-fibres firing, for observations of their behaviour would then become irrelevant.

What must be claimed is that statements about a person's pains accurately based on observations of his cerebral activity will always be correct. Yet this too is unsatisfactory. No doubt observations of my cerebral activity could make me withdraw a claim that my C-fibres are firing; but no such observations could lead me to withdraw the statement that I feel a pain when as a matter of fact I do. And this may happen on an occasion when observations of cerebral activity indicate that no pain is felt. The point here is not that a situation of this sort is likely to arise, but that the possibility of its occurrence remains open.[1] Moreover if I am debarred from speaking of pains and restricted to a physicalist language, as we have imagined, no observations of my cerebral activity could force me to retract the statement that *it seems to me* as if my C-fibres are firing when as a matter of fact it seems to me that they are. Once again the reason for this is that observations which give other people a right to say how I feel do not give them the authority in the matter that my own feelings give me.

Underlying this rejection of moderate scepticism is the principle that each person is in a special position with regard to the verification of claims made about his own states of mind. And this gives a hard-line sceptic the opening he needs. There is no consolation, as before, in pointing out that the facts of mind could conceivably be different, for no conceivable alteration in our experience could produce a state of affairs in which one person can tell whether someone else feels a pain in the way in which that other person can. But, according to a hard-line sceptic, exactly this would have to be achieved before we can speak with certainty about the mental states of others. The difficulty about this variety

[1] See Baier (viii), Smart (ix) and Rorty (xx), in *The Mind-Brain Identity Theory*, ed. C. V. Borst (1970). Could this case always be ruled out on the grounds that the subject does not understand the meaning of 'pain'? The identification of pains and cerebral states presupposes that the meaning of 'pain' is understood in *some* cases, e.g. those by which cerebral states gain their credentials to be connected with pains at all. Against an established correlation if there is no observational error we might decide that the subject is mistaken about the meaning, but in the process of determining that there is a correlation we cannot always say that he is mistaken. Ultimately it is a contingent matter whether we rule out a case on such grounds.

of scepticism is its irremediableness: the obstacle to certainty could not be overcome by *any* means, logical or contingent.

At this stage the arguments of Malcolm and Strawson appear as an attractive and successful defence of what we know to be true. If we assent to their arguments how much of a sceptic's paraphernalia should be discarded? Pretty clearly the first item to go is the erroneous conclusion that certainty about other people's mental states is impossible; and we must accept Strawson's point that it could not be the case that statements like 'That person heard me speak just now' or 'That person understood what I said' have no legitimate use. This commits us, at any rate, to the verdict that a sceptic's conclusion is false. But we are not thereby committed to saying the same about a sceptic's premise. Once again it is worth taking a leaf out of Moore's book. He unreservedly accepted that he knew to be true much that a sceptic claimed he could not know; yet he recognised that his position was only the opening move in the complicated game to follow, and expressed the strongest reservations about philosophical accounts of *how* he knew the statements which he did know. In this he left two options open: one could claim that a sceptic's conclusion had been correctly (or incorrectly) derived from a false premise, or that the premise is true but the conclusion does not follow. The latter is close to Wisdom's own view, and the problem is to discover what this premise is.

To what could a sceptic refer as proof of his conclusion? A correct general answer is the peculiarity that although a person's behaviour is (in principle) open to the observations of everyone a person's mind is not. Now the sort of thing to which this formula refers is, for example, this: suppose I do in fact feel a pain, or silently plan my holiday in my mind. I can be sure *on my own* that I feel pain or that I'm thinking of my holiday, without questioning or paying heed to what other people say or do. Yet if I believe for whatever reason that *you* feel a pain or are thinking of your holiday, I cannot be sure of this on my own but must notice quite a bit about your actions and circumstances. And if I can be sure of my state of mind on my own, i.e. in a way in which I cannot be sure of the states of mind of other people, I am free to suppose that other people cannot be sure of my state of mind exactly in the way I can. Or I am free to reflect that if I believe that you are thinking of your holiday then your thoughts (whatever

P

they are) give you a better reason to confirm or reject my belief than any thoughts of mine could give to me. These appear to be facts about mind that are correct no matter what happens. Noticing this a sceptic will argue that if they were *not* correct then one person could perform the impossible by judging a statement about another person's mind in all the ways that other person can.

Wisdom has argued that if there is something in this claim that misleads there is also something true. But what could this be? The claim suggests, and is intended to suggest, that I am at a disadvantage or in some way handicapped in my assessments of other people's minds. This seems odd because the disadvantage here is not like the disadvantage of being in a place too far away to hear someone speak but more like the handicap which prevents a person from being in two places at once, an event whose occurrence is inconceivable. What has happened, Wisdom diagnoses, is not only that the category of 'facts' is being modified by a sceptic to include logical truths but also logical truths disguised in such a way that their admission seems plausible. In short, a conceptual property characteristic of the procedure for verifying a particular class of statements has been presented as some sort of contingent impossibility. In his premise a sceptic is disclosed as assuming it to be *necessarily true* that other people are not in the same position as myself when it comes to verifying statements about my state of mind; and that, accordingly, if I can be sure about another person's state of mind I cannot, at any rate, be sure of this in the way in which that other person can. And this expresses the principle that statements about mind have an asymmetrical logic.

Should this principle be accepted? Wisdom answers: 'The asymmetrical logic of statements about the mind is a feature of them without which they would not be statements about the mind, and that they have this feature is no more a subject suitable for regret than the fact that lines if truly parallel don't meet.'[1] If Wisdom is right the principle of asymmetry must be acknowledged if discourse about mind is to be possible at all. And surely this is the case. If this principle did not obtain the referring use of expressions about mind could not be understood, since no distinction could be drawn between references to minds and references to behaviour; and if this were so we would be deprived of a

---

[1] 'A Feature of Wittgenstein's Technique,' *PAS* supp. vol. 1961, p. 10; see also 'Symposium: Other Minds' in *Other Minds*.

class of expressions necessary to the conceptual scheme in terms of which we describe other people and ourselves. An example will help here. Imagine that a drug has been discovered which temporarily alters a person's colour vision. In an experiment a person is shown a chart containing some coloured patterns. He first studies the chart; after being given the drug he looks at it again and is asked whether he notices any difference, and he says he does. Now if someone conducting this experiment comes and tells me that the subject noticed a difference after being given the drug, what can I understand him to mean? Not that he noticed a difference in the chart, for there was none. Not that there was a difference in the subject's behaviour, for there was none apart from his saying that he noticed a difference. Nor can it mean only that the subject said that he noticed a difference, for in the absence of any difference in the chart what the subject said would be unintelligible—unless I allow that the subject *could* notice a difference even if no one else can. And to acknowledge this is to assent to his special position. In order to make any sense at all of what I have been told I must allow that the subject is in a position to report a difference in a way in which it could not be reported by other people.

What emerges is that the final line of demarcation between statements about behaviour or physical circumstances and statements about mind is drawn by our presupposing an asymmetry in the latter though not in the former case. If I predict that a person who is in pain will feel differently after having an anaesthetic no doubt both of us will look forward to changes in his feelings and behaviour. But we do not, obviously, look forward to these events in quite the same way: I should expect *for* him a change in his feelings, whereas he would expect this *for himself*. Although I may be in a position to judge whether my prediction has been fulfilled from his subsequent behaviour, it would be logically incoherent of me to expect for myself the experiences he antici-pates; and it is these which give him a right to say whether my prediction is true. This is not to conclude that I have no right to judge, but only that I cannot confirm my prediction about a change in his feeling in all of the ways open to him.; my judgement, unlike his, is necessarily limited to an observational basis. Indeed to say that a statement about mind has an asymmetry in its veri-fication is to say in part that it is ascribable both on the basis of observation and not on this basis and that both ways are perfectly in order, as Strawson has claimed. What is ruled out is the idea that only one of these ways will do.

If we accept the principle of asymmetry to what are we committed as a consequence? It might be objected that the principle is unacceptable because it inevitably leads to scepticism and that this is too great a price to pay. The answer is that no such conclusion follows. By combining the results of Wisdom's discussions with those of Malcolm and Strawson we are in a position to see that this answer could not have been wrong. A sceptic's premise that a person cannot judge the mental states of someone else in all the ways the latter can is necessarily true; and in our conceptual scheme a sceptic's conclusion that the concept of certainty could not apply to judgements that a person makes about the minds of others necessarily is false. Therefore *necessarily* the derivation of a sceptic's conclusion from his premise is mistaken. And this discloses not only why scepticism about other minds cannot be correct, a conviction substantiated by Malcolm and Strawson, but also the justification for Wisdom's insistence that what a sceptic *means* is right.

Yet more than loose ends remain. If *knowledge* of statements about other minds is possible we are obliged to agree that one person is in a logically special position with regard to the truth of the statements said to be known. And this, perhaps, is a cause for some misgivings: would not the final court of appeal be the avowals of the person himself, which could be untruthful reports on which we have no further check? One way to answer this question is to adopt a sceptic's strategy of recommending that the ordinary use of 'know' be restricted in the interests of strict accuracy to a person's knowledge of his own mind, in the belief that a person who (e.g.) feels a pain could have no conclusive reason to doubt the truth of the statement that he does. Wisdom sees a sceptic as holding up knowledge of one's own mind as a paradigm for knowledge of the minds of others and then pointing out the consequence that the latter is impossible; a sceptic would, as we noted, persuade us to adjust our usage and call only this impossible sort of knowledge 'real knowledge of the mind of another'. Pretty clearly this reversion to scepticism is drastically wrong; for one thing, what makes our normal and unmodified usage of the word 'all right as it is', as Wittgenstein said, is simply the fact of its being normal.

Yet there is a grain of truth in this misdirected recommendation. As before, it is worth paying heed to Wisdom's warning that in a sceptic's most perversely mistaken moments he is apt to be driving at something illuminating and important. A close look reveals this recommendation to be a caricature of the adjustments we make as a matter of course in the changing contexts of our ordinary talk about minds. If asked what a particular person thinks or feels, in some contexts *nothing* could bring me to say I know, or am certain, about the answer; and I would have no qualms in saying *only that person* could know. To start with an artificial but polar case, suppose I ask you to think of a number between one and seven and guess that you are thinking of seven. You reply that you are thinking of five. How firmly do I stand corrected? I expect you to tell the truth and believe you are. Yet there is something troublesome about the whole affair. If you questioned me in the same sort of way then while I probably would answer truthfully, temptation being what it is I might not; and if I succumbed to temptation I could be certain that you do not know the number I actually picked. The peculiarity here is that the two situations are similar and in the latter case *I know you don't know*. How, then, when the situation is reversed, can I do more than accept what you say and leave it at that without claiming that I know?

In refusing to go too far I acknowledge rather than modify or alter the ground rules and conventions of ordinary talk. We are not, commonly, prepared to take a stand about being certain of the thoughts and feelings of others when fortified by the knowledge that in a parallel situation others cannot be certain of our own. Should I comment on the salty taste of the soup you have just warmed up and you, tasting it, say you cannot taste a trace of salt, I could not convincingly say either that I know you are fibbing or that I know you are right. I am certain of the fact that it tastes salty to me but you, perhaps, are not; beyond giving my word, or showing that there is no motive for me to fib and in general encouraging you to be confident about my statement, I can do little or nothing to show you that what I say is true. And if you accept what I say, although I may know that you are right, had I been disingenuous, and successful in my attempt to persuade, I could have known that you were wrong. Realizing this, in accepting *your* statement about not tasting the salt I simply take it to be true, to be said in good faith and so on, if there are no apparent reasons to the contrary. More than this is not expected: in such contexts the normal traffic of conversational business runs smoothly only on the understanding that questions of certainty beyond acceptance in good faith do not arise as ordinary issues. It is not always appropriate to state either that one knows, or that one does not.

This caution which comes from realizing that in comparable contexts sometimes other people cannot be sure of one's own feelings and thoughts is an adjustment peculiar to discussions about mind. It might be objected that we make similar adjustments when we are not talking of minds: the fact that other and better informed people do not know of a cure for the common cold, or why my roof persists in leaking, will make me cautious about saying that I do. Yet by assiduous effort I might, or could in principle, place myself in a position to know. And this is just what cannot be done in the cases above: no effort in turning up further facts and no reflection on those already turned up could put me in a position to be certain. To state the obvious: sometimes a person cannot convincingly speak of knowing, of being absolutely sure about, what another person is thinking or feeling, and *not* because he lacks any information which he conceivably could have.

If this sounds like scepticism in a new disguise notice that it is not the whole or even the larger part of the story. For it is clear to everyone that sometimes one *is* absolutely sure. Imagine a child who wakes in the morning with toothache.[1] His cheek is inflamed and he complains of the pain; however on being told that he will be taken to the dentist there is an immediate change in his attitude and he now says he is perfectly well and that the pain has gone. We know that the child fears a visit to the dentist from the scenes he made last time and that he complained of the pain up to the moment of being told where he would be taken. There is no question that we are right in overriding his avowal, seeing through his disguise and saying we know it still hurts. How, in these circumstances, could it make sense to say that one does *not* know? Cases going in this direction are easily multiplied. I can be *sure* that you (e.g.) do not like the tie I gave to you even though you

---

[1] I believe this valuable example comes from Renford Bambrough.

politely say you do: you never wore it, you gave it to the dustman. I can be sure that you would not have missed this important engagement unless you really did feel rotten; or that your having a headache was a convenient fiction for missing that other one. I can be sure of your discomfort if you tell me that eating those apples made you sick, and you *are* sick. People are, after all, capable of paying close attention to avowals and actions and to inconsistences between them, to motives for concealing and revealing feelings and to what can and cannot be brought off in the way of the display or concealment of one's emotions. If there are cases where one cannot know there are plenty of cases where one can.

These too are peculiar. When a person judges how I feel, often I can be sure not only that he is right but also that he knows he is right, and if I have attempted a disguise, that my defences have been breached. Generally, though not of course always, I can be sure that *you* know my state at the moment, e.g. if you commiserate after I have just misaimed and bruised my thumb with a hammer. Now if, as frequently happens, I come across someone else in circumstances like those in which I have had, or would have had, no doubt that other people are sure of how I feel (or have successfully penetrated my disguise), then if there is nothing in the circumstances adverse to my judgement I will not hesitate to say that I know how, or what, that person feels. Unlike the cases we took earlier, I recognize from my own position in comparable situations that the possibility of my being certain remains open and convincing, and that a special excuse, for which no evidence is forthcoming, would be needed to make a more guarded opinion at all plausible.

For obvious reasons I cannot be sure of another person's feelings, to take a sceptic's premise, *in the way he can*; but pretty evidently this does not imply (and would not normally suggest) that I cannot be sure at all. There is, to repeat Strawson's point, more than one way of being sure. 'Real' knowledge of the mind of another person is not peculiar in that it becomes unattainable as soon as a person is in a position to claim it, as Wisdom's sceptic would argue; but peculiar in that although there is only one way of being sure open to me, e.g. what Strawson has loosely noted as 'observation of the subject', *sometimes* I cannot know in that way *no matter what I do.* And this is the feature of which a sceptic's recommendation is a disastrous caricature.

We have noted that the kind of cautionary adjustments normally anticipated in this sort of context are abandoned in contexts where caution would itself be suspect. And these are contexts in which I can say 'I know' and be right. In such cases my claim to know (for example, that a person had a painful feeling when the hammer struck his thumb) is perfectly in order given (a) that there is nothing untoward about the circumstances and (b) the fact that I keep within the bounds of normal linguistic practice. There are said to be snags here, of course. It cannot be true that I know that someone else feels pain when he does not: he might previously have been given an anaesthetic, there might be something unusual about his nervous system, he might be pretending, and so on, all pointing to the truth that no matter how much I know about him I never know all there is to know that could bear on my claim. I never, in Wisdom's words, 'know the endless pattern of it all'. And this *is* fatal to my knowing what he feels, but only if there is a cogent case for a sceptic's alterations to our usage of 'know'. The answer remains that there is not. A sceptic, according to Wisdom, 'misdescribes our usage of "know" and misdescribes it in a self-contradictory way' by demanding that when I say 'I know' it is at least necessary that I am in a position to know in a way not open to me and that I must command an infinite amount of information. Now, to put one's feet on the ground of normal operations, this stipulation bears little resemblance to what I *am* committed to when I say 'I know', namely that I must be in a position to know *in the way I can*, by observation of the subject; that what I know must be the case, have really happened or actually be going on, and that I must be able to tell that I am right about these events. We have discussed, and found empty, the objection that I cannot tell that I am right unless I could report these events in the way in which I can report experiences of my own. But what of the objection that I cannot tell whether I am right because a mistake is always, even if remotely, possible?

This last ditch protest does not go very far. Undoubtedly there are *some* things that may enter my calculations as real possibilities of error (e.g. Was he too drunk to feel the blow?) and if I cannot eliminate them I cannot know. On most occasions no such real possibilities arise; yet there remain enormous numbers of questions with potentially adverse answers which, in the light of the particular circumstances, do not make the grade even as conjectural reasons for doubt (e.g. Has he been hypnotized? Or even, is he pretending?) although I freely admit that their happening is logically possible. It is these to which this objection points with the claim that irrespective of the circumstances of the case it is not logically inconsistent to say that my judgement is false. And this is impossible to deny: but once again a platitude has been given as a reason for a conclusion it fails to support. However much we strain its implications this truism does not have the consequence that my judgements are, or may be, mistaken, but merely that my judgements about other people's minds are not necessarily true. It is safe to say that no one ever thought they were.

We are likely, at this stage, to come round full circle and resurrect the initial obstacle by reflecting that what this last objection means is not that my judgements about the feelings of other people lack logical necessity but that they do not necessarily follow from the reasons I could have for making them. By now it is painlessly evident that they do not; and that the absence of a demonstrative connection is one factor in favour of characterizing the relationship here as one of 'logical adequacy' or of talking in terms of the connection's being 'conceptual'. In spite of its penumbra of obscurity this characterization is not far off the mark. Suppose that S is 'He winced when the hammer struck his thumb' and P is 'He felt the blow'. We ask whether S entails P, on which a good deal appears to depend; and prepared with the question 'Is it self-contradictory to assert S and deny P?' cast one eye on the possibility of pretence (etc.) justifying a negative answer, in turn preparing the way for a causal account of the relation. Yet a look at what actually happens in contexts where statements like these are made shows how artificial this exercise is. A person who says 'He winced so he felt the blow' need not for a moment suppose that S entails P, or that S is a causal sign of P; but that, given S, if no cogent excuse can be found for hesitating about P, it is *completely unreasonable* not to affirm P straight away; the question of whether there is an entailment or a causal inference in this case simply does not arise. Three (true) things can be said: first, in the circumstances P is the most rational and accurate judgement one could make, irrespective of the relation between S and P; second, it follows that even if the relationship between S and P were a standard one, its being standard would not be the reason for P's being rational and accurate; and third, to reject P on the (sole) grounds of the relation's being non-standard would be a clear mistake. The trouble starts when, forearmed with the conviction that the relationship should be approached and dealt with in terms of the standard operators of entailment or causal inference, we find that neither fits, and that there is no technical idiom tailored to meet the situation. Our reaction should be to describe *what we find*; this may mean setting aside the traditional thesis that there is involved in all such cases a procedure of inferring from some (outer) state of affairs to some (inner) state of mind; and that our practice is rather more analogous to that of deciding about the facts, say, in a court of law. Suppose that an employer failed to attach the usual guard to a machine and in consequence a workman was injured. Knowing the circumstances we ask, does this amount to, is this a case of, negligence? Our 'evidence' is wider than merely the particular facts presented in court; for in deciding the question we view these facts against a background of comparable situations providing a picture of what negligent actions are like; thus equipped we decide whether, or how, the case in question fits into the structure of negligent behaviour. In this a verdict of negligence is not *entailed* by anything at all; and to take the circumstances as a *causal sign* of negligence would be incoherent. The lesson here is that the presence of these relationships is not a standing requirement for the making of correct decisions. If this analogy is sound we can with a clear conscience describe the connections between S and P as being neither necessary nor contingent. Presumably any argument impairing P would have to be more certain than the judgement it claims to defeat; and the lack of a standard connection in this case is not (could not be) such an argument.

Yet the effectiveness of discarding the standard models in favour of a non-necessary conceptual relationship may seem greater than it is. Initially the idea was posed as the centrepiece of a general answer to the problem of other minds which, in turn, was disclosed to have a complexity rendering this strategy not wrong but inadequate. For the grounds of scepticism include not only the premise that judgements about mind are not deductive or inductive consequences of judgements about actions and their circumstances, but also the logically richer premise that judgements about mind have an asymmetrical logic and the latter do not. To provide an answer compatible with both the first premise and common sense, as Malcolm and Strawson pretty much do, is to have won a battle but not the war. For this does not explain why statements about mind provoke a sort of scepticism different from that suggested by the first premise, and why the asymmetrical logic of statements about mind which promotes that scepticism could not impair our knowledge of them. 'Unless we understand this,' Wisdom remarks, 'we cannot understand why people have so persistently clung to the model for the logic of the soul which gives rise to scepticism not only about the mental acts of others but also about their aches and pains, feelings of quickened heart beats, sensations as of voices, daggers, snakes.'[1]

[1] 'The Concept of Mind', *Other Minds*, p. 237.

X

THE RELEVANCE OF WISDOM'S WORK FOR THE PHILOSOPHY OF SCIENCE: A STUDY OF THE CONCEPT OF SCIENTIFIC EXPLANATION*

ARDON LYON

This was not what Mr. Bulstrode said to any man for the sake of deceiving him: it was what he said to himself—it was as genuinely his mode of explaining events as any theory of yours may be, if you happened to disagree with him. For the egoism which enters into our theories does not affect their sincerity; rather, the more our egoism is satisfied, the more robust is our belief.

GEORGE ELIOT: *Middlemarch*.

M Y AIM is to show how certain aspects of Wisdom's work can help us with problems in the philosophy of science. I first describe some of the relevant aspects of Wisdom's work, and then attempt to apply his insights to the much discussed question of the nature of scientific explanation.

I. *Wisdom's Philosophy*

One source of philosophical confusion, according to Wisdom, has been the view that 'there is knowledge of each thing only when we know its essence'[1] and that the essence of any thing X is given by producing a definition of 'X' in terms of a conjunctive-disjunctive relationship between characteristics A, B, C, . . . etc.:[2] or again the view that if C is neither a necessary nor a sufficient condition of X, then it follows that it is not necessarily connected with X.[3] Wisdom points out that a characteristic X can be related *a priori* with a characteristic C without the presence of either entailing the presence of the other. This insight gives rise to an

* I am extremely grateful to Renford Bambrough, Joan Ganz, David Hirschmann, Imre Lakatos and Stina Lyon for reading earlier versions of this paper and for providing many helpful criticisms and suggestions.
[1] Aristotle, *Metaphysics*, 1031b7, tr. W. D. Ross. From W. D. Ross (ed.), *The Works of Aristotle*, Vol. VIII, Oxford at the Clarendon Press, 2nd edition, 1928.

[2] See A. J. T. D. Wisdom, 'Metaphysics and Verification', *Mind*, Vol. XLVII, N.S. No. 188, 1938. Reprinted in *Philosophy and Psycho-Analysis*, Basil Blackwell, Oxford, 1953: see especially p. 82.

[3] See A. J. T. D. Wisdom, 'Other Minds IV', *Mind*, Vol. L, N.S. No. 199, 1941. Reprinted in *Other Minds*, Basil Blackwell, Oxford, 1952: see especially p. 107.

account of 'meaning' which incorporates an improved version of what Wittgenstein had to say about 'criteria'.[1]

The second aspect of Wisdom's work that I want to consider will have to be described in rather more detail. It concerns some of the things he has said about the nature of philosophical problems in general. I shall illustrate these by referring to a central philosophical puzzle that will turn out to be relevant to our discussion of scientific explanation—the problem of scepticism. A radical sceptic may claim that there can be no such thing as knowledge. A milder sceptic may claim that knowledge about some particular class of entities is impossible: he will contrast unfavourably some feature or features of those things he claims we cannot know, with some feature or features of those things he claims we can know: for example other minds compared with material bodies, material bodies compared with sense-data or Forms, laws of nature compared with particular statements, or contingent statements compared with necessary statements. Various philosophers try to combat these more or less paradoxical sceptical conclusions, by claiming for example that they are disproved by common sense, or by ordinary language, or even that they are examples of meaningless, nonsensical metaphysics. Wisdom has never been seduced into such views.

According to Wisdom, most metaphysical claims, if taken at face value, are simply false. But they are more interesting if not taken at face value. In that case, they use certain expressions in other-than-ordinary ways, and so may come to express tautologies.[2] But these tautologies are not empty or idle tautologies.

---

[1] I have tried to deal with some problems which arise from this account of meaning, and to indicate some earlier versions of the thesis, particularly in Dugald Stewart, in two articles: 'Criteria and Meaning', *Studium Generale* 22 (1969), pp. 401–426, and 'Family Resemblance, Vagueness, and Change of Meaning', *Theoria* 34 (1968 Part I), pp. 66–75.

[2] Wittgenstein also sometimes said this. But even as late as in the *Investigations* he sometimes puts forward the view that they were meaningless, or that other-than-ordinary uses must be misuses, or both. For example, of the sentence 'Only I can know whether I am in pain', he wrote: 'In one way this is false, and in another *nonsense*. If we are using the word 'to know' as it is normally used (and how else are we to use it?), then other people very often know when I am in pain' (my italics); *Philosophical Investigations*, Basil Blackwell, Oxford, 1953, § 246. Renford Bambrough has brought to my attention a similar but even later passage on p. 221e of the *Investigations*: this was not written until after 1946, when Wisdom wrote "We can't know the weight of thistledown" [may express] an eternal truth—because it's a tautology in that natural development of ordinary language to which we are encouraged in its proof'—*Other Minds*, p. 218. See also ib. p. 208 for various interpretations of 'We cannot know . . .' statements.

They embody various conceptual revisions, and conceptual revision can be desirable or undesirable or even both, since in conceptual revision something is lost and something is gained. Suppose a sceptic says that we cannot know whether any propositions about material objects are true, on the ground that any particular proposition p we assert, being contingent, may conceivably turn out to be false. His conclusion does not follow logically from what has been said, without the premise 'We cannot know the truth of any statement that might conceivably turn out to be false'. If he is using the word 'know' in its ordinary sense, then both this premise, and his conclusion about material objects, are false, since we do not ordinarily use the word 'know' in such a way that we can never know the truth of any statements that might conceivably be false, or the falsehood of any statements that might conceivably be true. But his claim can be interpreted as embodying a recommendation to use the word 'know' in this unusual, eccentric way.

A sceptic may well be unclear, when he says 'We cannot know that p', whether he is intending to make an *a priori* or an empirical claim. But what he says may well come to express a necessary truth because of the way he uses the word 'know': at first he may suggest that we would have knowledge of material objects if we had, say, some sense-faculty which we unfortunately lack; later he may say that nothing actual or conceivable would *for him count as* 'knowing that some statement about material objects is true'. It will then be impossible to 'know' the truth of such statements, come what may. His recommendation is not *just* a linguistic recommendation, since it is produced with a purpose and a point: it reminds us how different are the verification procedures relevant for ascertaining the truth or otherwise of claims about the material world (or about other minds, or about laws of nature, etc.) from those relevant for ascertaining the truth of claims about our sensations, or about numbers. Similarly, the radical sceptic says that knowledge is impossible, and this claim, which looks on the surface like an extraordinary insight or an extraordinary blunder about what we can as a matter of fact know, may come to express a necessary truth because of the way he uses the word 'know'. Wisdom has taught us that it is a mistake then to try to *combat* this claim, as many philosophers do, by attempting to show that it is false: for it simply is not false. Neither is there much point, usually, in the 'ordinary language' philosophers' blanket accusation that the metaphysician is misusing language: he uses it abnormally, as do the scientist and the poet, and we have to look at individual cases in order to find out, in each case, whether or not this is a good idea.

It is not quite correct to say that the sceptic *produces* a good or bad linguistic recommendation, or that he *recommends* conceptual revision, for he does not (normally) say, for example: 'Let us use the word "know" in such a way that there can be "knowledge" only about that about which it is impossible to be mistaken.' He simply goes ahead and (sometimes!) uses the word 'know' in that way: he makes statements which can express necessary truths because of the conceptual revision which he effects upon the word 'know' and its cognates. One of the advantages of the radical revision, which entails that the set of things which are 'known' is necessarily empty, is that it reminds us that there is no conceivable knowledge claim about which it is absolutely pointless to entertain some doubt at some time or other, even though it may usually be impractical and pointless to do so. One of the disadvantages of the conceptual revision practised by moderate and radical sceptics alike is that it fails to make the useful distinction between 'knowledge' and 'belief' in the ordinary senses of these words which we ordinarily and with some purpose do make; the distinction between, for example, 'I know that the population of England is greater than the population of Sweden' and 'I believe that the population of London is greater than the population of Sweden'.

Conceptual revisions cannot be right or wrong, true or false: they can only be more or less illuminating or misleading, better or worse for various purposes. No doubt for most purposes the disadavntages of the sceptic's revisions outweigh the advantages. And indeed sceptics, in common with other metaphysicians, often fail to realize that what they are doing—when looked at in the most sympathetic light possible—is something which embodies conceptual revision. They think they are using words in the old ways: after all, if they were *simply* using words in a new way, then there would be nothing to get steamed up about. As one might put it: if by 'knowledge' they do not mean *knowledge*, then there is nothing very exciting about telling us that there is no such thing. The answer to this is that they use the word 'knowledge' in a new

but not in a completely new way. The sceptic, who may think—
if he thinks about the matter at all—that he is using the term
'knowledge' in the old way, produces arguments to show that we
cannot have 'knowledge'; but then each of his arguments must be
either invalid or resting on at least one false premise. However, at
various stages of his argument he tends to use the term 'knowledge' in a more and more restricted sense. Such arguments do
indeed show that we cannot have knowledge in his new sense; and
there are features about the concept of knowledge which per-
petually tempt us to restrict its application in one way or another.
Unfortunately, many philosophers, not understanding what has
been happening, try to show that the sceptic's conclusion, using
his new terminology, is false, when in fact it expresses a necessary
truth.

As an example of a philosophy which denies the sceptic's
conclusion, let us take phenomenalism. The moderate sceptic
may point out that the evidence we have for the existence of
material objects comes to us in terms of either (a) appearances, or
(b) sensations.[1] It is a necessary truth that statements in terms of
the evidence (E-statements) do not entail the conclusions (C-
statements) which they are normally taken to support. In order to
block the sceptic's conclusion which he draws from this necessary
truth—namely, the conclusion that we cannot have knowledge
about C-statements—Berkeley and the phenomenalists wrongly
deny the necessary truth, when what they ought to do is to question
the advisability of contracting the term 'knowledge' so that we can
only 'know' the truth of statements which are entailed by indubitable statements—especially since the E-statements are anyway not
indubitable! But although Berkeley and the phenomenalists are
wrong, it does not follow that their work is valueless, since it
reminds us that there does not exist any other sort of evidence for
our conclusions about material objects.

There are many examples of philosophical claims which seem
absurd until looked at in this light, along with the theories which
are put forward to counter these claims; and so in philosophy one
tends to be pulled first one way and then another, never being
satisfied that any theory is correct, unless one happens to have

[1] We need not go into the question whether these come to the same thing, or
into why such a sceptic probably thinks, quite wrongly, that we cannot be
mistaken in our knowledge-claims about how things appear to us, or about our
own sensations.

overlooked a mistake in the argument put forward by its protagon-
ist. This at least partly explains why so many philosophical
problems tend to seem insoluble. Going through the pros and
cons of particular cases, one comes to see, not which theories are
right and which wrong, but what is to be said for and against the
various protagonists' ways of looking at things. This has been
done with unsurpassed brilliance by Wisdom in his series 'Other
Minds'. If read with intelligent sympathy, this work supremely
achieves the aim of helping us to reach that degree of understanding whereby

> . . . the metaphysical paradoxes appear no longer as crude
> falsehoods about how language is actually used, but as
> penetrating suggestions as to how it might be used so as to
> reveal what, by the actual use of language, is hidden. And
> metaphysical platitudes appear as timely reminders of what is
> revealed by the actual use of language and would be hidden
> by the new. . . . As we all know but won't remember, any
> classificatory system is a net spread on the blessed manifold
> of the individual and blinding us not to all but to too many
> of its varieties and continuities. A new system will do the
> same but not in just the same ways.[1]

II. *A Metaphysical Problem in the Philosophy of Science: The
    Nature of Scientific Explanation*

Let us now see whether Wisdom's approach can be applied to
a topic within the philosophy of science. Scientists often attempt
to explain why things behave in the way they do, and very often
they succeed in this project. Aided and abetted by philosophers of
science, they then sometimes attempt to say what scientific
explanation consists of. This certainly seems reasonable: if we
don't know what scientific explanation is, then we are liable to get
into a muddle if we try to produce examples of it, and it is indeed
sometimes claimed that a whole class of enterprises that are
thought by some people to provide scientific explanations, for
example within psychology, necessarily fail to do so. Thus

---

[1] *Philosophy and Psycho-Analysis*, pp. 100–101 and 119. I have here pointed
out that metaphysical statements are not exactly 'suggestions as to how [language]
might be used': they are (interpretable as) necessary truths which *embody*
suggestions as to how it might be used. In his later work Wisdom has suggested
that we now have to counterbalance the earlier (penetrating but false) claim that
metaphysical statements are 'really' verbal recommendations.

Q

perhaps we require a definition of the term 'scientific explanation'.

If two people disagree about whether something is a scientific explanation, it may be that they both use the term 'scientific explanation' in the same way, and disagree about whether the case under consideration has the features required in order for it to be an instance of the agreed term 'scientific explanation'. On the other hand, they may disagree about what is required for something to be a 'scientific explanation', and this *may* be because they use the term in different ways. Just as some philosophers contract the usage of the term 'knowledge' compared with the way it is used by other philosophers, or by men in the street, so we can see the same phenomenon at work in the philosophy of science. Now we should stop and ask: if X uses the phrase 'scientific explanation' in one way and Y uses it in another, is one of them just wrong, or what? Surely, we might think, what some people regard as scientific explanations simply are *not* scientific explanations, and this can and sometimes does lead to bad science, or to non-science masquerading as science.

Some philosophers and scientists just go on seeking a definition of 'scientific explanation' without in the least stopping to ask what they are doing. But those who are more cautious may pause and consider the matter. In the editor's introduction to a recent book of readings in the philosophy of science we find the following:

> . . . the dominant conception of the nature of philosophy in the English-speaking world [is that] philosophical problems are not empirical . . . [But] the analytical philosopher has to seek actual material on which to reflect. . . Let me give an example from the philosophy of science of (implicit) reliance on psychological or sociological phenomena. . . .[1]

There follows a quotation from Braithwaite's *Scientific Explanation*, concerning what it is for a generalization to be a law of nature. Certainly Braithwaite's claim, that a true generalization is not to be regarded as a law if it is based merely on direct evidence, but only if it has also been deduced from a wider or higher-level well supported generalization, is itself extremely odd. But what is relevant here is that Nidditch goes on to ask how such an account could be justified otherwise than by an alleged consensus?

[1] P. H. Nidditch (ed.): *The Philosophy of Science*, Oxford University Press, 1968, pp. 5 and 6.

> ... Once it is granted that the philosopher's data are empiric-
> ally accessible, it looks as if the status of the philosophical
> theories about them must be not quite non-empirical. ... [1]

The 'data' of the philosopher that Nidditch has in mind are
presumably (a) those things normally spoken of by scientists as
'laws', and (b) the views of scientists concerning what it is for
something to be, for example, a law of nature—for only this latter
could account for his reference to 'psychological and sociological
phenomena'. Now should we consider all scientists (a 'consensus'),
or only the best ones? But how are we to ascertain who are the
best ones, or whether for example psychoanalysts are scientists?
When one considers the views that various philosophers have put
forward about scientific concepts, it is quite clear that usually they
have not been carrying out a programme of the sort Nidditch
envisages. Although Braithwaite writes as though he is executing
naturalistic reportage, saying, for example, that 'this corresponds
to the way in which, generally speaking, we use the notion of
natural law',[2] if one were to interpret what he is doing in that
light, it would hardly merit serious consideration. For the example
Braithwaite examines is the generalization 'All men are mortal';
and it is surely true that hardly any scientist would consider this
to be a law of nature, no matter how it was established. Braithwaite's views are only worth considering when interpreted as an
account of what scientists and others *ought* to consider to be laws
of nature, explanations, etc., from the point of view of empiricist
philosophy: in the case of laws because he has the typical empiricist's horror of counterfactuals. One can attack Braithwaite's theories
by attacking their empiricist basis. Alternatively, and more
feebly, one can attempt to counter his conceptual revisionism by
pointing out what various scientists do consider to be cases of
natural laws or of scientific explanations, etc.; but this pointing
out is in general worth not much more or less than the parallel
case of pointing out what in accordance with ordinary language
are considered to be cases of knowledge or of free will, etc., when
faced with revisionary metaphysics about those concepts. Let us
therefore now consider the arguments that have been produced in

[1] *Ib.* p. 6.
[2] R. B. Braithwaite, *Scientific Explanation*, Cambridge University Press,
1953, p. 302.

support of some famous views about the nature of scientific explanation.

1. *Duhem—A Case of Moderate Scepticism*

I call Duhem a moderate sceptic because although he thinks there are cases of explanation, he does not think there can be cases of *scientific explanation* by appeal to physical theory. This should be compared with the moderate sceptic who thinks there can be cases of knowledge, but always of necessary, never of contingent truths. On the first page of *The Aim and Structure of Physical Theory* we are told that

> To explain (explicate, *explicare*) is to strip reality of the appearances covering it like a veil, in order to see the bare reality itself.[1]

No argument is provided to persuade us that this is what explanation always consists of: we just have to take it or leave it. We are then told that the theories of physics never do inform us about 'the bare reality itself', and thus they never explain. Unfortunately at no point in his book are the reasons shortly and simply stated as to why physical theories do not give us information about 'the bare realities'; but it is clear enough why Duhem thinks that this is so. He produces many examples of theories about the nature of atoms, fields, etc., which have later had to be given up. What his argument comes to is that since we can never verify that our theories indubitably do describe 'the bare realities', and since very often mechanical models are produced which the authors do not even intend us to consider as descriptive of an underlying reality but only as 'aids to thought', it follows that it is a mistake to think that such theories ever describe the underlying realities: according to Duhem, what they do is to 'summarize and classify the laws of observation'.[2]

But of course what is said to follow quite obviously does not follow, any more than from the fact that some of our claims to knowledge are false, it follows that all of them are. From the fact that the simple kinetic theory of gases entails Boyle's Law and various other statements which very roughly describe the behaviour

---

[1] Pierre Duhem, *The Aim and Structure of Physical Theory*, tr. Philip P. Wiener, Princeton University Press, Princeton, 1954, p. 7.
[2] *Ib.* p. 277. From an appendix, 'Physics of a Believer'.

of gases, it follows, surely, that it is reasonable to think that gases do consist of anyway *something* *like* extremely tiny extremely elastic particles. From the fact that a modified kinetic theory entails Van der Waal's equation, which more accurately describes the behaviour of gases, it follows that it is reasonable to think that gases consist of particles which, for example, take up some space. We now know that molecules are not particles, but what we think they are like makes it comprehensible that they should behave like particles. The kinetic theory, as indeed any theory, does not tell us for certain what they are like, but it tells us what they may well be like; and from the fact that we cannot be sure that it does approximately describe the 'underlying realities', it certainly does not follow that we can be sure it does not. From the fact that chemists incorrectly posited the existence of phlogiston and physicists incorrectly posited the existence of the aether, etc., it does not follow that we never have any reason whatsoever to believe that *any* theories are right in positing the existence of the entities which at face value they purport to describe.

Duhem thought that there are analogies between different scientific theories not because they describe underlying realities having similar structures, but because we tend to create 'artificial constructions' (p. 277) which classify things in such a way that they may provide 'useful instruments of research' (p. 101). But he remained unhappy about this account, mainly because it is difficult to see how a mere classification of phenomena can lead us to make predictions which we can test by experiment. If the predictions are correct, surely this is the most amazing luck, on his view? And if they are incorrect, why should we mind? We can just eliminate the predicted phenomena from our classification; that is, restrict the scope of the theory in a purely conventionalist manner. Reflection on this fact leads Duhem away from his tendency towards purely conventionalist positivism, and into saying that some classifications are more 'natural', less 'artificial' than others. One would think that, from Duhem's point of view, this must be a distinction within the realm of human psychology: but no—apparently the more natural classifications are those which provide 'an increasingly clearer reflection of realities which experimental method cannot contemplate directly' (p. 270). But if we can get increasingly clear reflections of realities —and how, on Duhem's view, could we have any reason to think this was happening?—then some of our 'reflections' might presumably be absolutely clear and correct, even if we can never be absolutely certain which. Still Duhem would perhaps not call such theories explanations, presumably because they do not and cannot provide what his definition of 'explanation' requires, namely, that we should *see* the bare reality itself: for 'the objects which are the source of this reflection escape visibility' (p. 104).

What can one say about a man who claims that every physical theory which has been thought to provide an explanation necessarily fails to do so? It is not just that such theories have so far *in fact* failed, but that, according to his definition, they could not but fail. If we point out that his definition of 'explanation' does not cover what are ordinarily thought of by scientists as 'explanations', this does not trouble him, since he thinks that scientists are simply mistaken about this matter. If Duhem is thought of as giving an account of normal scientific usage of the word 'explanation' then of course he is wrong; but presumably he would reckon he is providing us with a clearer insight into the nature of explanation than that provided by the normal working scientist: he thinks he is telling us what explanation *really is*, from which it follows that physical theories do not provide explanations, but classifications and descriptions. But—to put the matter rather misleadingly— explanations do not simply exist independently of our concept of *explanation*. Different usages of the term 'explanation' by different people will imply that different things are rightly called 'explanations' in accordance with those usages, just as different usages of the word 'gentleman' by different people will imply that different people are rightly called 'gentlemen' in accordance with these various usages.

All we can do is give accounts of these different usages and then by discussion and argument decide which of them are preferable for different purposes. We cannot force a person to give up his usage, but it is perfectly legitimate to point out that a person's usage is based on an illogical argument. He may not mind about this: after all, it is perfectly true in philosophy as in science that 'there is no doctrine so foolish that it may not some day be able to give birth to a new and happy idea' (p. 98). However, to follow Wisdom's suggestion, if we have shown that the proposed conceptual revision is based on a confusion, and if also we cannot find anything very much to be said in favour of the revision and much to be said against it, then it is reasonable not to use the proposed concept but another one. Of course in the case of someone so first rate as Duhem there is something to be said in his favour. Duhem's moderate scepticism about the possibility of explanation, that is, radical scepticism about the possibility of scientific explanation in physics, draws to our attention the fact that physical theories which all the competent scientists of the day have believed to be true accounts of an 'underlying reality' of atoms or waves, etc., which explain the behaviour of macroscopic phenomena, have often turned out to be false. But it blurs over the fact that some theories are extremely well-confirmed and may be true while others, given our present evidence, no longer have anything to be said in their favour. Furthermore, we can describe all this in the way I just have, rather than by making the paradoxical claim that physical theories never provide explanations, on the ground that any particular theory one considers might turn out to be false.

2. *Less Radical Scepticism—The Familiarity Model of Scientific Explanation*

The two most popular models of scientific explanation since the turn of the century have been the familiarity model, according to which we explain by comparing the unfamiliar with the familiar, and the generalization model, according to which (1) we explain the occurrence of various phenomena by showing that their occurrence follows from some general law or laws along with 'initial conditions', and (2) we explain laws by showing that they follow from more general laws or theories.

N. R. Campbell was the great proponent of the familiarity model, because he thought he could show that the covering law model never provided explanations of laws. His reasoning was as follows:

> I do not believe that laws can ever be explained by inclusion in more general laws. . . . To say that all gases expand when heated is not to explain why hydrogen expands when heated; it merely leads us to ask immediately why all gases expand. An explanation which leads immediately to another question of the same kind is not an explanation at all.'[1]

[1] Norman Campbell, *What is Science?*, Methuen and Co., Ltd., 1st edition 1921, p. 80. In *Physics: The Elements*, first published in 1920, which contains

But this is simply a mistake. It is a necessary truth that it is always possible to ask for an explanation of a state of affairs A which it is claimed explains why there is a state of affairs B; but it certainly does not follow from this that A does not explain B. It may not be possible at the moment or indeed at any time to explain A, but that is another point.

Suppose we see a Moslem taking off his shoes on entering a mosque, and we ask why he did so. It might be thought that the reply that he is a Moslem and all Moslems take off their shoes on entering mosques does not provide an explanation of why that particular Moslem removed his shoes, because it 'immediately leads to another question of the same kind', namely, why all Moslems take off their shoes.[1] But of course this is a different question. The reply does explain why he took off his shoes; it aligns his behaviour with that of other members of a group to which he belongs, and it cuts out alternative explanations such as that his feet ached or that he wanted to get his shoes cleaned. To take an example from physics: we might answer the question 'Why does this unforced body carry on travelling with the same velocity instead of slowing down?' by replying that all unforced bodies remain in a state of rest or uniform motion in a straight line. They do not, as one might think, tend to slow down (*pace* Aristotle on earthly horizontal motion), while the particular body we are considering overcomes this tendency because of some peculiar method of producing energy while suffering some chemical breakdown.[2]

Campbell did indeed think, in *What is Science?*, that laws can

---

much earlier views which for various reasons he was unable to 'correct', Campbell held that laws could be explained *either* by showing that they were examples of more general laws (Ch. V), *or* by reference to theories (Ch. VI). I think it fair to say that he thought even then that the second type of explanation is vastly superior to the first, which has to be hedged around with many qualifications (see *Physics: The Elements*, p. 117).

[1] I have, I believe, taken this example—which seems to me a pretty forceful objection to the generalization account of explanation—from a work in the philosophy of science that I have read at some time. But I have unfortunately been unable to trace it. Someone might put the objection like this: 'If I don't understand p, and you try to explain it by proffering q, I will be no further enlightened if I don't understand q'. But this fails to distinguish between understanding p, or understanding q, and understanding why p or why q is true.

[2] This remark indicates, but no more than indicates, (*a*) part of what is wrong with the claim that the equation 'F = ma' is normally used in such a way that it is true by definition, and (*b*) why Aristotelian physics, with all its teleology, does provide explanations of motion.

be used to explain individual 'events and changes' (p. 78), or even sets of such events and changes, but he thought they could not be used to explain other laws. And it does seem that the only argument he produced for this conclusion is just mistaken. Since he thought that the other main way of explaining is by comparing the unfamiliar with the familiar, he concluded that scientific explanations of laws must always make reference to theories, theoretical entities, or models which thereby compare the unfamiliar with the familiar. If, after we have pointed out that his argument is invalid, he were still to insist that only by comparing the unfamiliar with the familiar do we get real explanations as opposed to preliminaries for explanations, what can we do about it? For even if he accepted that his original argument was invalid, he still might stick to his conclusion, since he might just feel uncomfortable about the idea that laws can be explained by laws: after all—he might feel—the latter are just more general examples of the former, and so 'just as incomprehensible', in fact more so.

We might point out in reply that some models refer to things with which—at least at some stages of our scientific career!—we are extremely unfamiliar, or that the advance of science has cared little about feelings of discomfort. But to this a Campbellian can simply reply that this only shows that we have not yet produced a proper explanation of those phenomenal laws. In other words, he might so narrow the concept of 'explanation' that it is a necessary condition of something's being an explanation of a law, in his sense of the word 'explanation', that the explanans refer to entities with which we are familiar: if we cannot do this, we cannot understand the law. We can either deplore or applaud this move. The sensible reply would, surely, go something like this: 'If we can explain laws in terms of theories describing entities of the sort with which we are familiar, then well and good. If not, then it is often sensible to go on trying; but there is no a priori reason why the 'ultimate constituents of the universe', if there are such things, must be entities of the sort with which we are in fact familiar from our everyday experience. So it is not in fact very sensible to refuse to call anything an 'explanation' of a law unless it makes reference to the ordinary and the familiar, and science has made great advances by not doing this. If your account of 'scientific explanation' is meant to be a complete account of what are in fact often considered by scientists to be cases of scientific explanation, then of course it is incorrect. If on the other hand it embodies a conceptual revision, then it cannot be *wrong*, only more or less admirable. It is admirable to encourage us to provide explanations of the sort you favour, but less admirable to refuse to allow that anything else could explain why any particular laws are true. And incidentally it is admirable to emphasize 'how theories differ from laws, as you do, but not admirable to overemphasize this matter, since laws are usually 'theory-laden' too.'

3. *The Covering Law Model of Scientific Explanation*

One type of conceptual revisionist may claim that although we never explain laws by referring to real, underlying (theoretical) entities—since there are never any good reasons for believing that such entities exist, or anyway not in the manner posited by the theory (Duhem and Mach)—nevertheless to show that laws are deducible from theories *is* to explain the laws (Mach, but not Duhem).[1] Contemporary philosophers who favour the so-called 'covering law' model of scientific explanation usually take the term 'covering law' to refer to either laws or what we have so far called 'theories', the latter being looked upon as statements which can refer either to familiar things, or to unfamiliar things, or perhaps even to nothing at all.

In one of the most famous papers on this subject, Hempel and Oppenheim divide an explanation into two parts: the *explanandum*, which is what is to be explained, and the *explanans*, which is what is adduced to account for the explanandum. They then argue that a scientific explanation must have the following four characteristics:[2]

---

[1] For example: 'The atomic theory plays a part in physics similar to that of certain auxiliary concepts in mathematics; it is a mathematical *model* for facilitating the mental reproduction of facts. . . . But it is not necessary to regard these . . . mathematical helps . . . as anything more than mental artifices. . . . The theoretical investigation of the mathematical possibilities . . . has . . . nothing to do with the question whether things really exist which correspond to these possibilities. . . . This is the case, too, with *all* hypotheses formed for the explanation of new phenomena.' Ernst Mach, *The Science of Mechanics*, 9th ed. tr. Thomas J. McCormack, The Open Court Publishing Company, La Salle, Illinois, 1960; pp. 589 and 590.

[2] Carl G. Hempel and Paul Oppenheim, 'Studies in the Logic of Explanation', *Philosophy of Science*, 15, 1948. Reprinted in Carl G. Hempel, *Aspects of Scientific Explanation and Other Essays in the Philosophy of Science*, The Free Press, Collier-Macmillan Ltd., New York, 1965, pp. 245–291. What they in fact say (p. 247) is that they are going to give 'some general characteristics of scientific explanation', but four sentences later: 'If a proposed explanation is to be *sound*, its constituents have to satisfy certain conditions . . .' (my italics). I

R1. The explanandum must be a logical consequence of the explanans.

R2. The explanans must contain general laws, and these must actually be required for the derivation of the explanandum.[1]

R3. The explanans must have empirical content.

R4. The sentences constituting the explanans must be true.

Although the above conditions are copied verbatim from Hempel and Oppenheim's original article (apart from leaving out their expository comments), both there and in later work it is stated that R1 is actually not a necessary condition of scientific explanation. An explanation having all four characteristics is called 'deductive-nomological' (D-N): where, however, at least one of the laws in the explanans is statistical rather than universal, and furthermore the explanans probabilifies rather than entails the explanandum (R1), the explanation is called 'inductive-statistical' (I-S).[2] Hempel also points out that for explanations of empirical states of affairs, of either the D-N or the I-S variety, R3 is redundant. For it is impossible either to deduce or show the (relative) probability of an empirical statement on the basis of *a priori* statements alone.

Thus R1 is not a necessary condition for something's being a scientific explanation, and R3 is redundant. Now why should we accept R4? There have been lots of theories put forward which certainly have been accepted as explanations which have later turned out to be false; according to Hempel and Oppenheim this means that what were thought to be explanations were not really explanations at all, not even wrong ones. Normally we speak of explanations being correct or incorrect, right or wrong, but if Hempel and Oppenheim's account were correct, then there could not be such a thing as an incorrect scientific explanation.

Why were they tempted into this view, which seems so very implausible? The answer may be that if someone gives what we might call an incorrect explanation, then we are often inclined to

---

discuss in the main body of the paper some of the peculiar consequences of this unfortunate prevarication concerning what exactly they are trying to give an account of.

[1] The second part of the sentence means simply that the explanans must not contain redundant law-statements. If $L_1 \rightarrow L_2$, then $L_1 \wedge R \rightarrow L_2$, for any random R we may choose and which clearly is not part of the explanation of L_2. But see also p. 247 below.

[2] *Ib.* pp. 381 ff. So-called 'deductive-statistical' explanations have statistical premises entailing statistical conclusions.

say that it *doesn't* explain what happened. Suppose I see someone go into a shop, and ask why he went in. I may be told: 'He wanted to buy a tie.' Suppose that in fact he went in not to buy a tie but to see his girl-friend. Then there is a tendency to say that what I was told does not explain why he went in, because he did not want to buy a tie. Thus there is a tendency to use the term 'explanation' in a manner similar to that in which we use achievement words such as 'see' and 'proof'. We are sometimes inclined to say that, for example, if there are no ghosts, then it must always be false to say of any man that he saw a ghost.[1] This is a tendency that can be resisted and often is. Thus it might be said that the claim 'He wanted to buy a tie' provided *an* explanation, but the wrong one. All we can do here is to report these conflicting tendencies, and then decide which way we are going to use the word in some particular context, and for what reasons.

In fact there are excellent reasons for not making it a necessary condition of something's correctly being called a 'scientific explanation' that the sentences which purport to provide the explanans must be true. For there is much to be said in favour of the Popperian claim that we can never know whether law-statements are true, and if we accept this, then if we used Hempel and Oppenheim's concept of 'explanation' we would never know whether a purported explanation was an explanation or not. Furthermore, it would mean that there would be nothing which we could ever correctly call an 'incorrect explanation': there would just be 'explanations' and 'purported explanations'. This would be very awkward; it is much more convenient to refer to correct explanations, incorrect explanations, and things which some people might claim to be explanations but which in fact do not provide explanations at all, not even wrong ones. For, as we shall see, one aim of Hempel and Oppenheim's programme was to tell us what scientific explanations 'really are', so that we can ascertain whether a group of suspicious characters, for example functional

---

[1] See Gilbert Ryle, *The Concept of Mind*, Hutchinson's University Library, 1949, pp. 149–153, 222–3 and 238. There is an even greater inclination to use the word 'proof' as an achievement-word, and Hempel and Oppenheim may well have been influenced by this. If I want to give a definition of (say, deductive) 'proof', then my account should not include misproofs: 'misproofs are not proofs'. On the other hand we might say that So-and-So's proof contained an error that was overlooked for centuries. The more obvious the error, the greater is the inclination (with hindsight!) to put quotation marks around the word 'proof'.

hypotheses in anthropology, can ever provide scientific explanations, even if sometimes (what I would call) incorrect ones.

I have tried to give a sympathetic account of why Hempel and Oppenheim may have thought that it is a necessary condition of something's being a scientific explanation that the explanans statements be true. It must be admitted, however, that the reasons they gave in their paper are very muddled. For what they said was that obviously a 'sound explanation' must satisfy 'some condition of factual correctness' (p. 322). This is true but irrelevant; they started off by attempting to give an account of 'scientific explanation' but immediately slipped over into trying to give an account of a 'sound' or 'correct' scientific explanation. But not all scientific explanations are either sound or correct.[1] They rejected the weaker view that 'the explanans has to be highly confirmed by all the relevant available evidence rather than that it should be true' (p. 322), because if the explanans is at one time highly confirmed and later disconfirmed 'we would have to say that the original explanatory account was a correct explanation, but that it ceased to be one later'. About this I can only repeat that to say that 'the original explanatory account' was an explanation is normally to make a different claim from that made in saying that it was 'a correct explanation': if we now show that one or more of the original explanans-statements is false, this shows that it is not, *and never was*, a correct explanation, but does not show that it used to be an explanation but no longer is one. It is an explanation which it used to be, but no longer is, reasonable to accept as correct.

Hempel has never recovered from this extraordinary confusion. In his magnificently clear and detailed later paper 'Aspects of Scientific Explanation' (1965) he writes: 'If the explanans of a given D-N explanation is true, . . . we will call the *explanation true*'.[2] Although he does not actually say so, presumably this implies that if the explanans is not true, we have a 'false' explanation, which is an advance on the view that we have not got an explanation at all. We might prefer to speak of correct and

---

[1] cf Are all proofs valid? Then there is no such thing as an invalid proof! This sounds odd, but then so does talk of an 'invalid deductive proof'. See previous footnote.

[2] Carl G. Hempel, 'Aspects of Scientific Explanation', in *Aspects of Scientific Explanation and Other Essays in the Philosophy of Science*, p. 338. All the remaining quotations in the above paragraph are from the same page of Hempel's article. For further details see ibid., pp. 273, 383, 396, 397, 400 fn., 402 and 403.

incorrect explanations, rather than true or false ones, but this point need not detain us. Next, we learn that 'one factor in appraising the *soundness* of a given explanation will be the extent to which its explanans is supported by the total relevant evidence available' (my italics). Thus what are in fact false explanations can presumably be 'sound' at some particular period, because it is reasonable to accept them in the context of the scientific beliefs in which they are put forward. So far so good. 'Finally, by a *potential D-N explanation,* let us understand any argument that has the character of a D-N explanation except that the sentences constituting its explanans need not be true'. But we do not need the concept of a potential D-N explanation since, if we accept the account given so far, it is simply equivalent to 'explanation'. This confusion leads Hempel to say that 'we use the notion of a potential explanation, for example, . . . when we say that the phlogiston theory, though now discarded, *afforded an explanation* for certain aspects of combustion' (my italics). This means that what used to be a (relatively) sound—but of course false—explanation, has now turned into a 'potential' explanation because we know that some of the explanans statements are false! The fact that Hempel says that the phlogiston theory '*afforded* an explanation' shows that he thinks that although it used to be a (perhaps sound) explanation, now it is really no longer an explanation at all. It is a 'potential' explanation, and the inference is that some but not all potential explanations are explanations. But this conflicts with the idea that explanations can be true or false. Or do false explanations stop being explanations once we *know* they are false?

It is perfectly easy to get out of this muddle. We can speak of correct and incorrect explanations, depending, among other things, on whether the explanans statements are true. If the relationship between the explanandum and the proposed explanans is of the correct type, and if we have good grounds for believing that the explanans statements are true, on the basis of the evidence we have available to us, then it is more or less reasonable to accept, until contrary evidence appears, that the explanation is correct. There does not seem to be much more that needs saying about these particular conceptual points, but I will now try to show that this account fits in well with normal scientific practice.

It is well known that false statements are not deducible from true ones, whereas true statements are deducible from (suitably chosen) true or false ones. Thus any lawlike statement of the form 'All A are C' is deducible from 'All A are B' and 'All B are C', and we can easily produce substitution-instances to give T→T, F→F, and F→T. Thus factual claims or empirical theories which we now believe to be true, and which in fact are true, are deducible from theories which might later be shown to be false. Indeed, laws which we now believe to be false are shown in schools to be deducible from laws or theories which we now believe to be false, and which are said to explain them: for example (simplified) Kinetic Theory explains Boyle's Law, and Newton's Laws explain Galileo's Law of falling bodies.[1]

There might be two counters to this. First it might be said that although (simple) Kinetic Theory and Newton's Laws are false, they are or anyway were highly confirmed by experimental evidence, so they can count as explanations. But this does not help Hempel's position, since simple Kinetic Theory is *now* highly disconfirmed and known to be false, but we can still use it *now* to explain Boyle's Law (which is known to be false). The second counter might be this: although perhaps, strictly speaking, both simple Kinetic Theory and Newton's Laws are false, nevertheless it is very misleading just to call them 'false', since they are approximately true, and hence they explain the approximate truths of Boyle's and Galileo's Laws respectively. And Hempel's point can be construed as the claim that no one would accept that a theory explained anything if he knew at that time that it was *absolutely* false.

But we can think of a case where the alleged 'facts' to be explained are not facts at all (or probably not facts), the statements to be derived from the explanans are presumably completely false, and the theory being put forward to explain them is completely

---

[1] Or, to put it more accurately, from Newton's Laws we can deduce that the acceleration of a body freely falling in a vacuum is independent of its mass. It will vary with the mass of the earth and inversely with the square of the distance from the centre of the earth, but these can be considered approximately constant. Paul Feyerabend, in 'How to be a Good Empiricist', reprinted in Nidditch, op. cit., follows Duhem in pointing out (p. 20) that 'Newton's theory is inconsistent with Galileo's law', and concludes that in scientific practice, theories are used to explain laws which they contradict. This leads to a proposed methodology of chaos. But we need not put the matter quite so drastically: Newton's Laws explain why Galileo's Law is approximately true, and indeed explain why it is *only* approximately true, and to what extent. Compare the use of Newton's Laws to explain why Kepler's Laws are (only) approximately true, and the discovery of new planets.

false as well. At a time when Darwin believed in the inheritance of acquired characteristics, he suggested that cells produce minute granules, which he called 'gemmules', which circulate throughout the body and can enter the sex cells and then be transmitted to the offspring. Galton showed that gemmules do not circulate in the blood of rabbits, but Darwin did not think this was a fatal objection to his theory, 'which manifestly applies to plants and the lowest animals'.[1] And Galton retained the gemmule theory, assuming that gemmules exist in an hereditary material called 'stirp', which was supposed to be distinct from the body cells. How is this matter referred to by a working scientist *now*? L. C. Dunn describes it as follows:

> . . . in order to explain some cases of the inheritance of acquired characters, Galton had to assume that some cells give off gemmules which get into other cells and even into germ cells.[2]

We might be tempted to say: 'Nothing *could* explain how acquired characteristics are inherited, since they are *not* inherited. Only if they *were* inherited could anything explain *how* they were.' But Dunn apparently is not so tempted, even though of course he believes that Lamarckism is false. Furthermore, so far from the gemmule theory ever having been highly confirmed, there was even at the time no evidence for it whatsoever—apart from the fact that it would explain how acquired characteristics were inherited! Thus we have a clear case of a working scientist and historian of science describing something as an explanation, where the explanans is not confirmed at all, is now highly disconfirmed, and is believed by the author—more than this, known, surely— to be false.[3] So does it provide an explanation or not? And to answer this question, do I have to make a survey of the linguistic habits of scientists?

[1] Charles Darwin, *Variation of Plants and Animals under Domestication*, 1876, Vol. II, p. 350. Quoted in L. C. Dunn, *A Short History of Genetics*, McGraw-Hill Book Company, 1965, p. 37.

[2] *Ib*. p. 38.

[3] It is not necessary here to discuss whether we know absolutely for sure that acquired characteristics are not inherited. It is of course conceivable that we might one day find ourselves in the same position as Darwin himself, who at one time thought that evolution could be explained solely in terms of natural selection, and then later thought it had to be explained by the inheritance of acquired characteristics *as well*. The history of science is littered with examples of discarded theories which have made a come-back; but I am assuming here that both the explanandum and the explanans are completely false, and known to be so. If this example is not acceptable, then we can take another.

But what on earth hangs on these examples and how people might describe them? Some people would consider that they are cases of explanation, and some would not. The word 'explanation', as used in science, has a meaning which varies between different language-users. We can point out these different usages: how can we say which is 'correct'? We often say 'There are two alternative and incompatible theories to explain these facts', or 'There are two possible explanations for this'. Some people would say that possible explanations are not explanations any more than possible cats are cats: they are explanations only if what they claim is true. Others might say they are explanations only if they are highly confirmed. But the latter would be very odd: since theories can be highly confirmed yet false, is it not more reasonable to say that they should only be *accepted* as *correct* explanations if they are highly confirmed? Thus what we can do is to point out the advantages and the disadvantages of the various usages of the term 'explanation', and then, if we wish, decide which concept is the most convenient one to adopt for various purposes, depending on whether the advantages outweigh the disadvantages or vice versa. I take it that this is a central tenet of Wisdom's metaphilosophical advice, together with the reminder that we should not forget the advantages and disadvantages of the usages we have for the time being rejected. Since it is in discordance with at least some common scientific practice, and there seems to be little to be said in its favour, I would therefore propose that we drop both Hempel's R4, the requirement that the sentences constituting the explanans be true, and its weaker version, that they be highly confirmed by the available evidence.

It is most interesting to see how Hempel and Oppenheim set about their task of deciding that all cases of scientific explanation must have the features R1—R4. They took four examples of things which just about everyone would agree to be cases of scientific explanation,[1] and 'from the preceding sample cases . . . now abstract some general characteristics of scientific explanation'.[2] They notice that their examples have in common the

---

[1] One of their examples is that the undulatory theory of light explains the phenomena of refraction. It is worth while reminding ourselves that Duhem would not have agreed that this was an example of explanation, as I have indicated above.

[2] 'Studies in the Logic of Explanation', from page 247 of the reprint of *Aspects of Scientific Explanation*.

R

features R1—R4. They then look at various other statements which are sometimes said to be explanations, and conclude that since they lack one or other of the features R1—R4, they cannot really be explanations! But obviously, it would be equally reasonable to conclude that the features R1—R4 are not common (and necessarily common) to all scientific explanations. Their methodology assumes the essentialist thesis that there must be something common to all cases of explanation, which provides the rationale for our correctly calling them 'explanations'; something common apart from their being explanations. This thesis has been successfully criticized by Wisdom and Wittgenstein. Hempel and Oppenheim's argument is of a type often used by philosophers: since it leads to a narrowing of the concept under scrutiny it is a piece of mild conceptual revisionism, or what we might call 'mildly sceptical metaphysics'. It may not be immediately apparent that this is all their argument comes to, because it is hidden in an undergrowth of technicalities, persuasively framed questions, and appeals to that paradigm of all sciences, physics, the standards of which hardly any poor philosopher dare question.

Perhaps the most shocking example of this conceptual revisionism due to persuasive (or unpersuasive) definition is provided by Hempel and Oppenheim's claim that

> teleological assumptions, [even] while . . . endowed with empirical content, cannot serve as explanatory principles in the customary contexts. Thus e.g. the fact that a given species of butterfly displays a particular kind of colouring cannot be inferred from—and therefore cannot be explained by means of—the statement that this type of colouring has the effect of protecting butterflies from detection by pursuing birds.[1]

Now it is not at all clear how this example differs relevantly, if at all, from those that Hempel and Oppenheim consider to be *incomplete* explanations. One of their examples is that of a car overturning on a road because a tyre blew out while the car was travelling at high speed. Naturally, 'on the basis of just this information, the accident could not have been predicted':[2] but

[1] *Ib.* p. 256.
[2] *Ib.* p. 249. Here again, we find an ambivalent attitude between (a) such accounts don't provide explanations at all, and (b) they provide explanations, but incomplete ones. For they say (a) 'Many explanations which are *customarily* offered, especially in prescientific discourse, lack this predictive character,

the idea is that if we had been given a *complete* account of the initial conditions—the speed of the car, conditions on the road, skill of the driver etc.—along with complete, general, causal laws, if any such exist, then we could have *deduced* (condition R1) that the car would turn over. As I have remarked, it is not at all clear why, given a *complete* account of initial conditions—butterflies with various markings, the existence of predators, and the relevant laws of evolution, if any such exist—we could not have deduced that there would now exist butterflies with the specific markings they now have. But this is not my main point, which is that even if the explanandum could not have been inferred (deduced) from the proposed explanans, then the most we may validly conclude is that Hempel and Oppenheim's proposed definition of 'scientific explanation' does not provide necessary and sufficient conditions for picking out all and only the things which are considered by various scientists to be examples of scientific explanation. Hempel and Oppenheim drew the conclusion that the counter-examples to their definition are not 'real' explanations, but are at best psychological aids or 'heuristic devices'. But this conclusion cannot be validly drawn from the available premises: it requires the further premise that their definition is 'correct'. And in any event they held that there are statistical explanations, in which the explanans does no more than provide some probability for the conclusion.

In a later work Hempel examines the nature of functional hypotheses in biology, sociology, psychology and anthropology. Such hypotheses claim that a feature is present in a system or organism so as to produce a certain end or result of a type required to keep the system or organization functioning in a certain way. Hempel sometimes writes as though such hypotheses can never provide explanations, and sometimes as though they can but that they are never very satisfactory.[1] He thinks one difficulty is that even if they do explain to some extent why some trait or property is present in some organism or social group, they do not explain why some *alternative* fails to be present which would perform the

---

however' (p. 249) (my italics), and (b) 'In some cases, incomplete explanatory arguments of the kind here illustrated suppress parts of the explanans simply as "obvious".' (p. 250).

[1] C. G. Hempel, 'The Logic of Functional Analysis', first published in Llewellyn Gross (ed.), *Symposium on Sociological Theory*, Harper & Row, New York, 1959. Reprinted with some alterations in *Aspects of Scientific Explanation and Other Essays in the Philosophy of Science*, pp. 297–330; see especially pp. 308, 318, 324, 327 and 330.

same function. I think it would be fair to reply that there is presumably only a finite number of ways of producing the required end, and so we might be able to deduce that, if the system survives, some feature (rather than any other which might perform the same function) has some probability of being present. In other words I think, while Hempel apparently does not, that the problem of alternative possible traits or properties can be dealt with under the umbrella of I-S explanations. Thus we need to examine explanations which only provide some probability for the occurrence of the event or phenomenon to be explained. About this type of argument Hempel seems to me to be seriously mistaken.

Hempel claims that if we want to explain why Henry has mumps we might point out that he has played for several hours with a friend who later got mumps, that he had not suffered from mumps before, etc., and that under such conditions 'the disease will be transmitted with high statistical probability'.[1] The same example except with different actors suffering from a different illness is discussed in Hempel's later, introductory book, *Philosophy of Natural Science*, where the explanatory schema is put in the following form:[2]

The probability for persons exposed to the measles to catch
the disease is high
Jim was exposed to the measles

== [makes highly probable]
Jim caught the measles

Hempel thinks that an explanans only provides an explanation 'though of a less stringent kind than those of deductive-nomological form'[3] if the explanandum is given a high probability. But the fact that Jim was exposed to the measles will explain why he caught it even if—as is probably the case—very few people who are exposed to measles catch that disease.[4] The reason is that exposure to measles can *cause* its transmission, in the way that exposure to cancer cannot. To say that a burst tyre caused the car to turn over is to say, roughly speaking, that the bursting of the tyre was followed by the car overturning, and that if the tyre had not burst but other factors had remained the same, then the car

---

[1] *Ibid.*, p. 301.

[2] Carl G. Hempel, *Philosophy of Natural Science*, Prentice-Hall Inc., New Jersey, 1966, p. 59.   [3] *Ibid.*, p. 68.

[4] See Arthur W. Collins' excellent article 'The Use of Statistics in Explanation', *British Journal for the Philosophy of Science*, Vol. 17, No. 2, August 1966.

would not have turned over.[1] This is perfectly compatible with burst tyres being followed by cars turning over on very few occasions indeed, and thus with the explanandum statement 'The car turned over' being given only very low probability by the available evidence. If the system is completely deterministic, then if we had all the relevant evidence (initial conditions plus general laws), we would be able to deduce the explanandum statement. The more evidence we have, and the more laws we know, the more *fully* can we explain what has happened, and the more certainly can we predict what will happen. But with evidence which gives only low probability to the explanandum, we can still give a *partial* explanation of why the event occurred,[2] and this Hempel denies. Once again, we find the tendency in Hempel to equate 'explanation' with 'complete and correct explanation' or, when this won't do, then with 'nearly, or more or less complete (and correct) explanation'. One can appreciate the rationale behind this move and yet question its overall desirability.

If we have an indeterministic system, then there do not exist any universal laws completely governing the situation, not even unknown ones. There are only 'ultimately' statistical laws. It is presumably impossible ever to be certain that there do not exist ultimate deterministic laws governing statistical, apparently indeterministic behaviour. But suppose that the laws governing the emission of α-particles from radon^{222} are ultimately statistical in character. We want to know why an α-particle is shot out of a particular atom within the period t_1-t_2. Then the explanation may be that it is a radon^{222} atom, and radon^{222} atoms sometimes give out α-particles. The probability that it does so between t_1 and t_2 may be extremely low, since the half-life of radon^{222} is 3.825 days. We might describe this by saying: there is no explanation why during the period t_1-t_2 this particular radon atom gave out one particle as opposed to none or two.[3] Nevertheless, the explanation of why the atom gave out an α-particle is that it is

[1] For a more accurate account see my 'Causality', *British Journal for the Philosophy of Science*, Vol. 18, No. 1, May 1967.
[2] This is particularly so in the case of causal explanations. Non-causal statistical explanations are discussed in the next paragraph.
[3] Radon^{222} decays to polonium^{218} by emitting an α-particle. Polonium^{218} has a half-life of 3.05 minutes, giving out an α-particle plus an electron. So an atom which starts out as radon might give out two α-particles during a reasonably short time interval. Radon is formed from radium^{226}, which has a half-life of 1620 years, so it is *very* unlikely that a particular radium^{226} atom will give out an α-particle during a smallish time interval. Nevertheless, we might

radon, and this is what radon atoms sometimes, although actually comparatively rarely, do. This is of course a quite different matter from the *necessary* truth that if the probability of a radon[222] atom decaying within 3.825 days is one-half, then the probability is very high that *about* half the atoms in a given macroscopic lump of radon[222] (i.e. containing very many atoms) will have decayed after 3.825 days. But it is *this* high probability which Hempel says (p. 392) allows us to explain why about half the atoms in a lump of radon have decayed after 3.825 days.

This case is not relevantly different from what are presumably completely deterministic systems about which we use probability statements because of our ignorance of the initial conditions. Thus if the probability of a particular die turning up an ace is 1/5, then, given normal initial conditions, 'This die will not turn up an ace' has probability 4/5. According to Hempel we can explain (incompletely) why a particular throw of the die did *not* turn up ace, because the explanandum will be highly 'probabilified' by the explanans. We could have predicted 'It won't be an ace' with some confidence. But according to Hempel we cannot explain, not even incompletely, why a particular throw did turn up ace. Let us think, however, what we would reply to someone who asked why we got an ace on some particular throw. We might say something like: 'Well, in throwing the die randomly, you get aces sometimes—namely, in about 1/5 of the throws—and this just happens to be one of them'. Presumably a request for a *further* explanation of why we got an ace would be a request for the unknown initial conditions regarding the exact manner in which the die was thrown, along with the relevant dynamical laws.[1] Note that in none of the (partial) explanations we have been considering of various occurrences in the life history of dice or

---

explain why an atom gave out an *a*-particle by pointing out that it is a radium[226] atom. Furthermore, even if there is no explanation why radioactive atoms give out particles just when they do, it does not follow that there is no possible way of accounting for the fact that different elements have such differing half-lives.

[1] All this should be compared and contrasted with what Hempel says about I–S explanations in *Philosophy of Natural Science,* pp. 58–69, and *Aspects of Scientific Explanation,* pp. 376–412. Explaining why 'The nth throw was an ace' is quite a different matter from explaining why *about* 1/5 of all throws come up ace, and Hempel deals almost exclusively with the latter sort of explanandum. *Given* that the probability of getting an ace is 1/5, we can show mathematically why (*a*) the probability of getting aces in exactly 1/5 of a long series of throws is higher than the probability of getting any other proportion, even though each of these probabilities is very low, and also (*b*) why the probability of getting *approximately* 1/5 aces in a long series of throws is rather high.

radioactive atoms has a causal explanation been provided. I am inclined to think that it is rather misleading to express causal and non-causal explanations in arguments of the same form.

If we return to the case of the overturning car, we might now think: 'Yes, we can provide a (partial) explanation of why it turned over, namely, by pointing out as many of the causal factors as we can, which contributed to the accident'. Would this be to provide a *scientific* explanation of the accident? But 'scientific' as opposed to what? As soon as one asks this, one is struck by the question: Is there something called 'scientific' explanation as opposed to other sorts of explanation? Towards the opening of his essay 'Aspects of Scientific Explanation' Hempel states that:

> A scientific explanation may be regarded as an answer to a why-question, such as : 'Why do the planes move in elliptical orbits with the sun at one focus?' . . . (There follow several other examples ending with) . . . 'Why did Hitler go to war against Russia?' (p. 334).

The last question is thus mentioned at the outset as one which requires a *scientific* explanation as an answer. But isn't this highly odd?[1] When do we ask for scientific explanations, as opposed to other sorts? One area where this typically happens is in religious contexts. Someone might say that the rivers of Egypt turned red because God wanted to tell the Pharaoh to free the Israelites, and what God wants to happen (usually) does happen. Whether or not we think this theological explanation is nonsensical because unverifiable, we might reply that we would like a scientific as opposed to a theological explanation of the event, if such an explanation is possible. What is required is a naturalistic, causal explanation. Now is it just irrelevant to mention that to ask for a scientific explanation of an invasion, a car accident, or even a particular occurrence of the measles—as opposed to an epidemic —would be very odd? Assuming that these are all of a pattern with typical scientific explanations, Hempel *frames* them all in the

[1] It is true that Hempel had written on the previous page: 'The terms 'empirical science' and 'scientific explanation' will here be understood to refer to the entire field of empirical enquiry, including the natural and social sciences as well as historical research'. But this simply underlines my point: even if historians *never* provide correct explanations of a type different from those *sometimes* provided by scientists, it doesn't follow that they all have something in common, let alone something in common which makes it reasonable, without gross conceptual revisionism, to call them all 'scientific'.

same pattern, so that the explanans must either entail or at least highly probabilify the explanandum.

Now I would like to put the matter this way: is there any reason to think that all explanations produced by scientists, in scientific contexts, are scientific explanations, any more than that all explanations produced by historians, in historical contexts, are historical explanations? Hempel, of course, is inclined to think that there are no essential differences between historians' explanations and scientists' explanations. But even if this is true, it does not follow that they are all scientific. There are different sorts of explanation, relevant in different sorts of context, depending on what it is about the subject matter under consideration that we wish to have explained. If we are interested in finding out what are the features of explanations—as opposed to pseudo-explanations—which scientists produce, then we can list such features. We should not assume at the outset that any one or indeed any set of these features is necessarily either common or peculiar to all scientific explanations, let alone to all explanations produced by scientists. It does not follow that it is impossible to distinguish between explanations and non-explanations, or between scientific and non-scientific explanations, any more than from the fact that there is no feature that would be used to explain the meaning of the word 'lemon' that is necessarily common and peculiar to lemons, that it is impossible to distinguish lemons from non-lemons. Thinking that there must be such features distorts the accounts that are sometimes given of what it is to be an example of the concept being discussed.

We have seen that, for a reasonable concept of 'scientific explanation', neither Hempel and Oppenheim's R1 nor their R4 is logically necessary, and that if R1 were necessary, R3 would be redundant. Even R2 is not necessary, if explaining what caused some particular occurrence should be considered an example of scientific explanation—and it seems that in some situations it should. Are R1—R4 jointly sufficient? As Hempel has realised, there are several criticisms that can be made of his definition, of a purely formal kind.[1] These are of a type, however, that make

---

[1] The references to these can be found in *Aspects of Scientific Explanation*, p. 489. Actually Hempel states in the penultimate paragraph of *Aspects* that his 'explicatory analysis has not even led to a full definition of a precise "explicatum"-concept of scientific explanation; it purports only to make explicit some especially important aspects of such a concept'. But it is clear he hopes that a

scientists run a mile from philosophers of science, and I want to point out here that from a much more practical point of view his account does not provide logically sufficient conditions. For if we consider any law of the form 'All A are C', it is deducible from a random 'All A are B' and 'All B are C', and it is not too difficult to think up examples of B which will provide a highly confirmed, and indeed true, proposed explanans. An example would be:

(1) All metals conduct electricity
(2) Whatever conducts electricity is subject to gravitational attraction
∴ (3) All metals are subject to gravitational attraction.[1]

No one would regard (1) and (2) as providing an explanation of (3): they are just irrelevant to its truth. Metals are not subject to gravitational attraction *because* they conduct electricity: non-conductors are subject to gravitational attraction to just the same degree. Hempel and Oppenheim do say (in R2) that the general laws in the explanans 'must actually be required for the derivation of the explanandum'. But by this they mean that these laws must not be redundant for the particular deduction under consideration: they do not mean, as one might think, that there must not be any other way of deducing the conclusion from true general laws. In any event, this would not save them, for we have just provided such a deduction, and so if we were to put this interpretation on their words, it would mean that it would be impossible to explain why metals are subject to gravitational attraction, which it is not. Furthermore, it is at least plausible to think that there can exist alternative correct explanations for various scientific laws.

It would seem desirable to eliminate these counter-examples by purely formal means which refer only to structural relationships between the classes of entities referred to in the explanans; but there are reasons for believing that this cannot be done. For the moment all I can say is that an explanation of a law L must make reference to some *relevant*—for example, causally

---

definition in terms of necessary and sufficient conditions will be forthcoming once various purely formal difficulties have been overcome; and in the same essay he objects (p. 432) to one suggested feature of scientific explanations, viz. reduction to the familiar, on the grounds that it is neither necessary nor sufficient.

[1] The truth of each of these statements, like the truth of any lawlike statement, has to be taken with a few sacks of salt, because of both its range of application and its reference to theoretical entities. My objection is hardly novel: compare for example Aristotle's *Posterior Analytics* I, 6 and 7.

relevant—phenomena; either to phenomena of which the phenomena referred to in L constitute a sub-class, or to phenomena in a theory or theories from which L is deducible. And we can explain particular events either (1) by listing some of their causes, or (2) by showing that their occurrence follows from some laws of nature and initial conditions. But we do not have to be able to deduce that they will occur, or even to show that their occurrence is highly probable on the basis of what we know. Finally, I should mention that I have not said anything here about the pragmatic aspects of scientific explanation, because I do not believe that scientists *qua* scientists, as opposed to *qua* teeahers, need to concern themselves with this matter.

I have tried to indicate how two features of Wisdom's philosophy might be used to gain a better insight into a problem discussed by philosophers of science. This type of examination could equally be applied to many other topics, for example to the Popper-Kuhn controversy concerning the nature of science and of scientific advance. I cannot hope to have done anything like justice to the range and subtlety of Wisdom's work, a work that enables us sometimes to see each philosophical problem for what it is, so that 'the individual is restored to us, not isolated as before we used language, not in a box as when language mastered us, but in "creation's chorus".'[1] For it seems to me that, when the power and scope of Wisdom's work become more widely and deeply appreciated, it will not appear inappropriate to place it alongside that of the greatest philosophers of all periods.

[1] *Philosophy and Psycho-Analysis*, p. 119.

XI

SHARED GUILT

HERBERT MORRIS

'It is those that cannot connect who hasten to cast the first stone.' E. M.
FORSTER, *Howard's End*.

FATHER Zossima's brother in *The Brothers Karamazov* says
to his mother, 'Little heart of mine, my joy, believe me,
everyone is really responsible to all men for all men and for
everything. I don't know how to explain it to you, but I feel it is
so, painfully even. And how is it we went on then living, getting
angry and not knowing'. These are richly suggestive, troubling,
words. Their precise meaning may elude us and we may yet have
a sense of their profound significance, a sense that beneath them
lies insight that cuts through to something essential about the
nature of morality and human beings. We shall, I think, feel most
at ease with the claims that we are responsible *to* all men and *for*
all men, for they immediately suggest familiar claims about
morality—the one, that a wrong we do to any man is something
for which we must answer to every man, the other, that we have
moral duties to others by virtue of their humanity and not some
other fact about them, for example, their sex or nationality. These
claims are, of course, worth examining. But clearly it is the claim
that 'we are responsible *for everything*' that is most difficult to
understand, that is most intriguing; and it is therefore this claim
that most interests me. It seems clear that our attention is to be
focused upon responsibility for what is seen as evil and not for
what is seen as good, but where do we go from there? This essay
is a record of my attempt to flush out its meaning and to come to
grips with the truth there might be in it. I begin by setting out a
number of rather likely responses to the claim that we are responsible for everything. I then consider separately several different
lines of argument that might be offered in its support. I conclude
with an assessment of the claim in the light of the responses there
have been to it.

I

When we read the words 'everyone is responsible for everything', we may be perplexed, as perplexed for example, as when for the first time we come upon the view that material objects do not exist. Can anyone really believe that you and I are responsible for everything, even those things of which we have not the least knowledge? Are we responsible for all that which, had we known of it, we should have done what we could to prevent? After putting such questions to ourselves we may be prepared, without much additional reflection, to judge that nothing intelligible is meant by such persons. We may feel that, while words are used with which we are familiar, persons who say such things do not—they cannot really—believe what it is that the words convey.

There will be those, of course, who respond to the claim that we are responsible for everything with no perplexity at all. They admit to understanding it by judging it to be obviously false. There are those things for which we are and those for which we are not responsible, and it is clear that we cannot be responsible for most of the things that have gone on, are going on, and will go on. People who take this line seem to have a firm grasp of when it is that a person is responsible for something. They evaluate claims of responsibility by appeal to a model of responsibility which we may label 'individual responsibility' or 'personal responsibility'. This model has a hold on many persons and it is worth bringing out its characteristics, at least briefly, without further delay. This can best be done by noting typical ways in which responsibility is denied by some person for some occurrence where the occurrence is acknowledged to involve harm to some human being.

First, a person may claim that he was not involved at all in some harm's coming about, and that it was another who was responsible. Second, a person may admit a causal connection between his body and some occurrence, but nevertheless deny that he was responsible, for he may argue that the movements of his body were not under his control or that he was unconscious when the movements took place. Third, a person may deny responsibility in what came about by questioning the existence of a causal connection between his admittedly voluntary conduct and the occurrence. Thus, if he were to stab what he took to be a live human being and the knife were in fact entering what had only seconds before become a corpse, he would not be responsible for killing a human being. Fourth, the result which has come about may be one that would not have come about but for the individual's conduct and still, if the result were only remotely connected with the conduct or if it came about too accidentally or because of the intervening act of another human being, there would be no responsibility for the occurrence. What lawyers might call 'proximate cause' seems essential, then, for responsibility. Finally, to conclude this bare sketch of an elaborate mode of life, a person might admit that he was responsible for some harmful occurrence and reject the appropriateness of his being blamed or *held* responsible, for he may argue that he was without fault. That is, he may argue that his conduct met standards for proper conduct in the circumstances. On this view of the matter to properly be held morally responsible for some harm requires a causal and proximate causal connection between a person's faulty conduct and some harm. Now, if this is the model that we have —perhaps only vaguely—before our minds when someone says that 'we are responsible for everything' we naturally think that what he says is false.

We may react to the view that 'we are responsible for everything' in still another way. The claim may strike us as similar to other claims that appear to be straightforwardly about the world but which, as we soon discover from the array of defences presented for them, really involve modification of the concepts that enter into the claim. We may come at this view of what is going on in the following way. Imagine, we might say, a man who felt guilty over suffering by anyone, anywhere, and at any time. He would seem to have feelings appropriate to the belief that he was responsible for everything. But this man would remind us of those with whom we are already familiar, perhaps even remind us of ourselves, persons who feel guilty in circumstances where it is inappropriate to feel that way and about whom we say, 'they suffer from neurotic guilt'. But the inappropriateness in neurotic guilt is not merely the result of the fact that a person believes something to be so about the world that is not. It is not, for example, that the man feels guilty over having killed someone and his belief is erroneous. In such a case we say to him, 'Look, relax, you didn't kill him and you ought not to feel guilty about doing so'. Learning of his mistake the man may cease to feel guilt over the death. But the neurotic would react differently. He appreciates that he hasn't killed anyone and he persists in feeling guilty, so he tells us, over the person's death. Here we may believe that the inappropriateness of the feeling ties in with a restructuring of the conceptual links between fault, responsibility, guilt, and feeling guilty. Well, if something conceptual is afoot with neurotic guilt, what shall we say of 'we are responsible for everything' a claim which, if taken seriously, would lead to feelings of guilt of the most astoundingly neurotic kind?

If there is conceptual revision, it does not appear to be such a modest revision of one or more moral concepts as is going on, for example, when someone says of sexual intercourse without love that it is prostitution and of sexual intercourse with love that it is chastity. The claim seems to imply a revision in the concept of responsibility which is incompatible with the very idea of morality, for moral offences seem pre-eminently ones in which the conditions of fault obtain.

If conceptual revision is involved it appears to have still another feature. 'We are responsible for everything' has a partner at the other extreme: 'None of us is responsible.' These claims, at opposite extremes, may be regarded by some as involving not just revision of concepts central to morality but a shift that empties these concepts of usefulness. With these claims, as with 'all of us are mad' and 'all of us are selfish' we may be impressed by the lack of consequence of contrary cases. Everything is accommodated by the proponent of these views. But if we are responsible for everything, surely, an objector will argue, there is no longer any service being performed by the concept of responsibility. There is no point to our having the concept, for distinctions captured and thought important are erased. It is one more case where insulation from refutation is purchased at the too great price of informativeness and usefulness.

There are, then, these typical philosophical responses to the putting forward of a paradoxical claim: 'nonsense', 'false' and 'empty'. But there are other responses which reveal that considerable indignation is aroused by the claim. The view is surely put forward with the suggestion that it is an advance in moral thinking, that insight is being provided and that desirable moral conduct will follow acceptance of its truth. But is it not simply a mistaken moral point of view, one that has evil implications? Is it not a return to a morality, if we should be willing to call it that, beyond which we have advanced? Does it not remind us of what Ezekiel found unacceptable?

> What mean ye, that ye use this proverb
> concerning the land of Israel, saying,
> The fathers have eaten sour grapes,
> and the children's teeth are set on
> edge? As I live, saith the Lord God,
> ye shall not have occasion any more
> to use this proverb in Israel.

> The soul that sinneth, it shall die.
> The son shall not bear the iniquity of
> the father, neither shall the father
> bear the iniquity of the son: the
> righteousness of the righteous shall
> be upon him, and the wickedness of the
> wicked shall be upon him.

We may feel indignant, then, for what is morally false is put forward as morally true.

In fact, the claim that we are all responsible for everything, particularly when tied to narrower cases, say, being told that as whites we are responsible for the condition of the black man, responsible even for the evils perpetrated before our birth, produces not just intellectual disagreement, not just critical analysis but unquestionably, in the case of some people, considerable anger, sometimes anger of such intensity that we may become suspicious and wonder what nerve the claim has touched. There may be various reasons for this anger. Many of us feel already weighted down with guilt where normal conditions obtain, and it is understandable that we should not appreciate the suggestion that the magnitude of the burden be substantially increased. There are also those who see any claim leading to expanded responsibility and inevitable feelings of guilt as merely increasing the amount of breast-beating and bemoaning what is past, a looking backward that increases suffering but does not attend to the tasks before us.

Finally, there are those who believe they have the right to judge others and they become disturbed by views that make

questionable the exercise of their right. In fact, they are as angered
by the view that no one is responsible as by the view that we all are.
For they think responsibility, guilt, and blame important concepts
and believe that often others and not they are responsible and
should be blamed. But if we are all responsible, or if none of us is,
then it seems as if we are all precluded from blaming. 'Judge not
lest ye be judged.' Anger may be aroused, then, for feelings
regarded as legitimate are blocked and do not have the outlet they
now have.

It is clear that the claim 'we are responsible for everything'
may anger us and that even more limited claims about our responsibility, when we think we are innocent or perhaps when we wish
to hide our guilt from ourselves, will arouse anger. But I think
that for some persons it will be a troubled anger. We know too
well that the paradoxical reveals the hidden. And underlying our
bewilderment, our anger, even our contempt, may be a feeling
that these recorded responses to the claim that 'we are responsible
for everything' are inadequate, and that some insights not yet
revealed underlie the claim.

There is something else that may add to the uneasiness some
of us feel, even after all objections are put forward. We have
feelings that we do not reject so quickly as we reject feelings
labelled 'neurotic guilt', and yet they seem to be feelings no less at
odds with certain moral criteria. For example, a man may take
pride in the accomplishments of his countrymen when all he
appears to share with them is his nationality. A black man may feel
pride where before he did not because of his beliefs about the
accomplishments of other black men, ones who lived before he
was born. And do we not feel shame and think it appropriate, at
least sometimes, over actions of our country with which we have
not been involved? Again, to think of Jews as a class may bring
to mind a mode of thinking we abhor and that led to unspeakable
horrors. But may not the Jew think of himself as different and
take pride in his being different? Here, then, there is a sharing and
an experiencing of an emotion that people may not react to with
the anger and vehemence characterizing the claim about responsibility and what are taken to be its implications for being and feeling
guilty. Why should this be?

I started with a claim that not even the man putting it forward
felt capable of explaining. Some of these objections brought to

light that this claim has the power to arouse strong emotion. And it evidently does this because, being a moral claim, it seems to have implications for the kinds of persons we are, the conduct we should and should not engage in, the feelings we should, but do not, have. And now, as I see it, the ground is laid for seeing what features of our moral life may have led persons to make this claim.

II

One man, out to kill another, succeeds by stabbing the man to death. He is tried, convicted and punished for murder. He is responsible for the man's death; he is held legally responsible or liable for the man's death; he is adjudged guilty of murder. Another man, with precisely the same state of mind, engages in precisely the same acts, but by coincidence the man into whom he has thrust his knife has, unknown to the actor, died seconds before of a heart attack. About this would-be killer, we would not in the law, or indeed in everyday judgments outside the law, say that he was responsible for the man's death; and in the law he is not *held* liable or responsible for the man's death though, on some theories of attempt, he would be guilty of attempted murder. But were we convinced that the man did all that he believed necessary to kill, I think we should be tempted to make the following moral judgments: he is guilty; he is as guilty as if he had succeeded in killing; and, finally, we might also be tempted to say of him that morally he is a murderer or, at least, no different from a murderer. Students of the criminal law are familiar with discussions that deal with punishing less severely the man who attempts and fails through some fortuity than the man who succeeds. It is clear that a major problem posed by the differential punishment of attempters and consummators is the apparent lack of a moral difference between the two classes of men.

I want now to draw some distinctions relevant to the theme of this paper, several of which have been stimulated by thought about this case of attempted homicide. First, we shall want to keep separate, though they are obviously related, the concepts of responsibility for harm and being held responsible or blamed because of some wrong or offence. When a person is responsible for harm this ordinarily implies a causal relation between that person's actions and some harm. When a person is held legally responsible, this ordinarily implies the decision to impose a

S

generally recognized deprivation upon the person because of some defined wrong. Similarly, when a person is blamed, a negative attitude is expressed toward the person because of some wrong. The law sometimes permits persons to be held responsible even though they are not responsible for harm, witness the case of being held responsible for attempts. And, of course, we all the time blame persons though they have not succeeded in causing harm.

The second distinction is that between being responsible for something that has occurred and being responsible for the performance of some task in the future. The one is retrospective; the other is prospective. Consider, for example, this passage from Freud:

> Obviously one must hold oneself responsible for the evil impulses of one's dreams. In what other way can one deal with them? Unless the content of the dream (rightly understood) is inspired by alien spirits, it is a part of my own being. If I seek to classify the impulses that are present in me according to social standards into good and bad, I must assume responsibility for both sorts; and if, in defence, I say that what is unknown, unconscious and repressed in me is not my 'ego', then I shall not be basing my position upon psychoanalysis, I shall not have accepted its conclusions and I shall perhaps be taught better by the criticisms of my fellow men, by the disturbances in my actions and the confusion of my feelings. I shall perhaps learn that what I am repudiating not only 'is' in me but sometimes 'acts' from out of me as well. (*Collected Papers*, V, 156.)

The retrospective responsibility urged here by Freud is clear. The prospective responsibility is to deal with the dream material as one's own and not as something alien to one. Indeed, the entire analytic process can be seen as a subtle combination of these types of responsibility, for it requires for success a person's assuming responsibility for change and this is partly, at least, dependent upon recognition of one's retrospective responsibility for the way one is.

The third distinction is that between being responsible in the sense of being morally liable to answer or respond, equivalent to being guilty, and being held responsible. Many persons are morally answerable for wrongdoing without being in fact held answerable.

There is, next, a distinction between 'being guilty *of*' and being a guilty person. Being guilty *of* does not admit of degrees. One is or is not guilty of some wrong. But being a guilty person does admit of degrees. We think, for example, that, other things being equal, a murderer is more guilty than a thief, that, other things being equal, one who intentionally kills is more guilty than one who kills negligently. Now if we examine our attempter and consummator, there is a temptation to say that, while they are guilty of different offences or wrongs, they are equally guilty persons, that the upshot of their conduct does not bear on their degree of guilt. On this view, what is determinative of the degree of guilt is the state of mind with which a person acts and the value of the interest he threatens. But this line of thinking fails to distinguish sufficiently a person's blameworthiness and a person's guilt, both of which admit of degrees.

Let us turn to our attempter again. Suppose that a moment after he stabs what he assumes to be a live human being he is overcome with remorse and with feelings of guilt. Then he discovers that he has not killed the man. We can imagine a sigh of relief. The blood is not on his hands. The remorse vanishes. He does not feel as guilty, that is, the intensity of the pain associated with his guilt feelings is lessened and this reflects a recognition on his part that he is less guilty. Why is this so? To be guilty is, among other things, both to owe something to another and to be the justified object of their hostility. But what we owe, what we must do to make amends, is a function partly of what has actually been done. And the hostility that people feel is partly determined by the hurt they have actually suffered. So, the fortuity of not having killed puts our attempter in a position where he arouses less hostility and where he has less to do to make amends. He is, to be sure, still guilty—for reasons I shall soon go into—but his guilt is less than that of the consummator. Both are, however, equally blameworthy, for our moral assessment of their characters as manifested in their conduct does not treat as relevant the fortuitous upshot of their acts.

What is the relevance of all this to the claim 'we are responsible for everything?' First, the claim, quite clearly, should not be interpreted to mean that all persons are causally connected with all evil deeds and all harm. Second, the claim should not be interpreted to mean that all men are guilty of each and every offence that has been committed. The phrase 'for everything' should be understood as meaning 'for all types of wrongs, harms, evils'; it does not mean, then, that we are responsible for every instantiation of the type. Third, the point of the claim is that we are all responsible in the sense of being morally answerable for or guilty with respect to every type of wrongdoing. Now why are we all in this position?

Let us consider just the value of human life and wrongs related to it and let us look again at our last step attempter. He is as blameworthy as the man who kills. He is also a guilty person. But this carries the proponent of the claim that we are all responsible for everything only a short distance. For, while the man causally disconnected from death in my example may be guilty and as blameworthy as a murderer, it is simply not true that all men stand to the death of human beings in the same relation as men who have done all in their power to kill and who have only failed through some fortuity. What is true of these men is that they intend to kill; they do all in their power to kill and only some fact irrelevant to moral judgment of their persons, say, some unknown intervening agent or unknown circumstance, distinguishes them from the man who kills. But it is precisely these important facts that make these men guilty and that distinguish these men from most of us. And so examples of men doing all they believe necessary to kill hardly touch most persons, for an insignificant number of men fit the description of those who have done all they believe necessary to kill. It might be granted, then, that if 'we are responsible for everything' is interpreted as I have interpreted it, and if the world were composed entirely of persons such as our attempter, the claim would be true. But the world just is not that way.

Let us consider, next, a man who intends to kill, who takes substantial steps towards killing and who then abandons his project because he fears being caught—the man he seeks to kill is guarded by the police. How does he stand legally and morally? In the law he is generally treated as a man who has attempted to kill and his abandonment is not a defence. Such a case does not satisfy even the proposed liberalized abandonment rule of the American Law Institute's *Model Penal Code*, for the man cannot be said to have 'voluntarily renounced his criminal project under circumstances manifesting renunciation of his criminal purpose'. And it seems clear that if the man is one who held back primarily or solely because of fear of apprehension, there are no marks to be placed on the credit side of his moral ledger sheet. It may even be claimed that 'in the eyes of God' he is indistinguishable from the last step attempter. Suppose just for the moment that this claim is granted. Those who hold out against the claim 'we are all responsible for everything', now interpreted as 'we are all guilty', will still find it an exaggeration for, while the class of those who have intended to kill and who have taken substantial steps toward this end and then turned back out of fear may be larger than the class of those who have gone the whole way, few additional persons, hardly all of us, fit into this class of attempters.

The class of the guilty widens considerably when we consider a man's character and what he desires to do. Suppose that a man desires to kill. Suppose he firmly believes that were he to possess Gyges' ring, with its capacity to make him invisible, he would kill. All that holds him back is fear. Is he any less guilty than the man who turned back at a later stage because of fear? It is precisely here that we can imagine the proponent of our extreme view pressing forward. The man has not formed an intention to kill, but his reasons for restraint are not morally creditable ones and he is not, just because of a decision not to proceed, excluded from the class of the guilty. Indeed, morally, does such a man differ from the killer? If he does not, is not the class of those who must admit to sharing the guilt associated with murder enlarged considerably?

We have travelled some way from our killer and our last step attempter to the man who desires and turns back out of fear alone or, for that matter, any reason that is not a morally creditable one. If we believe that all such persons are guilty and if we accept as warranted the view that most, if not all human beings, do on some occasions desire to kill, desire, indeed, to do a range of acts that constitute harm to others, and that it is a rare human being who has always, given such desires, restrained himself for morally creditable reasons, then we shall perhaps find the claim, as so interpreted, more plausible than before. This is, I think, one possible line of defence for the view 'we are all responsible for everything' and it needs now to be evaluated.

To begin with, someone may suggest that there is a significant moral distinction between, on the one hand, the class of those who do everything they believe necessary to succeed and those who succeed, and on the other hand, classes ranging from the substantial step attempter back to those who merely desire and do not form the intention to kill out of fear. What is true of the latter classes and not the former is that, if we are dealing with free agents, there is always the possibility that, were such persons to continue and the policeman no longer around, they would turn back for morally creditable reasons. Let us call this change of mind for morally creditable reasons 'a change of heart'. Now, if we grant that a change of heart is possible, even in the case of a man who firmly believes he will go on to kill, we cannot say, and the man who himself has the desire or even the intention cannot say with certainty, that he will take steps to kill and that no morally creditable reason will bear on him and lead to a change of heart. Indeed, we cannot even say this about all those individuals who do all that they believe necessary to kill, for, in some cases, they can by subsequent conduct intervene and prevent harm from resulting. The person who has poisoned a cup of coffee can empty it before it is drunk.

The merit in this suggestion is its drawing our attention to differences in degrees of guilt. The claim 'we are all responsible for everything', at least on the basis of the kinds of cases we have been considering, should not depend on the truth of 'we are all equally guilty', for we are not. But the suggestion I have set out is neither clear nor, on either of two possible interpretations, correct in the explanation offered for differences in degrees of guilt. Is it being claimed that the mere possibility of a change of heart makes one less guilty than one who has not had such a change and who has gone the whole way? But why should a possibility bear on one's guilt? We are tempted to say at this point, 'It's only if he in fact will have a change of heart that he is less guilty than one who has not'. But perhaps then the claim is that the person might be as guilty; it is just that neither we nor he can know whether or not he is. This position seems wrong too, wrong because it fails to give sufficient weight to what a man has actually done. A man's going farther simply makes him more guilty than one who has not gone as far even if the one who has travelled less distance will in fact not have a change of heart. With each step one takes toward the ultimate end an opportunity to forbear is left unseized and more guilt is added, the quantum of stain increasing as one moves to the end. It is not the absence of a change of heart but the distance travelled that bears on guilt. Neither the last step attempter nor the consummator has had a change of heart, yet they are not equally guilty.

Let us now consider those classes of persons about whom we can say 'They have accepted desires to do acts that are wrong'. As I employ the concept of accepting desires these are either persons who form intentions to realize their desires or, if having desires, they do not form such intentions, fail to do so for reasons that are not morally creditable. Are such persons guilty at all? What do we think of such persons? What, too, we may ask, do they themselves feel and for what reasons? We think of them, I believe, as guilty, at least to some degree. And it is clear, I think, that persons who accept desires may feel guilty because of their mental posture.

What might account for and justify one's having a feeling of guilt with respect to a state of mind in circumstances where harm to another is not evident? Freud's explanation is that the infant equates the intention or wish with the deed because of its belief in the omnipotence of thought. One may also be reminded of Jesus' remark that the man who lusts after a woman has already committed adultery with her in his heart. Jesus here is, I think, closer to the truth than Freud, for there is reason for guilt with respect to desires and intentions apart from a primitive belief in their causal efficacy. It is important to see that certain mental states are in themselves destructive of valued relationships. They are destructive because the relationship is partly defined in terms of feelings and thoughts.

Consider a man who has a valued relationship of reciprocal trust and fidelity with his wife. Now suppose that this man at some point forms the intention to commit adultery. If the man commits adultery and the wife learns of it, we can readily see the harm to her. But suppose the wife does not learn of the husband's infidelity, for there has been none. She only learns of his intention. Here too we can see harm. But suppose she doesn't learn of his intention. The relationship has still been damaged, for it is defined partly by each partner being prepared to exercise restraint out of love and respect for the other. The man's intention reveals that he is no longer prepared to abide by this condition. It is understandable, then, that he may feel guilt, understandable that, after a change of heart, he may wish to confess what he desired to do, what he formed the intention to do, in order thereby to restore a relationship he sees himself as having damaged.

To be sure, our relationship to others in society is only rarely that of love or friendship. It ought however to be a relationship, and responsible persons so understand it, in which there is reciprocal care and trust and respect. A man who accepts a desire to do an act harmful to another has a state of mind incompatible with a relationship among human beings that is valued by all responsible persons. He is, given his state of mind, no longer trustworthy; and his state of mind reveals a lack of care and respect for his fellow men. Certain states of mind constitute wrongs, then, for these states are themselves incompatible with morally required relationships between human beings.

Now suppose that we have all been guilty of such wrongs. Suppose we have harboured malicious intentions. What are the consequences? Is this guilt which we have all shared one for which it is possible to make amends? If we have by our thoughts separated ourselves from this ideal, only partially realized, community of responsible persons, how do we atone, how do we become *at one with* that community again?

Let us turn attention first to those who have accepted desires to do acts harmful to others but who might yet have a change of heart. Their guilt implies, I believe, the assumption of responsibility, a prospective responsibility, to renounce their desires and to labour toward being persons who, in caring for and respecting others, are themselves worthy of the care, trust and respect of others. The significant point is that a relationship of a valued kind has been ruptured by a state of mind; it can be restored by the person acquiring the appropriate state of mind.

What, however, of the man who goes the whole way. There are those in this class who succeed and those who fail. Let us first compare those who fail with the class of those who intend and who make substantial steps in furtherance of their intention. It is a mistake, I believe, to treat, as the American Law Institute's *Model Penal Code* would have it, these different classes of attempters in the same manner. The man who intends and who takes substantial steps has ruptured a relationship. He has also, perhaps, increased the risk of an actual invasion of the specific interests of other human beings by his steps in furtherance of his intention. But when we deprive such persons of their liberty, it is not primarily as punishment for wrongdoing, but as a preventive measure. Punishment in such cases does not perform its essentially moral task of restoration. A person's apologizing and renouncing his criminal purposes would be sufficient to restore his relationship with others. If he does not renounce his criminal purposes, preventive reasons can explain his continued incarceration, but it is not the case that a deprivation is being visited upon him for wrongdoing and that with this deprivation he pays off some debt to society.

It is otherwise, I believe, with the man who has done all that he believes necessary to realize his criminal purpose but who fails. He has ruptured a relationship of trust and respect for which he might make amends in the manner I have described. But he has done more and he owes more. Punishment of such a man is peculiarly appropriate, for it deprives him of any unfair advantage he has acquired as against all responsible persons in society. The picture I have in mind is as follows.

There are rules in all societies compliance with which provides benefits for all persons. These benefits consist in non-interference by others with what each person values, such matters as continuance of life and bodily security. Making possible this mutual benefit is the assumption by individuals of a burden. The burden consists in the exercise of self-restraint by individuals at a point where, were they not to exercise it, others would in the normal course of events be harmed. If a person fails to exercise self-restraint even though he might have, he relinquishes a burden which others have voluntarily assumed and thus gains an advantage which others, who have restrained themselves, do not possess. This system is one in which the rules establish a mutuality of benefit and burden and in which the benefits of non-interference are conditional upon the assumption of burdens. A moral equilibrium is, then, established.

Our man who goes the whole way but who fails through some fortuity upsets that equilibrium, for he has relinquished a burden which others have assumed which is a condition for the benefits of the system. He resembles the consummator in this respect, but he differs from the attempter who might yet turn back. This attempter has decided to relinquish the burden of self-restraint that is the condition for the benefits of the system, but he still has opportunity to exercise restraint. He doesn't as yet have, as does the man who goes the whole way, the unfair advantage that justice demands be taken from him. The man, then, who goes the whole way derives the benefits others do but, by relinquishing a burden others have assumed, he gains an advantage over them. Punishment, a deprivation occasioned by wrongdoing, deprives him of his advantage and restores the upset moral equilibrium.

What accounts for the differential punishment of the two classes of men who do all in their power to succeed, the unsuccessful attempter and the consummator? I suggested earlier that they were equally blameworthy but not equally guilty. The consummator owes more because he has taken and acquired more. He has not just the satisfaction attendant upon relinquishing the burden of self-restraint, but he has the satisfaction attendant upon realization of his desires. He has not only upset the equilibrium I have described but violated the rights of particular persons. He must then do something to re-establish the moral equilibrium resting on mutual exercise of restraint and he must do something to make amends for the particular harm to the individual.

There is one final matter that I want to raise before we move on to other types of cases that may be appealed to in support of the claim 'we are responsible for everything'. So far, I have sought to loosen up objections to the claim by interpretations of responsibility, blameworthiness and guilt. It is particularly important, however, to avoid too cramped a concept of what we are guilty of. It is clear that focusing, as I have, upon essentially legal examples of attempted homicide and homicide, has its disadvantages. The law has good reasons for attempting to define offences in relatively precise terms. But, of course, in doing this and in being guided by other principles that define the law's proper scope much that is evil is not encompassed within the law. Murder, legally, for example, requires a corpse and what enters into defining a corpse are physiological considerations. But morality is not limited in this way. There is a death in life, and when we look upon ourselves, our acts and our thoughts, few, if any of us, can escape the taint of blood. Nietzsche writes: 'One has not watched life very observantly if one has never seen the hand that—kills tenderly.'

III

Thus far I have attempted to bring out one way in which it makes sense, and might even be true, to talk of our all being guilty, our all sharing in guilt. I want now to turn to another class of cases where more is involved than our each sharing certain states that give rise to guilt. The individuals I want now to consider are labelled in law 'accomplices'. Part, I believe, of what underlies the claim 'we are all responsible for everything' is the view that we are all in one way or another accomplices in evil. This line of argument at some point dovetails with the one we have just examined, for persons may be guilty because of intentions which, if executed, would make them accomplices.

In these cases of shared guilt, it is acknowledged that there is an individual who is guilty of some wrong. In the law he is labelled 'a principal'. One shares the guilt associated with that wrong because of a relationship to the principal. There is a considerable body of legal material on complicity. Let us first turn our attention to this.

As our law is now constituted one who counsels, advises, or persuades another or who aids another in committing a crime is a party to that crime and since the abandonment of common law distinctions between principals and accessories, guilty of the same offence as the principal and subject to identical punishment. Encompassed within the law governing complicity are the following classes. First, there are those who advise or persuade another to commit some crime and who are parties to the crime without being causally connected with the ultimate harm. Complicity doctrine is not the ground of liability when a responsible actor gets an irresponsible person, say a child or insane person, to perform some deed that is contrary to the law. Likewise, if one gets a responsible person to perform an act proscribed by law either through coercion or deception one is directly related to the offence and once again complicity doctrine is not the basis of liability. There are, second, those who aid or assist another in the commission of a crime. The law generally requires that the person's purpose be to assist in the commission of an offence, though there is strong difference of opinion within the United States' Federal Courts whether or not knowingly facilitating the commission of an offence should be sufficient. The law, for example, will generally leave untouched the businessman who provides a commodity which he has good reason to believe or even knows will be used for a criminal purpose if the businessman can establish that he was indifferent to the commission of the crime and was just interested in his usual profit. New York, going further than has generally been the case, has created a new offence titled 'criminal facilitation' in which liability requires: (1) a belief that 'it is probable that' one is rendering aid to a person who intends to commit a crime, (2) that one engages in conduct which provides such a person with means or opportunity for the commission of an offence, and (3) that the person has in fact aided another to commit a felony. There are, next, those who aid the perpetrators in escaping detection, apprehension, conviction, punishment. There are other classes of persons which legal systems have sometimes singled out and treated as guilty, usually not of the offence committed by the principal actor, but of separately defined offences. These include: those who knowingly profit from the wrongdoing; those who stand by and do not make an effort to prevent the offence when they might have done so without risk to their own well-being; those who fail to take steps to prevent escape. The law leaves untouched those who merely approve and those who create by their conduct the general atmosphere in which crime thrives. This is a sketch of the legal situation with regard to complicity. What now are the boundaries of moral complicity?

First, I have so far in this essay limited myself to the states of mind of desire and intention. But it is important to realize that a person may be blamed for matters which he neither desired nor intended to bring about. One may, of course, be guilty of reckless or negligent homicide. One may be blamed for taking unwarranted risks. I raise this point now, for it is apparent that the law generally circumscribes liability for complicity by insisting upon purpose or at least knowledge. Legal liability is not imposed upon the man who aids another but does so recklessly or negligently. Those who wish to impress upon us our complicity in wrongdoing will wish, and correctly I think, to take into account a variety of states of mind that, associated with conduct, are a basis for guilt.

Second, they will move to expand the concept of complicity so that it encompasses all conduct for which one may rightfully be blamed that substantially contributes to wrongdoing. Thus, individuals may seek to bring out possible sources of our complicity in wrongdoing by bringing to our attention: unwise and repressive legislation which requires restraint over powerful impulses without any clear corresponding gain to society, the unwillingness of citizens to provide greater financial support for educating the young and educating and compensating the police, for improvement of prisons, for greater numbers of probationary officers, for improved facilities and programmes for juvenile offenders; they may point also to those many aspects of our culture that convey to persons generally an impression of indifference and positive distaste for the values of human affection and respect; they may point to all that leads to frustration, anger and discontent and that might be otherwise if people were less afraid and prepared to sacrifice more. The list is obviously long that enumerates the many things we do and fail to do that contribute to the existence of wrongdoing. Unless we are saints are we not guilty of involvement in at least some forms of conduct that promote wrongdoing?

Third, one may share guilt because one profits from wrongdoing. There are clear cases here, cases in which we believe that a person partaking of the results of some wrongdoing thereby associates himself with it, as when one accepts known stolen goods from a thief and uses them for one's own satisfaction. What is not clear is that we are all guilty with respect to all types of wrongs if this is the basis of our guilt. I turn now to one final point that may support the view that we all profit from wrongdoing of every kind.

It is important, I think, in coming to appreciate our subtle and not so subtle complicity in wrongdoing to understand what psychological investment we may have in it. This requires that we take into account a possible connection between shared guilt in the preceding section and shared guilt through complicity. What I have in mind has been much elaborated upon in psychoanalytic literature and in Sartre's richly textured *St Genet*. The criminal crosses a barrier which others desire to cross but do not. He gives in to impulses; others restrain themselves. This process involves a heavy cost in satisfaction to each person and is accomplished through the internalization of precepts and negative responses to their violation. Set up in us is a mechanism which aggressively responds to threatened and actual violations. If something like this is so, we can conjecture that the criminal services our needs in the following ways. First, he acts out what we only fantasize. We can derive satisfaction from identification with him. We can derive satisfaction from seeing our desires realized if only through the medium of another. Second, the criminal, while a vehicle for our satisfaction, among other things, also arouses envy and anger in us toward him. He has seized what it has taken us so much to forgo. Normally, we must forbear from expression of anger; we must not strike out but rather keep the aggression in. The criminal is someone, however, if only in an institutionally governed way that we can strike out against and regard it as acceptable. Here, we may say, our instinctual life is relatively unhampered. Third, the criminal also permits the aggression that otherwise would turn inward to be deflected outward. He, not we, is guilty. Finally, he perhaps services us in still another way. In giving in to what we all desire, he manifests what we too often do not, power and daring, a willingness to risk oneself for the satisfaction of strong desires. Both Stendhal and Nietzsche, among others, believed that criminals demonstrated that there was still a spark of life left in man.

If there were no criminals, should we have to invent them? If there is truth in the suggestion that we should, how much of human conduct is subtly devised to perpetuate the very existence of those of whom we say we are so longing to be rid?

IV

There is another class of cases where we may speak of 'shared guilt'. These cases do not support the view that 'we are all guilty with respect to all types of wrongdoing'. They do support the view, however, that we are all guilty of some evil. In Camus's *The Fall* the hero walking along the bridge hears the splash and does nothing. His guilt is apparent. It is here that pressure will begin to be applied by the proponent of the view that we are all guilty. How are you and I to be distinguished from Camus's hero? Are not you and I, in the lives we lead, omitting to do what we could to prevent suffering? Perhaps people in need are not within a few feet with their suffering vividly before us. What difference should that make? How shall we go about distinguishing between the child starving close by and the one starving in some more distant place? And shall we distinguish between a hand held out for food and one held out, perhaps less apparently, for compassion and understanding? I think that it may be admitted that if we could in fact prevent suffering and do not then we are

responsible for it. But, it will be argued, this does not mean that
we are at all blameworthy or that we have any guilt with respect
to what comes about. We all have obligations closer to home and
perhaps, if we each attend to these, more in the end will be gained
by all. Also life has more to it than attempting to rescue or assist
those in need. We have also our own lives to lead at some level of
intensity, joyfulness and beauty. A concept such as 'what can
reasonably be expected of one' may be used to block the claim
that we are guilty because we fail to prevent suffering we might
have prevented. The concept of guilt is linked to that of fault
and this concept is in turn linked to demands that may rightfully
be placed upon a man. These in turn connect with the reasonableness of a man's conduct. And it may be argued that it is at least
not unreasonable to act in ways that are not related to alleviating
suffering. There is some balance we must all strike. So the
argument will go.

In response, this may be said. It is clear that there are those
persons who have sacrificed more than we. When we reflect
on their lives, if we are sensitive and honest, we may be struck by
our weakness and selfishness. At this point, people may begin to
be genuinely troubled over their moral condition. First of all,
which one of us can say that he has always done what could even
reasonably be demanded of him? Have we balanced in an acceptable way living a decent human life and helping those who are less
fortunate? The grip of the claim 'We are all guilty' tightens here,
for it is no easy matter to determine where the line is to be drawn
when a concept as vague as 'reasonableness' is our guide; and we
may, naturally, feel anxious when drawing it that we have un-
warrantedly favoured our own interests over those of others.

Second, even if we have done all that could be expected of a
reasonable man, perhaps there is still more that we could have
done. I think of these remarks of Jaspers in *The Question of
German Guilt*:

> When our Jewish friends were taken away, we did not go out
> into the street and cry aloud until we also met our death. We
> preferred to remain in life for the weak, even if justifiable,
> reason that our death would not in any way have helped. It
> is our own fault that we are still alive. . . . It demands that
> we should take on us the consequences of being alive in such
> conditions.

270   HERBERT MORRIS

There are two types of situations that Jaspers presents to us in his book that he does not clearly separate. There is, first, the case of our failing to do whatever we can to prevent evil. There is, second, the case of one who has not necessarily failed, in any way but merely in remaining alive when others have their lives unjustly taken, but is guilty. An attachment to human solidarity, were it not for our weakness, would lead man to sacrifice his life though this would accomplish nothing but an affirmation of human solidarity.

A person may certainly feel in either of these cases what he will label 'guilt'. And if in fact one has guilt for not doing all that a saint, a hero, an angel would do, then surely 'we are all guilty' in this sense. But when Jaspers talks of fault and guilt in the circumstances in which he does, the idea of guilt, because fault conditions, normally associated with guilt, are absent, is merging into something else. He recognizes this by labelling the guilt 'metaphysical guilt'. I think this phenomenon may also be described as 'self-guilt' or 'guilt before oneself' or perhaps best 'shame'.

Its striking feature is that being metaphysically guilty does not imply a rupture in established moral relations with others. Thus nothing may be re-established by confession or repentance or forgiveness or punishment. Guilt, in standard cases, is linked to the idea of an imbalance occasioned by some wrong. A relationship with another or others has been damaged. It connects with ideas such as fault, restoration, confession, making amends, repentance, forgiveness, punishment, justice, excuse. It is all otherwise with shame. Fault is not essential to shame; we do not make amends for a shameful act. Nothing can be forgiven. Punishment is inappropriate and cannot serve as it does with some types of guilt to restore relationships.

There are two points that seem to me particularly important to emphasize here. First, in failing to do the extraordinary, we may feel that we are less than we would desire to be. Still, it is inappropriate for others to make any demand on us to have performed in that way. Second, our failure may be, not in neglecting to do the extraordinary, but in doing and failing to do things that, while ultimately involving harm to others, are most directly crimes involving ourselves, crimes that consist in one way or another in failures of integrity, failures to be and to act as our conception of ourselves dictates. There is a strong temptation to talk of guilt here—guilt before ourselves—rather than shame, for fault conditions do obtain in many instances, and it is our own choices that have turned us away from being ourselves. The impulse to talk of shame, in this type of case also, as in cases of not doing the extraordinary, comes from the inappropriateness in these cases of alleviating the feelings we have by conduct such as confession, making amends, asking forgiveness or receiving punishment.

V

We have looked at cases where there may be talk of guilt and we had before us the extraordinary and there was a temptation understandably felt to say that guilt and shame were there merging. We have also looked at cases where guilt may be spoken of and a rupture in a relationship with others is not involved but rather a break with one's self which gives rise to an obligation to return to or be what we believe we should be. In all these cases, whether the act we think of is one within the capacities of normal men or whether it calls for some extraordinary conduct, it is an identifiable individual who possesses in some sense a capacity to have behaved otherwise and has not. This partially accounts, I think, for the temptation to talk in these cases of guilt though, as I have tried to show, in some instances the concept is being stretched. There are cases, however, in which the pull on the concept of guilt is very severe indeed and where shame seems far the more appropriate concept. In these cases we feel shame for what others do where none of the reasons for sharing guilt so far brought out seem apparent.

What are the criteria for taking pride in and feeling shame over the deeds or characteristics of others? We connect ourselves in some way with others and when they act we see it reflecting not just on them but on us. They may be at fault and thus guilty. We are not at fault, but we still see their conduct as reflecting on us, reflecting perhaps on deficiencies we share with them. We want to hide from the view of others because we believe that what another person has done reflects on us because of our connection to this person. Suppose my own son does well; I may take pride in his accomplishments. If he does poorly, I may feel ashamed. There is here, we want to say, my involvement with what he is and, thus, how he performs partly and understandably reflects credit or discredit on me. But is it always this way? And when it is not, where one's efforts do not link up in some way with those of

T

others, is taking pride or feeling shame irrational? Something like neurotic guilt?

There are always bases for identifying oneself as being a member of a certain class, a thing of a certain kind. There are, for example, a variety of criteria relating to identifying oneself as a male, as an American, as a Catholic, a kind or selfish person, a human being. In identifying ourselves as human we think of characteristics we have that other animate things do not. We might think that to be human is to be rational or have the capacity for rationality. Or struck by the significance of the setting forth of values and what this implies, someone may identify being human with the capacity to feel guilt. When such a person comes upon a psychopath he may feel a strong temptation to describe such a person as an animal in the body of a human being. We look upon ourselves as members of a class and there are usually relatively well-accepted bases for so doing—though the criteria are, as in the case of 'human being' or 'person' numerous and complicated in character. Now, this is the reason why, when a member of a class of which we consider ourselves a member does something commendable, we take pride. It is in the family so to speak. It is saying something about us. And likewise for the ignoble. There is something, I think, to the feeling of being ashamed at being human when one reflects on the horrors perpetrated by our species and likewise for the pride in its accomplishments. One would rather be an animal when one hears sometimes of what mankind is capable of. One shares in the attributes manifested in some evil deed. If animals judged us, we should turn away in shame at what humans have done to them.

When Father Zossima's brother said 'we are all responsible for everything' we may feel that he was struggling to make some point about the appropriateness of our feeling shame, perhaps before God, because of the evil done by any human being, as if some defect in us were revealed by what any human being did. But I think what he found impossible to explain was our all being in fact guilty and as guilty as any wrongdoer who had ever perpetrated evil. It is not that what another does reflects upon us. It is that we are in fact the other. Mankind was a unity, a single child of God, and there was no separateness, the act of one being the act of all. He saw close connections to the point of a moral identity where we see significant disconnections. At the heart, then, of 'we are all responsible for everything' is a metaphysical belief about persons and actions similar to beliefs we ascribe to certain primitive societies which interpret the act of one member of a tribe as the act of each and every member of the tribe. Father Zossima's brother extends the unity of the family against which Ezekiel rebelled to the whole of mankind. And the implication of this, for him, is that any moral judgment of one by another makes in fact guilty and as guilty as any wrongdoer who had ever no sense. Why did he come to these beliefs? Was it because of a sense that there was evil within us all and that its manifesting itself in time in the acts of one person rather than another was essentially adventitious?

'We are all responsible for everything'. I have attempted to see how understanding might be furthered by examination of several different types of consideration that might lead to the claim. I first moved to interpret 'responsible for everything' as 'guilt with respect to all evil'. I next drew a distinction between being guilty and being *as* guilty. I then traced various routes to a view that we are all guilty. One route emphasized the commonality of impulses toward evil. Another stressed the degree to which we are all implicated in wrongdoing through complicity with others. Another stressed guilt arising from our failure to act. Still another attempted to draw attention to guilt before ourselves.

Interpreting the claim as I have what should our attitude be toward the objections raised at the beginning of the paper? A number of the objections are wide of the mark because 'responsible for everything' is erroneously interpreted as implying some causal connection between all persons and all harm. When the claim is interpreted as 'we are all guilty' a number of the criticisms may be deflected.

It might still be argued, however, that 'we are all guilty' deprives of usefulness the concept of guilt. I do not think that this criticism is valid. First, as we have seen, there are still degrees of guilt. Second, gaining an insight into our own moral condition may lead us to assume responsibility for becoming different, for becoming persons whom others can understandably care for, trust and respect.

XII

LITERATURE AND PHILOSOPHY

RENFORD BAMBROUGH

IN THE beginning was the Word (with a capital W). In the beginning was the Logos (with a capital Lambda). The Word is manifold, and in more than one way. First, it is twofold. Logos is both Speech and Reason. When Aristotle says that man is a λογικὸν ζῷον he means that man is the animal that speaks and reasons. From λόγος and λέγειν in Greek we have inherited logic, but also dialogue; not only syllogism, but dialectic.

The Word is Reason made flesh. Without reason the word is a noise or shape. Without words reason is a ghost.

The Word is also manifold because Speech is manifold and Reason is manifold. Each of them is both one and many, and the modes of utterance are modes of understanding.

But the duplicity of speech and reason is united in the Logos. The multiplicity of the modes of utterance is united in Speech, and the multiplicity of the modes of understanding is united in the power and the glory of the Reason.

When speech and reason were called λόγος the primal unity still hid the duality and multiplicity. Professor H. D. F. Kitto has said that the Greeks had no word for it—no word for *literature*. He might have added that the Greeks had no word for philosophy, or for history or science. The unity of understanding and of utterance concealed the distinctness of their modes. Plato's 'ancient quarrel' between ποίησις and φιλοσοφία is therefore a γενναῖον ψεῦδος—a useful fiction. It was because Plato was struggling to separate ποίησις from φιλοσοφία and poetry from philosophy that he found it convenient to represent them as separate and opposed. His struggle to separate them would have been unnecessary if he had not recognised that both in principle and in ancient practice philosophy and literature were modes of one substance. Parmenides and Empedocles were not poets who happened to be interested in philosophy or philosophers who chose to write in verse. Like Homer and Hesiod and Heraclitus and Herodotus they were Greeks who understood and uttered, thought and spoke. Plato's struggle was an internal struggle not because poetry and philosophy were at war in him but because they were united and he strove to tear them apart.

The Greeks had no word for literature because they still lived in a united Republic of Letters. The themes of literature are the themes of philosophy too: Man, God, Nature, Art; Will, Fate, Necessity, Chance and Freedom; Knowledge and Ignorance, Truth and Falsehood, Good and Evil. To learn about self-knowledge and self-deceit you need the help of Socrates and Oedipus; Bishop Butler and Freud and Hobbes and Hume, but also Proust and George Eliot and Henry James and James Joyce and James Baldwin; Sartre on *mauvaise foi* in *L'Être et le Néant*, but also Sartre on *mauvaise foi* in *La Putain Respectueuse*. I once met a philosopher from the Sorbonne whose doctoral subject was the idea of seduction in literature and thought, and I was surprised until I remembered Camus and his epigraph from Defoe: 'Il est aussi raisonnable de représenter une espèce d'emprisonnement par une autre que de représenter n'importe quelle chose qui existe réellement par quelque chose qui n'existe pas.' And this is a special case of Wittgenstein's remark about the value and the risk of seeing one thing as a limiting case of another. Wittgenstein was struck mainly by the risk, but his own contributions to literature and philosophy display the value, and help to explain why readers with no taste for literature are baffled by his obscurities and are so often at a loss to understand his clarities.

The Republic of Letters is disunited now, and it is therefore its continuing unity that must be emphasised. To emphasise this hidden unity is to provoke insistent stress upon its unconcealed variety, to be involved in a philosophical conflict about literature and philosophy. This conflict serves to suggest a unity of method between philosophy and literature that is just as important and just as liable to be forgotten as the unity of theme. The two main points of method that bind philosophy and literature into one republic are both expressed by Blake.

'*Without contraries is no progression.*' In philosophy and in literature the human understanding moves in dialectical paths, and it does so because of the nature of the tasks that are set before it in those provinces of the republic. Philosophy is the conflict of the obvious with the obvious. It is obvious that we are free agents and obvious that our actions have causes, and obvious that if we are free agents our actions cannot have causes and that if our actions have causes we cannot be free agents. It is obvious that there are many things that we know for certain to be true and obvious that the conditions and criteria that must be satisfied before we can know anything for certain to be true cannot and could not possibly be met. It is obvious that every conclusion needs a reason and that every reason is a conclusion and needs a further reason and so that no procedure of proof can ever come to an end that is not arbitrary and so that no procedure of proof is a procedure of proof. And it is obvious that you and I and Galileo and Pythagoras can prove things.

Moral conflict is often the conflict of right with right, of the obviously right with the obviously right, and this is what among other things explains and justifies the belief that a philosopher should have something to offer to the morally perplexed. Moral perplexity is structurally akin to philosophical perplexity and calls for the same dialectical procedures.

Tragedy is often concerned with moral conflict, and that to some extent explains and to nearly the same extent justifies the belief that tragedy is the conflict of right with right. A problem play is also a play about a conflict between something obvious and something obvious. (Even if every tragedy is a problem play, not every problem play is a tragedy.)

'The Holiness of minute particulars'. Blake's phrase is inscribed on the ark of the republic's covenant. T. E. Hulme's gists and piths are to the same effect: 'Something is always lost in generalisation. A railway leaves out all the gaps of dirt between. Generalisations are only means of getting about.' (*Speculations*, p. 230). These generalisations of Blake and Hulme are means of getting as near as their own justice will allow to a summing-up of the procedures of literary and philosophical dialectic. A dialectical conflict is normally a conflict between generalities, which are partial and distorting because they are generalities, and the process of resolving such a conflict is the process of examining more minutely and particularly the minute particulars concerning which the opposed generalities are in conflict. Such a method of reasoning is usually informal, and its typical informality serves to link it with literature rather than with the formal and generalising mathematical and natural sciences, and so to disguise from many of its exponents as well as from nearly all its critics the fact that it is a method of reasoning at all.

Such a method is not confined to literature and philosophy, and it may be practised with a high degree of formality, as may be seen in the operation of the adversary system in courts of law. The system stylises and institutionalises what is in outline the same dialectical procedure for discovering and displaying an informal and complex pattern of details without losing scope and generality. What it stylises and institutionalises is the method of *conversation*, a mode of speech and reason which is itself a plurality as well as a unity, ranging as it does from Odysseus in the tent of Achilles or Jesus with the elders in the Temple to the austerities or asperities or banalities of police interrogation, bus queue altercation, lovers' quarrel, Question Time, Proceedings of the Aristotelian Society or extraordinary general meeting of the Royal Society for the Prevention of Cruelty to Animals.

The dialectical or adversary system that is the *de jure* method of the law is *de facto* the method of philosophy and history and criticism, in general of the humanities—of what in reports of the General Board of the Faculties at Cambridge are happily called the *literary* subjects. It is their conversational character, their untidy informality, that lays them open to the suspicion of indiscipline and subjectivity, of not getting anywhere. A conversation seems to have achieved nothing if we cannot say what it has achieved; but the appearance of failure is often deceptive. (A man I see every day may change without my noticing that he has changed. I may notice the change and not be able to say how he has changed.)

In ordinary conversation we make many remarks that are trivial and obvious; it *is* cold for the time of year, but to say so may just be to pass the time of day. In ordinary conversation we often make remarks that are obvious without being trivial. It may be obvious that she loves me or that she loves me not, and still important to me that she should answer Yes or No. In conversational conflict between the obvious and the obvious, and therefore in literary and moral and philosophical conflict too, it is necessary for both sides to state the obvious; for each to re-affirm what the other knows but denies or forgets because it seems to conflict with what is also obvious and is nearer to the front of his mind. Plato's judgement was sound when he linked dialectic with *Anamnesis*, with reminding and recalling of what we know but still need to be told by ourselves or others. And reminders are usually of minute particulars, of forgotten instances to which some hasty generality is vulnerable. Let me illustrate the importance of reminders of instances by reminding you of instances.

In his exchange with Professor René Wellek on 'Literary Criticism and Philosophy' Dr. Leavis declines to state any norms or criteria or principles by which he judges works of literature. He hints that philosophy may have need of such machinery, but literary criticism is concrete and philosophy is abstract, and we must fear the blurrings and bluntings and muddlings and misdirections that are commonly the 'consequences of queering one discipline with the habits of another'. Most people, whether they are philosophers or not, are unthinkingly on Wellek's side. Leavis has been challenged by many critics who were not philosophers to define his terms and state his principles. The old Socratic assumptions die hard, partly because of the influence of Socrates but mainly because of the powerful plausibility by which they beguiled Socrates in the first place. Even Leavis in his answer to Wellek is defensive on the philosophical point, and is uncompromising only in the claim to have a discipline of his own that can dispense with philosophic apparatus.

I believe that Leavis is right on the philosophical point as well as on the literary point; right on the philosophical point because he is right on the literary point, and because that point is not just one about literature but about the nature of all criticism, about the nature of values, and about the nature of all the modes of utterance and of understanding. Always and everywhere we must worship the Logos in the holiness of minute particulars.

So when Leavis offers what he pertinently calls 'some elementary observations by way of reminder' he might well have said that philosophy could do with more of the habits of literature and criticism and that criticism could do with less of what critics often think are the grander habits of philosophy. The definition of tragedy has by this time turned into the tragedy of definition, and when critics parade their postulates and nail down their necessary and sufficient conditions for being a sonnet or a novel or an epic, or Romantic or pastoral or picaresque, they are aping the apes among the philosophers who from Socrates to Russell have played follow-my-leader and queered philosophy with the bad habits of philosophers.

But many philosophers, like most critics, have been too good at their job to practise what they have preached. The 'placing', the setting of instance by instance, that Leavis rightly represents as the concrete and intricate task of the critic, is sometimes well done and often boldly attempted even by critics who will tell you, because they will also tell themselves, that they are doing and ought to be doing something quite different. Even when they do go through the motions of the abstract gymnastics that their theories call for they are usually covering with only a thin disguise a more or less well directed attention to the despised particularities. The wild goose of definition is never captured, but the chase takes the hunter over just the rugged and uneven ground whose contours he needs to survey.

It is the same story in philosophy as in criticism. There too the role of abstraction and generalisation is to take one side in a dialectical pattern whose objective is always and whose achievement is sometimes to set out what in particular stands where and in what relations to this and that and the other thing. Leavis has said elsewhere that in the last resort a critical conversation comes to this: that one man says 'This is so, isn't it?' and the other answers 'Yes, but . . .'. In his answer to Wellek he does not make strong enough and wide enough claims for this technique of comparison, on which all reasoning and not just all critical reasoning is ultimately founded; though he does insist on the point that I most want to extend from criticism to all the modes of thought when he claims for his methods a 'relative precision that makes this summarising seem intolerably clumsy and inadequate'.

Professor Donald MacKinnon has warned philosophers in general of the dangers of an 'excessively cerebral' approach to literature and has rebuked Aristotle in particular for forgetting when he came to write on poetry that according to his own wider philosophy all knowledge must be of what is universal. But Aristotle in the *Poetics* is not so much forgetting that knowledge is of the universal as remembering that there are more ways than one of achieving a grasp of the universal. When he says that poetry is more serious and more philosophical than history, that it deals not only with what particular things Alcibiades did and what in particular happened to Alcibiades but with what is universal, he is fully faithful to his wider theory of knowledge and its modes. For as much as any of the great philosophers he saw and emphasised that only through the particular can the universal be apprehended, and that much at least of the value of knowing the universal consists in the fact that to grasp the universal is to grasp the particular. He is therefore near to Ezra Pound's conception of literature as a science: 'Art does not avoid universals, it strikes them all the harder in that it strikes through particulars.' (*Literary Essays*, p. 420). 'The arts, literature, poesy, are a science just as chemistry is a science. Their subject is man, mankind and the individual. The subject of chemistry is matter considered as to its composition' (p. 42). Pound may be unduly limiting the subject-matter of the science that is literature, but on the perils of the old bad dichotomies he says the right things one after another: 'Saxpence reward for any authenticated case of intellect having stopped a chap's writing poesy! You might as well claim that railway tracks stop the engine. No one ever claimed they would make it go.'

T. E. Hulme's respect for the gaps of dirty individuality between the generalisations did not inhibit and does not contradict his correspondingly emphatic claim for philosophy: 'From the outside it has all the appearance of a science. But this we might take as a piece of protective mimicry to ward off the multitude, to preserve it in its seclusion as the rarest of the arts.' Nor did he forget that the arts as well as the sciences have to do with knowledge and ignorance and truth and falsehood: 'I do not mean what Nietzsche meant when he said "Do not speculate as to whether what a philosopher says is true, but ask how he came to think it true". This form of scepticism I hold to be just fashionable rubbish. Pure philosophy ought to be, and may be, entirely objective and scientific.' (*Speculations*, pp. 17–18).

There is a hint of the influence of the old dichotomies in the demand that works of literature be judged by canons of strictly *literary* discrimination: the old dichotomies of form and content, feeling and reason, imagination and intellect, subjective and objective. A hint, too, of the essentialism about literature of which there is more than a hint in the insistence that to say what literature is is only or primarily to say what is distinctive about literature and not what is true both of literature and of some things that are not literature. It is the most tedious platitude, but one that needs to be asserted because it is sometimes denied, that to know the nature of a thing is to know both how it resembles other things and how it differs from other things; to know, as one revealing idiom puts it, what that thing is like.

At its most extreme the old dichotomizing becomes the destructive madness of I. A. Richards in *The Principles of Literary Criticism*: 'There are two totally distinct uses of language' (which are of course the scientific and the emotive). In the same sense there are two totally distinct universities, Oxford and Cambridge; two totally distinct species of animals, whales and wallabies; two totally distinct works of art, Rodin's Thinker and the Madonna of the Rocks. But there are ten thousand other works of art, animal species, universities, for these to be totally distinct from.

Here of course I parody and oversimplify. Nobody would be tempted to dichotomize away Harvard and the Sorbonne or the hedgehog and the fox, and it is not for nothing that Richards and others are drawn into the particular exaggerations that madden and destroy them, and which then have to be palliated by maddening exaggerations that would be destructive if they did not *ex hypothesi* meet with their saving antidotes. It is not just that the scale is different, that reason and emotion are vast categories rather than isolated instances in the realm of thought and language. What is more important is that the extremes of dispassionate reason and unreasoned passion, though sharply opposed and separated by three thousand miles, are closely akin and linked by intermediate states. And wherever one extreme may by slow degrees become its opposite there is scope and need for the same dialectical conflict of reminder against reminder: good and evil, selfish and unselfish, free and compelled, sanity and madness, ignorance and knowledge. These are all paradigm examples from the sphere of operation of that fundamental mode of thought and talk in which each says to the other, 'This is so, isn't it?' and each replies 'Yes, but. . . .' For they are all cases in which what is obvious is in conflict with what is obvious, and when the obvious conflicts with the obvious something that is obvious will have to be denied and something that is obvious will have to be asserted, and so we shall reach for the patent instruments of philosophy and literature, tools and weapons forged for the battling and building of the workers and warriors of the Logos: paradox and platitude.

We are nearly all, like Socrates, wiser in our practice than in our theory, and recognise in speaking and reasoning, as we may fail to recognise in generalising about speech and reason, that there is a time for platitude and a time for paradox; a time for being literal-minded and accusing another's paradox of being merely fanciful, and a time for being fanciful and accusing another's platitude of being merely literal-minded. But even here it is easy and unhelpful to stop at this general observation. What is difficult and valuable is to know in the concrete which barrel to fire and which stop to pull out. We at once recognise as parody Hopkins's reminder to Wordsworth that ordinarily it is the man who is the father of the child. We all set down as an idiot the editor who improves *As You Like It*, Act II, Scene i, lines 16–17, 'Books in the running brooks, sermons in stones', to the more sober and accurate sense of 'Stones in the running brooks, sermons in books'. But nobody is immune from the impulse to unseasonable literalness. Philosophers are beset by the sin of meeting a paradox only with a demonstration that it has 'unacceptable consequences'; with a demonstration, in other words, that it is a paradox.

Sometimes it is just this that needs to be said and shown. For it can easily happen that the author of a paradox does not recognise his paradox for what it is, and wants to have the benefits and take the risks of literally denying a literal truth. His reminder then calls for an answering reminder. One half-truth deserves another, and it takes two halves to add up to a unified apprehension. In rarer cases the paradox will not even be a half-truth and its perversity will need and deserve the literal-minded savagery that philosophers, with even-handed injustice, visit upon the deserving and the undeserving alike.

It is this to and fro and give and take that gives us vision in depth, whether in literature or philosophy or in the dialogue and dialectic of an ordinary day in an ordinary life. A stereoscope uses two pictures from different angles. You will not see the landscape in perspective if you never shift your point of view. The Parthenon or the Winged Victory of Samothrace cannot be presented in a photograph but only in a book of photographs, cannot be seen at a glance or even with a long steady gaze but only by going round in circles on the Acropolis or in the Louvre. If you want to see life whole you must not *begin* by trying also to see it steadily. When you have made the round trip several times you may be able to stand in one place and still see or remember all at once what at first could only be seen by moving from one partial view to another.

All talk of points of view and aspects and perspectives brings with it the risk of sliding into subjectivity. It can be made to seem that what something is like depends on how you look at it or where you see it from, and this is one of many but one of the most influential reasons why literature is said to have nothing to do with *knowledge*.

It is obvious that the look of a thing will be different if you look at it from a different angle. This seems to conflict with what should also be obvious, that what a thing is like from this point of view and from that point of view is all part of what the thing *is* like, and that if that is what we want to know we are not at liberty to choose part of it and represent it as being the whole. This is already shown by the cases of the statue and the temple, but a few examples that come nearer to the bones of contention may be necessary and should be sufficient to establish that nowhere in the wide scope of this principle is its application limited by any variation in subject matter or logical kind or degree of subtlety, difficulty or complexity.

A man once told me that the most beautiful sight he had ever seen was the breaking and burning of a Spitfire against a night sky. Though he knew that he was watching the violent death of a friend, the sublimity of the spectacle had impressed and continued to impress him, but also to trouble him. Was it right to have noticed the beauty in spite of the death and the destruction? Could it really have been beautiful at all when it was the scene and occasion of such a death? Was it beautiful, or was the beauty an illusion disguising the horror and the terror?

It is understandable that in such a case there should be some confusion of feeling, but there is no basis for the man's anxious concern that in recognising the beauty he was denying the horror, that there was a logical tension or contradiction between these two elements or aspects, and that he had to choose one of them and reject the other. A beauty may be a terrible beauty. A horror may be horrible and still sublime.

In T. S. Eliot's essay on Matthew Arnold there is a clear statement of a related point. Eliot writes that Arnold sets too much store by the advantage for a poet of living in a beautiful world: 'We mean all sorts of things, I know, by Beauty. But the essential advantage for a poet is not, to have a beautiful world with which to deal: it is to be able to see beneath both beauty and ugliness; to see the boredom and the horror and the glory. (*The*

Use of Poetry and the Use of Criticism, p. 106). Eliot himself shows more directly in his own work the recognition of the unity of opposites that led him to place at the head of *Four Quartets* two epigraphs from Heraclitus, for whom war and peace and summer and winter were one. The way up is the way down and the way forward is the way back—ὁδὸς ἄνὼω κάτω μία καὶ ὡυτή—but Heraclitus and Eliot combine apparent opposites again when they see that flux and variety and coming to be and passing away are not inescapable obstacles to knowledge and objectivity for those who have νοῦς as well as eyes and ears: τοῦ λόγου δ'ἐόντος ξυνοῦ ζώουσιν οἱ πολλοί ὡς ἰδίαν ἔχοντες φρόνησιν. The λόγος is one and the same for all men and in so far as any of us prides himself on having a private understanding of it his pride is its own reward in blindness and isolation.

The startling collocations and abrupt transitions of *The Waste Land* or *The Love Song of J. Alfred Prufrock* achieve by the same technique of shifting angles and elevations a stereoscopic representation of a multi-dimensional world or mind that is itself in motion and change, full of variety and contrast, and yet having a nature that can be accurately and precisely portrayed if the right projections are adopted and understood. And the critic who presents the presentation must also employ and not only understand the instruments, for the critical task is itself one of multi-dimensional description, sharing its structure with the task of the poet and the philosopher, for whom as for the geometer and the architect a depth is a multiplicity of surfaces.

Pascal muses on man the master of thought and language, emperor holding in united comprehension the vast finitudes and infinities of space and time and eternity—until he is distracted by the buzzing of a fly. When we ask, 'Which is the faithful portrait?' we show how little we understand of portraiture. Not even a map is expected or required to show all that a map could show in the sense of all that could be shown by all the multitude of maps of that of which it is a map.

Even from a jet aircraft, and when we know and remember the speed of its flight, the polar ice, the wastes of northern Canada, or the plains of Ohio, may seem magnificently or tediously endless. Air travel has reduced the size of the earth but it has also given us a sharper view of its vastness. And yet somebody who crosses the great plain or the unlimited desert, whether in a Comet or a train or a stage-coach, may know that he is also to be compared with the fly on the window pane, the microbe on the speck of dust. There is not here a *choice* of alternative aspects, but two slides in the same lantern-lecture, and if you miss one of them you have not seen the whole show or heard the whole story. Or rather, as Hulme rightly suggests, there is not and could not be a *whole* story, but that means that there is always more and more to learn and not that nothing can be known: 'The truth is that there are no ultimate principles, upon which the whole of knowledge can be built once and for ever as upon a rock. But there are an infinity of analogues, which help us along, and give us a feeling of power over the chaos when we perceive them. The field is infinite and herein lies the chance for originality. Here there are some new things under the sun'. (*Speculations*, pp. 233–4).

And every one of the infinite analogues is reversible; light may travel in either direction between any two things that are related by analogy. Even to point out an unnoticed difference between this and that may serve to help you in the overall placing either of that or of this. This can be illustrated by an example that has the further convenience of showing how much of the literary and philosophical mode of understanding of which I have been speaking is at home in spheres from which philosophy and literature are often thought to have been irrevocably banished.

We speak naturally enough of a flow or stream of traffic, though it may at first surprise us that terms and theories of fluid dynamics are applicable to the movement of anything so un-fluent as a ten-ton truck or an oil tanker. But then we may remember how surprised we were when we first learned something about the literal cases of liquids—about what we come down to if we pursue the chemistry and physics of waterfalls and kettles and the boiling ocean: these too consist of particles in motion. At once and at last we connect a paradox about buses and cars with a paradox about milk and water and by a shift of perspective permanently improve our grasp of how things literally are in the world of mountains and molecules; a shift of perspective more similar than we might have expected to the shift that puts into some of their right relations the huge desert and the tiny galaxy or man the monarch and man the microbe.

Eddington and Jeans with their double tables and swarms of bees did harm as well as good. With more insight and more care they could no doubt have done less harm and more good. But in the enterprise they were engaged in, as in all philosophical and poetical enterprises, the risk of harm is inseparable from the hope of good. What could not possibly mislead cannot lead or guide us.

'That was a way of putting it—not very satisfactory' (*Four Quartets*, p. 17). But anything that was a very satisfactory way would be a satisfactory way of saying something else. That is why the wrestle with words and meanings can seem at times intolerable:

> Trying to learn to use words, and every attempt
> Is a wholly new start, and a different kind of failure
> Because one has only learnt to get the better of words
> For the thing one no longer has to say, or the way in which
> One is no longer disposed to say it. And so each venture
> Is a new beginning, a raid on the inarticulate
> With shabby equipment always deteriorating
> In the general mess of imprecision of feeling,
> Undisciplined squads of emotion (pp. 21–22).

Eliot goes on to speak in other terms of what I have called the role of reminders in extending and deepening our understanding in literature, philosophy, morality and religion; of how much of what we need and strive to know has been known to others whom we cannot hope to emulate. Earlier he had written, in *Burnt Norton*, of the same intolerable struggle, a theme that runs through *Four Quartets* and through much of his work:

> Words strain,
> Crack and sometimes break, under the burden,
> Under the tension, slip, slide, perish,
> Decay with imprecision, will not stay in place,
> Will not stay still.

There is the risk here and in other passages of pining for what will have the stillness of the Chinese jar and still have the power of the slipping, sliding, perishing words to live and move and have a being that consists in and makes possible their expressing and communicating the shifting surfaces that are the depths and dimensions of the Word. Like Rudolf Otto on the inexpressible, Eliot seems at times to be aspiring after impossible modes of communication that would capture the truth on a blank canvas or a silent gramophone record. Kant once and for all rebuked such aspirations: 'The light dove, cleaving the air in her free flight, and feeling its resistance, might imagine that its flight would be still easier in empty space.' The stresses and strains and resistances are as indispensable to thought and understanding as they are to the Chrysler building or the Sydney Harbour Bridge. Eddington's table stands firm only while the bees buzz. And so we come back to Heraclitus and the union of opposites, the tension and stability of the bow and the lyre.

In thought and speech the tension is between the ambition to say all and only what is true and the urge to convey at any cost, even the cost of accuracy and completeness, something of what we see or glimpse or dream. The idea that what matters most to us is inexpressible will recur as long as men's minds are dominated by the disastrously simple models of expression that go with the bad dichotomies of which I have been speaking; for while those models grip us we are prompted to deny the status of modes of rational communication to all the means best fitted for the expression of our subtlest thoughts and most precise emotions. (Eliot's distinction between vague emotion and precise emotion does something valuable to atone for, if only because it so directly contradicts, his mischievous dogma that the philosophical poet expresses only 'the emotional equivalent of thought.')

Eliot's feeling that 'That was a way of putting it—not very satisfactory' was an appropriate feeling, and many of us on many occasions are more fully justified in feeling the same about our mumbling attempts to explain or describe or understand. When, like Eliot, we recognise that we have failed we may then, like Eliot, start again and try to do better, or we may, after many and grave failures, despair of ever succeeding, and may even come to think that what we had been trying to do cannot in principle be done. In either case we shall be likely, if we have succumbed to the tyranny of the traditional models, to see no alternative to an unsatisfactory way of putting it except a satisfactory way of putting it, and hence to miss in our theory the truth that our own best practice sets before us: that a series of unsatisfactory ways of putting it may succeed in conveying what none of them would convey by itself and what could not be conveyed by any *one* way of putting it.

We are often able to convey the truth without making any true remarks, to convey accurately and effectively what we cannot

U

express with literal truth and exactness. For what is conveyed in such a case is not another kind of truth but the ordinary truth. What is unusual is the conveyance, the vehicle that carries understanding from mind to mind. And to say that it is unusual is only to contrast it with what are dangerously taken by philosophers as the paradigms of speech. It is not to say that you will only rarely meet such vehicles on the roads.

The example that I have quoted from Eliot is typical of one very common means of conveying truth about a complex matter without saying any one thing that is true; one that consists in making a series of inadequate and untrue remarks and withdrawing each as soon as it is made. I may give you a useful idea of a man's face or character by making a number of comparisons that you and I both recognise to be far-fetched. That a face or character prompts this or that far-fetched comparison tells us something about the character or face, and that these are a selection of the far-fetched comparisons that it prompts will usually tell us more than the sum of what is told by the separate comparisons. The phenomenon we are here concerned with is a kind of solo dialectic, in which from the varied and perhaps conflicting remarks of a single speaker we derive knowledge or understanding comparable with what might be given by a consideration of the discordant testimony of two or many witnesses.

In *The Honest to God Debate* (p. 112) Professor Christopher Evans makes some comments about books of devotion that have a wider application: 'Such books tend to be lopsided. They are bound to be, because their authors feel so intensely what they have to say. Such books have to be put alongside one another so that they may rub off some of their lopsidedness.' When a book or a description or an explanation is partial or lopsided we are not to reject it but to supplement it with another or others that are equally lopsided and incomplete: 'One set of symbols is strong where another is weak, and is weak where another is strong. Some are good for one thing, others for another'. 'The Bible, I believe, uses a whole riot of symbols, and allows them to clash against each other, so that no single one of them shall dominate and capture us.'

That last symbol is also to be found in Wittgenstein: 'A *picture* held us captive.' But Wittgenstein saw more clearly and steadily the weaknesses of symbols than their strengths, and was inclined at least on some occasions to preach (though not to practise) a total renunciation of pictorial utterance. The remedy for enslavement to a picture is liberation from that picture. To be forbidden to use any other picture, or even the same picture again, would be to exchange one tyranny for another; and the two tyrannies are in secret alliance, since they both depend on the idea that the various pictures are mutually exclusive rivals and hence that if we use a picture at all we must choose one and reject all the others, whereas (as Evans explains) the various pictures or symbols contribute jointly to a unified apprehension that no single one of them by itself could provide or convey.

It is instructive to compare Wittgenstein's use of the 'duck-rabbit' drawing with the conclusions drawn by Philip Mairet from a similar picture that he prints in the introduction to his English translation of Sartre's *Existentialism and Humanism*. Mairet makes his drawing into an example of existentialist choice; what can be seen either as a black cross on a white background or as a four-petalled flower calls for a decision from the spectator, who is entitled to choose and to stand by an interpretation that is rejected by the next person to whom the identical pattern is presented. Wittgenstein makes equally clear that there are alternative ways of seeing the drawing, and also that one cannot, even after having seen both aspects, see the pattern simultaneously as presenting both its aspects. He presents and describes the phenomenon of 'change of aspect'. But the conclusion to be drawn from his discussion (even if he nowhere unequivocally draws it himself) is opposed to the lesson that Mairet tries to teach, and this time we cannot mediate between the parties by speaking of freedom of choice and agreeing to differ. Mairet's use of the double-aspect picture is mistaken, and Wittgenstein provides most of the material for the adequate account that he does not explicitly offer. The main point to emphasize is that the drawing does *as a matter of objective fact* present the two aspects between which the existentialist or voluntarist interpretation would require us to choose. A picture that is only a picture of a duck and a picture that is only a picture of a rabbit are both different from a picture that is both a picture of a duck and a picture of a rabbit. Somebody who insists that a duck-rabbit is only a duck or only a rabbit has either failed to see one of the aspects (and could possibly be taught to see it) or is perversely or from confusion of thought denying that there are two aspects to be seen.

My advice, like all advice, is easier to give than to take, especially in a single paper or lecture. My abstractions have been designed to defend the concrete. But the concrete can defend itself, and examples can be offered to defend and illustrate the power of examples.

When you go to New York for the first time you will be told that New York is not of course the United States. New York is different and special. If you then fly to the Coast you will be told that of course Los Angeles is special and San Francisco is if anything even more special and California is not America but something different. You will be told the same true story in the Middle West and the Deep South, on the Canadian border and in New Mexico. You can see the Rockies or the Grand Canyon or the White House or Hollywood and still not have seen America.

But when you have seen *all* these things and all the others that I might have mentioned have you still seen nothing of America? How else can you come to know or see America than by seeing or knowing first one of these things and then another?

A similar point is made by Wittgenstein's example of the books:

> Imagine we had to arrange the books of a library. When we begin the books lie higgledy-piggledy on the floor. Now there would be many ways of sorting them and putting them in their places. One would be to take the books one by one and put each on the shelf in its right place. On the other hand we might take up several books from the floor and put them in a row on a shelf, merely in order to indicate that these books ought to go together in this order. In the course of arranging the library this whole row of books will have to change its place. But it would be wrong to say that therefore putting them together on a shelf was no step towards the final result. In this case, in fact, it is pretty obvious that having put together books which belong together was a definite achievement, even though the whole row of them had to be shifted. But some of the greatest achievements in philosophy could only be compared with taking up some books which seemed to belong together, and putting them on different shelves; nothing more being final about their positions than that they no longer lie side by side.

The Blue Book, pp. 44–5.

I have made progress towards the solution of a jig-saw puzzle as soon as I put together two pieces that clearly go together, even if I can neither make sense of them as part of a picture nor put them in the place that they will occupy in the finished puzzle.

These examples are trivial but not negligible. They are some of the minute particulars of which the tapestry of human knowledge is composed, and it is woven, like every other tapestry, thread by particular thread.

The same examples serve to articulate the metaphor of 'placing' that Leavis uses to present criticism, as Wisdom has presented philosophy, as a process of comparison, of setting one thing beside another. 'This is so' and 'Yes, but . . .' are reminiscent of Wisdom's three fundamental operators: 'You might as well say . . .', 'Exactly so' and 'But this is different'. The last of these is the title of *Other Minds* II (p. 38), but the doctrine of this trinity is most fully and picturesquely taught in the Virginia Lectures of 1957 and in other places where he has spoken of 'Father's method and Mother's method'. When those lectures are at last available we shall have further and better particulars of the kinship between reason and rhetoric, science and poetry, logic and literature, that he has perceived more clearly and marked more strongly at each successive stage in the development of his thought. And in representing the nature of reason and the nature of rhetoric, as in representing the nature of God or man, truth or time or good and evil, his aim has always been what he says it is in this passage from his 'Note on the New Edition of Professor Ayer's *Language, Truth and Logic*':

And, after all, our ultimate object is not to find a complete simile for the logic of matter any more than the poet's object is to find a complete simile for what he describes. It is to see it for what it is. Philosophy is not only less like the discovery of natural fact than people once supposed, it is also less like the discovery of logical fact than they next supposed, and more like literature—which makes it again more like the discovery of natural fact, only now it is the rediscovery of familiar fact through the recall of familiar logic dressed in not merely unfamiliar but scandalous clothes.

Philosophy and Psycho-Analysis, pp. 242–3.

Blake attributes our common understanding to a universal poetic genius, but he knew as we all have reason to know how much in our efforts to gain or retain or regain a grasp of the familiar we need to depend on the individual poetic genius.

XIII

CHRONOLOGICAL LIST OF PUBLISHED WRITINGS OF JOHN WISDOM, 1928–1972

COMPILED BY JOHN LINNELL

1928

1. 'McTaggart's Determining Correspondence of Substance: A Refutation', *Mind*, Vol. XXXVII, pp. 414–38.

1929

2. 'Bentham on Division', *Psyche*, Vol. IX, No. 3, pp. 10–19.

3. 'Time, Fact and Substance', *Proc. Arist. Soc.*, Vol. 29, 1928–29, pp. 67–94.

1930

4. 'Interpretation and Analysis', *Psyche*, Vol. XI, No. 2, pp. 11–31.

1931

5. *Interpretation and Analysis in relation to Bentham's theory of definition*, Psyche Miniature, K. Paul, Trench Trubner and Co., 136 pp., London. This reprints item 4 (pp. 7–60) together with a final section entitled 'Paraphrasis and Fictions', (pp. 61–136).

6. Critical Discussion: 'Bentham's Theory of Definition', *Psyche*, Vol. XI, No. 4, pp. 79–83. A response to criticism by Ogden and Lockhart in the January 1931 issue of *Psyche* to the original article (item 4). It is followed by Max Black's comments on the original article, the criticisms and Wisdom's reply, pp. 84–7.

7. 'Logical Constructions I', *Mind*, Vol. XL, pp. 188–216. Reprinted in *Logical Constructions*, 1969, pp. 41–76.

8. 'Logical Constructions II', *Mind*, Vol. XL, pp. 460–475. Reprinted in *Logical Constructions*, 1969, pp. 77–96.

9. 'Note on Identity of Structure', *Mind*, Vol. XL, pp. 268–71.

1932

10. 'Logical Constructions III', *Mind*, Vol. XLI, pp. 441–64. Reprinted in *Logical Constructions*, 1969, pp. 97–126.

1933

11. 'Logical Constructions IV', *Mind*, Vol. XLII, pp. 43–66. Reprinted in *Logical Constructions*, 1969, pp. 127–56.

12. 'Logical Constructions V', *Mind*, Vol. XLII, pp. 186–202. Reprinted in *Logical Constructions*, 1969, pp. 157–77.

13. 'Ostentation', *Psyche*, Vol. XIII, pp. 164–77, reprinted in *Philosophy and Psycho-Analysis*, 1953, pp. 1–15.

1934

14. *Problems of Mind and Matter*, Cambridge University Press, 215 pp. Reprinted with new preface in 1963.

15. 'Is Analysis a Useful Method in Philosophy?' *Proc. Arist. Soc.* Supp. Vol. XIII, pp. 65–89 (Symposium with M. Black and M. Cornforth). Reprinted in *Philosophy and Psycho-Analysis*, 1953, pp. 16–35.

16. 'An Explanatory Note on the Elements of Facts', *Analysis*, Vol. I, 1933–34, p. 32.

17. Critical Notice: C. D. Broad, *Examination of McTaggart's Philosophy*, Vol. I, *Mind*, Vol. XLIII, pp. 204–24.

18. Critical Notice: C. H. Langford and C. I. Lewis, *Symbolic Logic*, *Mind*, Vol. XLIII, pp. 99–109.

19. Review of Max Black, *The Nature of Mathematics*, *Mind*, Vol. XLIII, pp. 529–31.

20. Review of S. Buchanan, *Symbolic Distance in Relation to Analogy and Fiction*, *Mind*, Vol. XLIII, p. 254.

21. Review of C. K. Ogden, *Bentham's Theory of Fictions*, *Mind*, Vol. XLIII, pp. 252–3.

22. Note: Lewis and Langford's *Symbolic Logic*, *Mind*, Vol. XLIII, p. 279.

1935

23. 'God and Evil', *Mind*, Vol. XLIV, pp. 1–20.

24. Review of M. Grant, *A New Argument for God and Survival*, *Mind*, Vol. XLIV, pp. 395–7.

1937

25. 'Philosophical Perplexity', *Proc. Arist. Soc.*, Vol. XXXVII, 1936–7, pp. 71–88, reprinted in *Philosophy and Psycho-Analysis*, 1953, pp. 36–50, and in *The Linguistic Turn*, ed. R. Rorty, 1967, pp. 101–10.

1938

26. 'Metaphysics and Verification I', *Mind*, Vol. XLVII, pp. 452–98, reprinted in *Philosophy and Psycho-Analysis*, 1953, pp. 51–101, without the 'I' in the title and without the words 'to be continued' which appear below the final paragraph on p. 498 of *Mind*.

27. Review of Sir W. Barrett, *Personality Survives Death*, *Mind*, Vol. XLVII, pp. 526–7.

1940

28. 'Other Minds I', *Mind*, Vol. XLIX, pp. 369–402, reprinted in *Other Minds*, 1952, pp. 1–37.

29. Review of K. Horney, *New Ways in Psycho-Analysis*, *Mind*, Vol. XLIX, pp. 351–3.

30. Review of K. Richmond, *Evidence of Identity*, *Mind*, Vol. XLIX, pp. 100–2.

1941

31. 'Other Minds II', *Mind*, Vol. L, pp. 1–21, reprinted in *Other Minds*, 1952, pp. 38–59.

32. 'Other Minds III', *Mind*, Vol. L, pp. 97–121, reprinted in *Other Minds*, 1952, pp. 60–86.

33. 'Other Minds IV', *Mind*, Vol. L, pp. 209–42, reprinted in *Other Minds*, 1952, pp. 87–122.

34. 'Other Minds V', *Mind*, Vol. L, pp. 313–29, reprinted in *Other Minds*, 1952, pp. 123–40.

35. Critical Notice: H. V. Dicks, *Clinical Studies in Pyscho-pathology*, *Mind*, Vol. L, pp. 408–14.

36. Critical Notice: W. Ellis, *The Isles of the Soul in Western Philosophy and Science*, *Mind*, Vol. L, pp. 414–9.

1942

37. 'Other Minds VI', *Mind*, Vol. LI, pp. 1–17, reprinted in *Other Minds*, 1952, pp. 141–58.

38. 'Moore's Technique', Contribution to *The Philosophy of G. E. Moore*, ed. P. A. Schilpp, 1942, pp. 421–50, reprinted in *Philosophy and Psycho-Analysis*, 1953, pp. 120–48.

39. Review of S. Anthony, *The Child's Discovery of Death*, *Mind*, Vol. LI, pp. 84–5.

40. Review of A. B. White, *Worry in Women*, *Mind*, Vol. LI, pp. 389–90.

1943

41. 'Other Minds VII', *Mind*, Vol. LII, pp. 193–211, reprinted in *Other Minds*, 1952, pp. 159–78.

42. 'Other Minds VIII', *Mind*, Vol. LII, pp. 289–313, reprinted in *Other Minds*, 1952, pp. 179–205, without the words 'To be continued' which appear below the final paragraph on p. 313 of *Mind*.

43. Critical Notice: C. H. Waddington and others, *Science and Ethics*, *Mind*, Vol. LII, pp. 275–82, reprinted in *Philosophy and Psycho-Analysis*; 1953, pp. 102–11.

44. Review of C. Morris, *Paths of Life*, *Mind*, Vol. LII, pp. 86–7.

1944

45. 'Philosophy, Anxiety and Novelty', *Mind*, Vol. LIII, pp. 170–6, reprinted in *Philosophy and Psycho-Analysis*, 1953, pp. 112–9.

46. Obituary Notice: L. S. Stebbing, *Mind*, Vol. LIII, pp. 283–5.

1945

47. Review of R. W. Pickford, *The Psychology of Cultural Change in Painting*, *Mind*, Vol. LIV, pp. 281–2.

48. 'Gods', *Proc. Arist. Soc.*, Vol. XLV, 1944–5, pp. 185–206, reprinted in *Philosophy and Psycho-Analysis*, 1953, pp. 149–68, in *Logic and Language* (First Series), ed. A. Flew 1951, pp. 187–206, in *Classical and Contemporary Readings in the Philosophy of Religion*, ed. John Hick, 1964, pp. 413–428, in *Contemporary Philosophy*, ed. J. L. Jarrett and S. McMurrin, 1954, pp. 239–52, and in *Religion from Tolstoy to Camus*, ed. W. A. Kaufmann, 1961, pp. 391–406.

1946

49. 'Other Minds', *Proc. Arist. Soc.*, Supp. Vol. XX, pp. 122–47, (Symposium with J. L. Austin and A. J. Ayer) reprinted in *Other Minds*, 1952, pp. 206–29, and with Austin's essay in *Philosophy in the Twentieth Century*, ed. W. Barrett and A. D. Aiken, 1962, vol. 1, pp. 774–821.

50. 'Synopsis of Paper: Other Minds'. Three alternative versions were supplied to J. W. Scott, editor of *A Synoptic Index*

to the *Proceedings of the Aristotelian Society 1900-49* in response to a synopsis made editorially and are all printed on p. 0201 of the *Index.* The second of these is printed with a few changes in *Other Minds*, 1952, pp. 230–31.

51. Critical Notice: Howe's *Invisible Anatomy*, Glover's *Psycho-Analysis*, Layard's *The Lady of the Hare*, and Sears' *Survey of Objective Studies of Psycho-Analytic Concepts*, *Mind*, Vol. LV, pp. 346–56, reprinted in *Philosophy and Psycho-Analysis*, 1953, pp. 182–94 with the omission of the last two sentences: 'We know that nature isn't always neat. We need to recognize that logic isn't either.'

52. 'Philosophy and Psycho-Analysis', *Polemic*, No. 4, 1946, pp. 37–48, reprinted in *Philosophy and Psycho-Analysis*, 1953, pp. 169–81, and in *Classics of Analytic Philosophy*, ed. R. Ammerman, 1965, pp. 285–295.

1947

53. 'Bertrand Russell and Modern Philosophy', *Politics and Letters*, Vol. 1, No. 1, pp. 75–82, reprinted in *Philosophy and Psycho-Analysis*, 1953, pp. 195–209.

1948

54. 'Note on the New Edition of Professor Ayer's *Language, Truth and Logic*', *Mind*, Vol. LVII, pp. 403–19, reprinted in *Philosophy and Psycho-Analysis*, 1953, pp. 229–47.

55. 'Things and Persons', *Proc. Arist. Soc.*, Supp. Vol. XXII, pp. 202–15 (Symposium with Professors D. M. MacKinnon and H. A. Hodges) reprinted in *Philosophy and Psycho-Analysis*, 1953, pp. 217–28.

1950

56. 'The Concept of Mind', *Proc. Arist. Soc.*, Vol. L, 1949–50, pp. 189–204, reprinted in *Other Minds*, pp. 220–235 and in *The Philosophy of Mind*. ed. V. C. Chappell, 1962, pp. 49–59.

57. 'Metaphysics', *Proc. Arist. Soc.*, Vol. LI, 1950–51, pp. i–xxiv, reprinted in *Other Minds*, 1952, pp. 245–65.

58. 'A Note on Probability', Contribution to *Philosophical Analysis*, ed. Max Black, 1950, pp. 414–20, reprinted in *Philosophy and Psycho-Analysis*, 1953, pp. 210–16.

59. 'The Logic of God', B.B.C. broadcast, reprinted in

Paradox and Discovery, 1965, pp. 1–22, and in *The Existence of God*, ed. John Hick, 1964, pp. 275–98.

1952

60.   *Other Minds*, Oxford and New York, 259 pp. Collection of items 28, 31, 32, 33, 34, 37, 40, 41, 49, 50, 56 and 57. Reprinted in 1956. Second edition with new preface, Oxford and New York, 265 pp., 1965. Reprinting of this edition in paperback by University of California Press in 1968.

61.   'Ludwig Wittgenstein, 1934–37', *Mind*, Vol. LXI, p. 258–60, reprinted in *Paradox and Discovery*, 1965, pp. 87–9.

62.   'Existentialism', *Cambridge Review*, Vol. 73, 1951–2, pp. 257–60. Reprinted in *Paradox and Discovery*, 1965, pp. 34–7.

1953

63.   *Philosophy and Psycho-Analysis*, Oxford and New York, 282 pp. Collection of items 13, 15, 25, 26, 42, 44, 46, 48, 51, 52, 53, 54, 55, 58, together with a previously unpublished article 'Philosophy, Metaphysics and Psycho-Analysis', pp. 242–282. This book was reprinted in Oxford and New York in 1964 and in New York and Berkeley, California in 1969.

1954

64.   'What is there in Horse Racing?', *The Listener*, 10 June, 1954, Vol. LI, pp. 1015–16.

1955

65.   Foreword to M. Lazerowitz, *The Structure of Metaphysics*, London.

1956

66.   'Religious Belief', *Cambridge Review*, Vol. 77, 1955–6, pp. 636–41 and 667–8, reprinted in *Paradox and Discovery*, 1965, pp. 43–56.

1957

67.   'Paradox and Discovery', The Howison lecture at the University of California, Berkeley, California, reprinted in *Paradox and Discovery*, 1965, pp. 114–38.

1959

68. 'G. E. Moore', *Analysis*, Vol. 19, No. 3, pp. 49–53, reprinted in *Paradox and Discovery*, 1965, pp. 82–6.

1961

69. 'The Metamorphosis of Metaphysics', *Proc. Brit. Acad.* Vol. XLVII, pp. 37–59, reprinted in *Paradox and Discovery*, 1965, pp. 57–81, and in *Studies in Philosophy*, ed. J. N. Findlay, 1966, pp. 213–40.

70. 'A Feature of Wittgenstein's Technique', *Proc. Arist. Soc.*, Supp. Vol. XXXV, pp. 1–14, reprinted in *Paradox and Discovery*, 1965, pp. 90–103.

1962

71. 'Mace, Moore, and Wittgenstein', contribution to *C. A. Mace*, a symposium edited by V. Carver, London, pp. 97–123, reprinted in *Paradox and Discovery*, pp. 148–66.

1963

72. Preface to paperback reprint of *Problems of Mind and Matter*, item 14.

1965

73. Preface to second edition of *Other Minds*, item 60.

74. *Paradox and Discovery*, Oxford and New York, 166 pp., collection of items 59, 61, 62, 66, 67, 68, 69, 70, 71, together with previously unpublished lectures and essays: 'Free Will', pp. 23–33, 'The Meaning of the Questions of Life', pp. 38–42, 'Price's *Thinking and Experience*', pp. 104–13, and 'Tolerance', pp. 139–47. This book was reprinted in Berkeley, California in 1970.

1969

75. *Logical Constructions*, New York, 181 pp., with an introduction by Judith Jarvis Thomson. A collection of items 7, 8, 10, 11, 12, introduction pp. 3–39, bibliography, pp. 179–81.

76. 'Eternal Life', in *Talk of God*, Royal Institute of Philosophy Lectures, Volume Two, pp. 239–50.

1971

77. 'Wittgenstein and "Private Language" ', in *Ludwig Wittgenstein: Philosophy and Language*, edited by Alice Ambrose and Morris Lazerowitz, pp. 26-36.

1972

78. 'Epistemological Enlightenment', Proceedings of the Pacific Division of the American Philosophical Association.

XIV

NOTES ON CONTRIBUTORS

D. A. T. Gasking, Professor of Philosophy, Melbourne University.

Judith Jarvis Thomson, Professor of Philosophy, Massachusetts Institute of Technology.

D. C. Yalden-Thomson, Professor of Philosophy, University of Virginia.

Ilham Dilman, Lecturer in Philosophy, University College, Swansea.

M. R. Ayers, Fellow of Wadham College, Oxford.

George W. Roberts, Associate Professor of Philosophy, Duke University.

J. M. Hinton, Fellow of Worcester College, Oxford.

Keith Gunderson, Professor of Philosophy, University of Minnesota.

R. W. Newell, Senior Lecturer in Philosophy, University of East Anglia.

Ardon Lyon, Lecturer in the Department of Social Science and Humanities, the City University, London.

Herbert Morris, Professor of Law, University of California, Los Angeles.

Renford Bambrough, Fellow and Dean of St. John's College, Cambridge.

John Linnell, Dean of the College of Arts and Sciences, Grand Valley State Colleges, Allendale, Michigan.

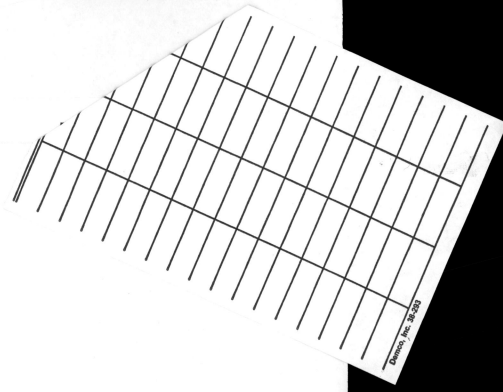